In this book, Chude Jideonwo joins the conversation on some of the major topical issues of the day. He writes delightfully about some of the big questions surrounding the expression of popular will. Does democracy throw up the right answer always? Chude asks impliedly, with sure-footed irony, "whose right is right?" Perhaps those who are left out of mainstream economics in the super-concentration of capital have a right to be right too?

A world in which a few prosper and many, many more do not, is a world in disequilibria. That reality introduces tensions into the very fabric of democracy. Unsteady benefits of development, non-inclusive economic growth and class tensions are today's reality in many societies. Jideonwo argues for more dialogue and for humility in understanding what is going on in reality when "inevitable expectations" do not materialize in elections. He does not accept fads and asks deep questions about some faddish conclusions about millennials, social media and more. His is a fertile mind that goes where it can go in search of answers, with no fear. In the process, he leads us to think about issues not just jump at superficiality. A lot of what he says is what many who champion Sustainable Development are also saying — our world is in need of holistic, multi-stakeholder approaches to economic development. We can no longer ignore the fact of the billions who are left to writhe in deprivati⁻   dignity. And if we try, they hit back — sometimes with "M   t elections, as Chude suggests.

Between the leading an   ımility, accountability and true connec   .equired totem posts of success, for ages. Wł   ₋ nard to achieve then? Chude does us all a service by d.   ₀ ⅈⅈⅈs vigorous views in this book.

– **Yaw Nsarkoh**
Executive Vice President, Unilever Ghana and Nigeria.

I'll be recommending this read far and wide both to friends across Africa and further afield because it shares a sense of urgent optimism about what this next generation of African advocacy entrepreneurs can and must achieve when they get organised, and as they move from influencing the outcome of elections to influencing the implementation of policy, and as they form networks to follow the money, from grassroots to tops, holding power accountable whoever holds it.

– Jamie Drummond
Executive Director, Global Strategy at ONE

The authors offers a fresh perspective on forces shaping African and global politics, including the information revolution and economic integration, and examines the ways in which activists can harness those forces to build citizen-led movements. As this book's introduction asserts, "[T]his is the most important job in the world – there can be nothing more important than helping a people find a voice, and a nation find its way." I'm with him. The reader will be too.

– Jane Wales
Former Special Assistant to President Bill Clinton and Senior Director of the National Security Council/ Chief Executive Officer, Global Philanthropy Forum

A uniquely brilliant and illuminating account of what it takes to build formidable political campaigns in Africa that against all odds resulted in resounding victories in the presidential elections of Ghana and Nigeria. The authors weave a uniquely African and fundamentally citizen-centered framework that disrupts the status quo and taps into the core aspirations of the people, the vast majority of whom are young and more networked than ever. The winds of change are upon us. This important clarion call for sustained civic engagement and political participation among the youth of our continent couldn't be more timely. It's a must read."

– Eddie Mandhry
Director for Africa, Yale University

Lively, provocative and, at heart, optimistic, this book will give you a different perspective on Nigeria and Africa, one written from the ground up, not from the usual 10,000 feet.

– David Pilling
Africa Editor, Financial Times

HOW TO WIN ELECTIONS IN AFRICA

WHAT ACTIVISTS, DONORS, SOCIAL
ENGINEERS AND CITIZENS CAN LEARN FROM
STATECRAFT INC'S SUCCESSFUL RUNS IN
NIGERIA AND GHANA
(+ PARALLELS WITH DONALD TRUMP)

CHUDE JIDEONWO,

WITH ADEBOLA WILLIAMS

Published in Nigeria in 2017 by Kachifo Limited
Under its Kamsi imprint
253 Herbert Macaulay Way
Yaba, Lagos, Nigeria
0807 736 4217
info@kachifo.com
www.kachifo.com

A catalogue record for this book is available from
the National Library of Nigeria.

ISBN: 978-1-54392-674-3

Layout: Akeem Ibrahim
Cover design: Victor Ehikhamenor

For the citizens of Nigeria and Ghana.
Thank you for convincing us that
Africa is finally ready.

CONTENTS

ACKNOWLEDGEMENT

Our company StateCraft Inc would probably not have been inspired as early as it was if Oronto Douglas (of blessed memory) hadn't tapped us to handle youth communication for the presidential campaign of Goodluck Ebele Jonathan in 2011. He gave us the most interesting professional challenge of our lives at the time and made us rethink our entire approach to our nation-building mission.

He deserves thanks.

As does Rotimi Amaechi, whose mandate to us in 2014 to run the entire campaign communication for Muhammadu Buhari finally validated our model, gave us wings to fly and created a force that is now continental.

The thinkers, doers and volunteers who have worked with us to deliver magic for clients past and present across the continent deserve thanks too. It is because of them that we are able to share these crucial lessons.

The entire team at RED has routinely delivered magic, driven by a keen appreciation of Africa's urgent nation building imperative. Thank you.

Remi Ogunkayo, who has led campaigns in Nigeria and Ghana, and is leading other present efforts, Isime Esene who gave it the first look-through, as well as Dami Adebayo, who helped with the crucial research for this project have been invaluable beyond measure.

Thank you also to our board members, Francesca Uriri and Tolulope Orekoya for looking through the drafts of this book and sharing crucial insights that made it even better.

Also many thanks to the outstanding writers and thinkers whose thoughts and research we relied on.

Above all, thank you to those who made it possible for us to even exist in the first place, top of the list of course are our parents, who believed passionately from day one.

Chude Jideonwo
March 2017
Lagos, Nigeria

INTRODUCTION

ON THE JOYS OF NATION BUILDING

W e had just finished a strategy meeting for a presidential candidate and the team had 96 hours to put together the strategic road map for his candidacy.

The next day however, a document arrived for me: an extensive strategy document prepared by my co-founder, Chude Jideonwo. He helped build the foundations of the company, but had stepped aside, focusing on leading the group and directly supervising content, but what he had heard and seen about the candidate excited him immensely: he had decided to build the document himself, weaving the history context and imperatives for that candidacy and for the citizens.

"If it was a non-nation client," I teased him, "you wouldn't have touched this document at all."

He didn't disagree. The light shone in his eyes, the cause made him alive. His bones were set on fire.

I know exactly how he feels. All of us who work at StateCraft Inc know exactly how he feels.

Political and government consulting in many African markets is a rolling stone of excitement. Because Africa is standing at the cusp of remarkable change, citizens discovering extensive powers, dictators losing their grip and establishments meeting their comeuppance, it is a time of great possibilities and opportunities like no other for citizenship and for political engineering.

It isn't easy to set up a revolutionary company in a society where nation building has often been left to civil society or political players, but StateCraftInc found the courage to pioneer, and its bold intervention in this space has cleared a path of new possibilities for a continent and its people.

Bringing professionalism to a field with dim lights, and surviving the primitiveness of many of our political and governance structures with private sector imperatives, requires both the bravery of purpose and the passion of conviction. Both of those have been easy because this is the most important job in the world – there can be nothing more important than helping a people find a voice, and a nation find its way.

There is no other way of saying it – the 2015 elections in Nigeria and the 2016 elections in Ghana were a miracle of history. No one expected them. They had all the elements of impossibility; all the factors that guarantee failure.

But they had the one thing that always guarantees change: citizens. Citizens of these nations took the reins of their destinies, and we were excited that the custodians of this transition trusted us to help smoothen these paths. We are equally honoured that custodians in East, West and Central Africa have also trusted us with these assignments, and we look forward to the changes that these citizens too will bring.

Therefore in winning these difficult, impossible elections we learnt timeless truths about the essential character of the African voter – truths that cut across the continent, and that we also understand and connect with viscerally because we have a stake in this continent's success. Unlike consultants who come into Africa from other climes, we are Africans, born in Africa, working in Africa; we understand the anger and the hope - our work is often personal.

It is those rare insights we have gotten as the only organisation with our breadth of experience that we are now sharing with a continent in urgent need of more success stories, and at a quicker pace.

The things we have learnt however, also have global resonance, and to ensure that a universal audience (fascinated as the world is by America's marquee contests) can connect with this work, we have drawn substantially upon careful study of global elections with a focus on upheavals in the United States and the United Kingdom over the past ten years. We draw constant parallels, in almost each chapter, especially with America's 2016 elections and Brexit's 2016 vote.

Because of globalisation, the work of the political and social engineer/strategist has become not easier, but simpler– the same trends of nationalism, populism and economic inequality cut across much of the open world. Citizens learn from, imitate and are inspired by commonalities now made apparent and transparent.

We are hopeful that these engineers and strategists will find the insight from Africa's famously opaque spaces useful, as well as students and professionals who seek to build careers in nation building, or build businesses that address the imperatives of social transformation.

To the latter especially, this is a love letter: Africa needs you, your skills and your passion urgently, today.

Adebola Williams
April 2017
Nairobi, Kenya

FOREWORD

Young Africans have come of age – in the most significant ways possible. The world resists this notion at its own peril.

For them democracy is not an alternative, democracy is the only option, despite the cynicism about capture by new and old political elite. Dictatorships and autocracies are dirty/abhorrent words that an increased number of civic-minded and empowered members of this generation are determined to wipe off from our political lexicon.

But how? Part of the answer to that is precisely what struck me about my experience with StateCraft Inc in their collaboration with the New Patriotic Party's (NPP) 2016 political campaign.

For them, the work that they do on political communication is not just a professional assignment, even if that should be enough since they know the turf and they secure the results. It is instead a mission; one that comes from a visceral sense of what Africa must do if it must thrive; if it must jettison its legacies of corruption and bad governance behind; if it must finally achieve its potential and free more than a billion people to live in decency and freedom.

StateCraft's deep insight from their work on the ground, in the streets, and at all levels of society has culminated in developing a powerful private sector tool for rebuilding and remodeling citizen's engagement and political behavior to confront the pervasive problem of bad governance and political capture across Africa.

Many would have heard of StateCraft after their remarkable work in the 2015 Nigerian elections in their crucial role in helping to unseat, as many have called it, a 16-year ruling party monopoly, to bring a much needed change into office Nigeria's current president, after three tries for that office.

The exact same happened for the NPP candidate in Ghana; where the symbol of the aspiration, Addo Dankwa Akufo-Addo had also made as many tries for that position, and the people were finally ready for this change to come.

StateCraft brought to Ghana during our 2016 elections that same passion and visceral understanding of what citizens wanted; a message of empowerment and a cry for change from corruption and plutocracy. Their model sharpened the sense of purposefulness of the diverse strategies including 'adopt a polling station', millennial engagement etc, and crystallised the outlines of a movement that brought success and has set Ghana on the course of revival.

Their mission continues, across Africa, giving voice to generational aspirations, and building networks of citizen-driven transformation, country to country.

This book is a testament to vision, hope and an unshaken belief in the capacity of many to change their own countries. Africa should pay attention. These are the beacons of a change that has only just begun.

Carpe diem!

Ken Ofori-Atta
Minister of Finance, Ghana

1

LEGACY DOESN'T MATTER
AS MUCH AS IT USED TO

This is how Jeb Bush figured it would happen in America's 2016 elections. His father had been president and a respected figure in the Republican Party. His brother had been a two-term president, parlaying his father's name and imagined legacy into electoral victory, and emerging – despite his failings – as an icon of the political right.

The media had been whispering about a Jeb run for at least the eight years since his brother left office, and for some, before (he was supposed to be the Bush brother who would be president). He had also been a successful governor of Florida, with an image as a bi-partisan wonk who made things happen and was destined for higher office.

In short: this was a man whose binder was full of legacy. He had everything ready to launch him into the presidency – the kind of thing that has routinely launched Kennedys and Clintons and Luther King Jrs into either office or national acclaim.

So when he got into the race for the Republican ticket, he was the immediate frontrunner, quickly raising a financial juggernaut that climbed up to $157,186,415 and securing the endorsements of a roll call of establishment players. As far back as November 2012, Politico.com already had the bold headline "2016 election: Hillary Clinton vs. Jeb Bush?"

The confidence was based on one thing only – his legacy, of political success, familial connections and governance chops.

But by the time he crashed out of the race – publicly humiliated by the upstart Donald J. Trump and routinely mocked by a shocked national press corps – with under eight per cent of the vote in the South Carolina primary polls, this much had become clear: the legacy he rode upon mattered to everyone else except the people who were most important – the voters.

Politicians have always been able to count on legacy. Not just in America, but across Western and Eastern Europe, and certainly in Africa, where both functional democracies and pseudo-dictatorships have largely depended on people with experience, capacity and networks in the military, in politics or in government at some level.

But voters don't care anymore. And nowhere is this more true than in Africa.

In Nigeria, voters pulled the lever for Goodluck Jonathan in 2011. It is easy to forget now, but he was the unlikeliest candidate for the highest political office. This was a man without a concrete political profile, not to talk of legacy. As deputy governor in Bayelsa, he was simply – even by his own telling – a placeholder, selected based on the perception that he wouldn't aspire, and wasn't qualified, for more.

He was chosen for Vice-President over more storied candidates like the fearsome Peter Odili who had been governor of Rivers and the adored Donald Duke who had been governor of Cross River, precisely because he had very little to say, no networks to speak of and presented no threat to any political force.

But for the Nigerian public, he represented something that his campaign strategists captured instinctively and powerfully, even if he ultimately didn't fulfill that promise: he was a "breath of fresh air".

All of the things that were typically considered weaknesses in politics, turned out to be his strengths.

When we signed on to manage campaign communication directly targeted at the youth demographic, his appeal was abundantly obvious to us; his lack of attachment to existing establishments and absence of a formidable record upon which to judge him being the centre of his appeal. "Goodluck Jonathan," we said in the theme of our messaging, "was a different kind of president."

What was more important to the voters, and what matters most today above all things is not the record of the past, but the promise of the future. Not what has happened in the past, but what will happen in the future.

When Goodluck Jonathan was mocked for saying "he had no shoes", politicians and journalists stuck in a time warp were missing the point that his international core messaging strategists had adapted from their own experience in other successful global elections: people were tired of the old and wanted the new. And this mental revolution has been building up steadily over the past two decades.

Writing for *Commentary*, Nicholas N. Eberstadt captured the ongoing disruption that establishment players didn't get in his essay, 'Our Miserable 21st Century'.

"On the morning of November 9, 2016, America's elite—its talking and deciding classes—woke up to a country they did not know. Whatever else it may or may not have accomplished, the 2016 election was a sort of shock therapy for Americans living within what Charles Murray famously termed "the bubble" (the protective barrier of prosperity and self-selected associations that increasingly shield our best and brightest from contact with the rest of their society)...

"Yes, things are very different indeed these days in the "real America" outside the bubble. In fact, things have been going badly wrong in America since the beginning of the 21st century.

"It turns out that the year 2000 marks a grim historical milestone of sorts for our nation...

"The warning lights have been flashing, and the klaxons sounding, for more than a decade and a half. But our pundits and prognosticators and professors and policymakers, ensconced as they generally are deep within the bubble, were for the most part too distant from the distress of the general population to see or hear it. (So much for the vaunted "information era" and "big-data revolution"). Now that those signals are no longer possible to ignore, it is high time for experts and intellectuals to reacquaint themselves with the country in which they live and to begin the task of describing what has befallen the country in which we have lived since the dawn of the new century."

Something had given way. People were not just frustrated by, but disdainful of the establishment, and their records of legacy that had only left rampaging income inequality, endemic government corruption and a collapse of security, across nations.

Legacy was no longer an assurance of effectiveness. It was now testament to complicity.

In 2012 having a legacy worked against Addo Dankwa Akufo-Addo. He was the politician who came from a great family, His father was a president and his grandfather was a king. He seemed like he had been born to be president. John Dramani Mahama, on the other hand, rose through the ranks to get to the role of president. He was thrust into the role because the president died in office. John Mahama won eight out of ten regions in his first presidential elections against Nana Akufo Addo.

By 2016 however, Mahama now had his own legacy. And it just didn't smell right.

This doesn't mean that legacy doesn't matter at all. Or that candidates with a legacy cannot win elections. It means that it is no longer an important determinant for credibility or support. If anything in fact, it is a burden.

The fresher you are – think Obama 2012 and Trump 2016 – the better. When people uniformly detest the political and governance establishments, participation in that consensus leaves you guilty until proven innocent. The new are not innocent, but they get the benefit of the doubt.

So, Muhammadu Buhari was a perfect vehicle for the message of change, because – by a stroke of luck – the only national legacy for which he could have been truly judged, was truncated by a military coup within two years of his leadership in 1985. His executive management of the Petroleum Trust Fund became the one-eyed man in the sea of blindness that was the years late dictator, Sani Abacha, laid waste to Nigeria.

A scant resume became a powerful testament. Many voters remembered the one-year as a period of calamity. The vast majority could only think about the three years that could have been.

One year matched against five years; that became the race between Buhari and Jonathan. The latter was burdened by legacy, a testament to ultimate complicity and culpability in the recent history of mismanagement and failures in Nigeria's leadership. The weight was so heavy, that even the positives of that administration became negatives.

Fruitlessly, Jonathan sought to rely on the legacy of infrastructural development: roads, schools, airports, rail networks. But legacy had become a treacherous thing. Where he spoke of airports, citizens heard of the corruption that attended the process. When he spoke of schools, citizens heard of waste in government spending.

His legacy became a single story of liability.

In fact, legacy becomes dangerous because in its entitlement, it loses sight of the issues that are driving voter concern and angst. The candidate is busy trying to prove why she deserves to be voted for – "The most qualified candidate in modern American history," Barack and Michelle Obama crowed about the ultimately losing Hillary Rodham Clinton – while the citizen is busy wondering how everything went wrong under her, and why she and her ilk are entirely bad.

Legacy often serves to drive a gulf between those who sit in public office and the issues that animate the voting public.

"Bush was on the wrong side of the most galvanizing issues for Republican primary voters," Politico famously noted.

Continuity has become a dirty word in a world where it appears to everyday citizens that there is more going wrong, than there is going right. Citizens are deeply suspicious of establishments, networks and consensuses.

The reason for the global distrust in institutions lies in this reality:

"Compared to one year ago, the level of trust that young Americans between 18 and 29 years old have in most American institutions tested in our survey has dissipated compared even to last year's historically low numbers," a 2014 Harvard Kennedy School poll noted. "For example, in the last 12 months, trust in the President has decreased from 39 percent to 32 percent, the U.S. military has decreased from 54 percent to 47 percent (the first time below a majority) and the Supreme Court from 40 to 36 percent. Below is a graph that charts the composite trust index (an average of six public institutions tracked using the same methodology) since 2010.

"The level of trust that young Americans have in the President and the U.S. Military has suffered the most over the last year. The growing lack of trust in the President comes from Democrats (64% trusted the President to do the right thing all or most of the time in 2013, today the number is 53%) and Independents (31% in 2013, 23% today) — and not from Republicans whose opinion has not changed in the last year. Thirteen percent (13%) of Republicans trust the President to do the right thing all or most of the time. These findings stand in contrast to the U.S. Military; over the last year, the military has lost trust across all parties (Democrats are down 6 points to 44%, Republicans 5 points to 63% and Independents down 8 points to 40%)."

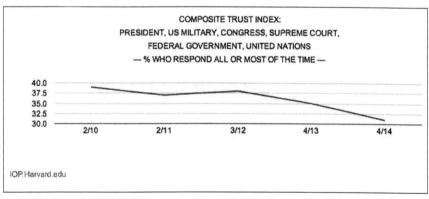

Figure 1: Composite Trust Index of Six Public Institutions in the U.S.

Institutions are the representation of the existing establishments and thus bear the brunt of the cynicism. Institutions reek of the past. The future may be inchoate and unpredictable, but at the very least it has no legacy to speak of.

Change is the only acceptable reality.

It has always been said about American politics that the candidate most able to paint a vision of the future, is the candidate that ultimately wins.

That American tradition is now a global reality.

"I serve as a blank screen on which people of vastly different political stripes project their own views," Obama famously wrote in *The Audacity of Hope.*

Blank slates that speak of a possible future are now more attractive than loaded pasts. Politicians who are burdened by the bygone need to learn the skill to focus solely, completely and unrelentingly on the future. All the voters want to speak of today is tomorrow.

2

CHANGE MATTERS. PERIOD.

"Don't tell people what you have already done for them," one of our team members presciently noted in a review meeting post another successful election project. "Tell them what you are going to do for them."

This is where many politicians stumble. This is where Hillary Clinton stumbled, first in the Democratic primaries of 2008 and then in the presidential elections of 2016.

"There has never been a man or a woman, not me, not Bill, nobody more qualified than Hillary Clinton to serve as president of the United States of America," Barack Obama said in rally after rally.

And he was right.

As an August 2016 Vox piece noted, "It's true Clinton has more foreign policy experience than most recent nominees. She's far more politically experienced than Obama was. And due to her time as first lady, she's even actually lived in the White House."

Thirty years of public life bore witness of her over-qualification, and she rightly boasted in these achievements often: work for the Children's Defense Fund, her fight for universal healthcare and women's rights as first lady, dogged battle for New York after the 9/11 terrorist attacks as junior Senator, and her globally celebrated gig as Secretary of State for her country, amongst others.

This was a woman who had dedicated her life to the cause of public service, and done plenty for her countrymen and women in the decades that she had committed herself to public life.

But when it came to the 2016 presidential elections, voters just didn't care for all the things she had purportedly done for them, many of them even seeing this repeated pitch as a sense of entitlement: "I have done all these things for you, and to reward me, now you should make me your president."

Voters said no. And not only did they say no, they swung in the totally opposite direction, instead selecting a man in Donald J Trump who had no history of working for anyone or any interest other than himself.

Pitching what you have done in the past no longer works. Its era has decidedly ended.

The same danger caught and destroyed the candidacy of Goodluck Jonathan for the Nigerian presidency in 2015.

"Buhari did not buy a single rifle when he was head of state," Jonathan said of his opponent who was Nigeria's leader for only one year as opposed to his five. He went on to list all of the things he had done for Nigeria, and for which Nigerians should presumably be grateful – everything from investment in youth enterprise to remarkable strides in agriculture.

Voters have two visceral reactions to this self-centered argument. First, they reject the assumption that they should assess the positives only while ignoring the negatives. And often, with career politicians, they find that the negatives outweigh the positives.

Second, voters seem to understand that dynamic a bit differently. This was a contract – citizens paid for their elected and unelected representatives to do a job. In return the representatives, in addition to being paid, get prestige, access, networks and power. To expect gratitude for the process of doing your job now increasingly appears to many citizens as perverse.

The only winning proposition, therefore, is for those who stand for public office to focus, not on what they think they are entitled to by rea-son of doing their jobs, but on what the citizens continue to be entitled to: a government that works for them.

Politicians who rely on the past will always lose the argument. Those who embrace the future will always win it.

This is why the message of change, always powerful in democratic context, has gained renewed urgency in the past decade. Voters, global-ly, are not impressed with the status quo, believing that they have been shortchanged by a club of self-centered elite and their collaborators. Even where they are, they believe they can get a better deal; they believe they deserve a better deal.

Change is the only message that can appeal to this aspiration.

The people of Ghana were tired of their economic situation as well as the incessant power cuts in 2016. This much was clear to anyone who spent time, as we did, focus grouping everyday citizens.

Yet the incumbent insisted on a message predicated on the infra-structure built in the past four years that didn't address the central is-sue of rising costs of living. It certainly didn't help that the people saw waste and corruption in these projects that the John Dramani Mahama government built, and built its campaign on. Citizens felt his opponent's campaign strategy of tying the corruption and waste to the economic sit-uation helped to drive the change agenda.

One of the enduring images of the campaign for us was when our candidate, Addo Dankwa Akufo-Addo went on a drive around town campaigning and as he passed by 'Dubai' (the new interchange Mahama had built) a crowd from that area followed him, singing his praises. This was supposed to be an area firmly in Mahama's corner because of the interchange that he just built.

But the people were tired. They wanted change.

They wanted change for the better No one votes for change into worse. Change means that, in an atmosphere of relentless optimism or idea of possibilities, voters believe that it is possible to get more and to be more.

They might project pessimism in everyday conversation, but voting for new candidates who promise better or different is a testament to hope. It is always a sign that voters believe there is the possibility for new outcomes, and anyone who is able to capture that aspiration, to project and channel its limitless energies, is almost certainly going to win any election.

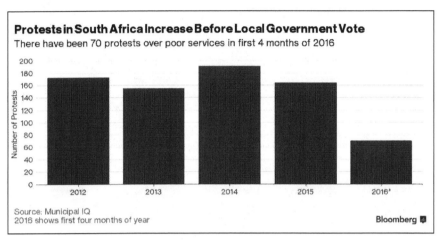

Figure 2: Protests in South Africa Increase Before Local Government Vote

Candidates, who are facing elections therefore, where they are vestiges of the past or current dispensations, need to find ways to connect their legacies to the promise of the future. This has become a non-negotiable reality of electoral processes and environments the world over, and especially in Africa.

That linkage of the past to the future is the only winning combination that can ward off the insurgent oppositions that fresh candidates bring. These fresh candidates might themselves not be entirely new, but if they are disconnected with the status quo, then they present the opportunity for newness, and a different direction. And in this lies the magnetism of their power and appeal.

Whilst it is of course true that government is hard and messy and needs time and patience for it to translate into concrete benefits for citizens, it is the duty of the politician or the political party to make that case.

Nothing can and should be taken for granted in a democracy. It is the duty of politicians to present themselves continually as the willing vehicles for the achievement of popular aspiration, no matter what their past achievements have been. They must reject the temptation completely to project any sense of entitlement to an already beleaguered citizenry.

Report cards of roads built must accompany humility as to roads left to be built; celebrations of airports constructed must be narrated alongside the enormity of the work left to do within the airports. In effect, the exuberance of past accomplishments must be tempered by the humility of the work that abounds to be done.

Citizens now regard governance as a work in progress; a continuum if you will. But they don't mean this as a continuity of present consensus.

Instead it is continuity in the way that the lives of the people can continue to improve, and the work towards that can be discharged by any willing party, be it a person already in office or a person who wants to be in office. Whoever makes the case better; whoever says they will advance this work in progress, or in some cases begin the work of progress, that is the person who wins the vote.

Change is a powerful message because globalisation, capitalism and democracy held such huge, expansive, lavish promises and each has delivered very little compared to the scale of the hope they engendered.

Citizens are caught in this vast expanse of what they see as nothingness, and they are now desperately pulling down systems, breaking down structures and pushing away traditions.

Only those who acknowledge the abundance of work that remains to be done, especially in African nations, need apply. Only those who understand the hunger for change deserve the job.

3

ANGER MATTERS, MORE THAN YOU KNOW

As a confederate culture, Africans don't routinely engage with emotions on an institutional level.

There is after all a reason why South Africa's elegant Truth and Reconciliation Commission prototype is rare still; Rwanda's brave annual contention with its genocidal history is novelty to visitors from the continent, and Nigeria delayed the release of the Biafra movie *Half of a Yellow Sun* from its cinemas to protect the supposedly fragile sensibilities of its citizens.

So it makes sense that research into our behaviours doesn't typically measure, as the rest of the world – or at least the West - does, our emotions.

Polls about Nigerians and the way they see governance routinely ignore a crucial dimension – everyone measures the tangible mostly, yet beneath the tangible attitudes towards corruption, mismanagement and insecurity lie the intangible reality that drives many of reactions and perceptions of government and governance on the continent: anger.

Take, for instance, the results of a May 2012 NOI Gallup Poll. The poll was about corruption, but in fact what it revealed were the emotions behind Nigerian decision-making.

"The results of a recent snap poll have revealed that incessant reports of high profile cases of corruption, particularly the pensions fraud scandal, make Nigerians really sad and angry," the poll noted. "Respondents were asked to express how they feel whenever they hear news reports regarding the increasing cases of corruption in the country. From the results, 52% of the respondents admitted that such reports made them sad, 36% said it made them angry, and 10% said they are tired of hearing about such stories; while 1% said they do not really care."

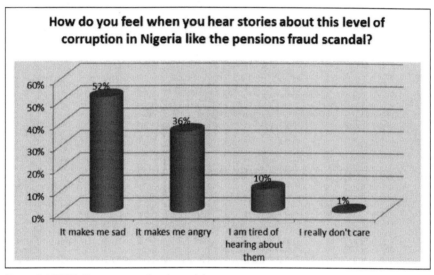

Figure 3: NOI Poll on pensions fraud scandal

It is important to note that when it came to 'I don't care', as a sentiment, only one per cent expressed a lack of strong emotion. That is deeply significant.

Often, Nigerians will say they are tired, but this is mostly a worldly-wise camouflage for the actual, consistent emotion: rage.

It's the same story with another poll on marriage.

"In response to the question of why there is increased domestic violence in the society," the NOI Poll reports. "6 in 10 Nigerians (60%) ascribed the recent increase in domestic violence to poverty. The respondents suggested that poverty has led many people into frustration and anger, and at the slightest provocation, people resort to violence as a means of expressing their frustration with their poor situation."

This is also a global reality.

In April of 2016, Americans reported anger with their government as the bane of their lives.

"Nearly 8 in 10 Americans (78%) said they are dissatisfied or angry with the federal government," an Associated Press–GfK poll found.

It's remarkable, the dichotomy between their anger and their personal lives.

"But at the same time, a greater percentage (84%) of respondents said they are enthusiastic or satisfied with their personal relationships, and 77% said the same about their career," the report notes. "64% said they are satisfied with their financial situation. Respondents said their anger is directed at the overall political system and career politicians who they say don't put constituents first."

People are angry about their governments.

"Those findings are consistent with a presidential election that has been defined, in many ways, by voter anger, as anti-Establishment candidates in both parties have found success by tapping into widespread frustration with Washington."

The co-founder of AOL struggled with this anger in a September 2016 piece announcing his endorsement of Hillary Clinton.

"I think I get why Trump has been such a potent political force this year," he said. "I am well aware that millions of people are angry about their prospects and fearful that the forces of globalization and digitization have left them behind. I also recognize many are frustrated by politics and feel we need an outsider to shake things up. But I don't think Trump is the answer, for those people or for the country."

His realisation turned out to be too late.

"Nearly 7 in 10 [American] voters said they were unhappy with the way the government is working, including a quarter who said they were outright angry," according to preliminary results of exit polls conducted for The Associated Press and television networks by Edison Research. "Three-fourths of those angry voters backed Trump."

And not just in America.

In June 2016, according to a USA TODAY/Suffolk University Poll, "Americans by an overwhelming 4-1 margin agree that the United Kingdom's vote to leave the European Union was a sign of anger and dissatisfaction that can be seen in other countries, including the United States. Just 16% call it an isolated referendum."

One of the respondents said: "I think it is an indication of a broader feeling among people around the world, where they are feeling more and more helpless about controlling things in their own countries. I do happen to believe the refugee crisis and immigration were important components of things that people were unhappy about."

Another said: "It shows that there are people that are definitely not coming up with others, people that feel like they are being left behind. I know that the similarity, the anger at government in general is similar."

"Anger fuels the U.K's brexit campaign," read a headline in the thick of the vote debate. "Growing public hostility toward politicians tightens the British vote on EU membership."

And then, after anger at government made the United Kingdom leave the European Union, anger at government yet continues unabated.

A UK Standard headline in January 2017: "Young people express anger over Theresa May's Brexit strategy, study finds."

In August 2016, the Guardian noted that anger was driving behaviour in South Africa's electoral processes.

"South Africans have shocked the African National Congress (ANC) in local council elections by handing significant gains to the opposition," it said in a piece titled 'South Africa's Local Election Shock Down to Anger'. "But it is clear from the low turnout in crucial areas that the outcome is less about voting for the Democratic Alliance (DA) than taking a stand against the ruling party."

This was the same emotion as in 2014, when NDTV reported: "Anger as South Africa votes."

In June of the same year, the Voice of America noted that South Africa's usually peaceful elections had suddenly taken a violent turn – and the unusualness of this strong sentient.

"Anger over ANC leadership driving latest cycle of violence," it surmised. "Despite South Africa's violent history, it does not have a history of violent democratic elections - in fact, the nation was hailed for its peaceful first democratic poll in 1994. Since 2010, ISS figures show, violent protests have risen - to the point where the nation sees an average of three protests every day.

"Steven Friedman, who heads the Center for the Study of Democracy, says it's fairly easy to pinpoint the source of the anger - and see why so many people are available to throw rocks in the middle of a weekday. South Africa's economy contracted severely at the beginning of this year. Nearly 27% of the population is unemployed. And more than two decades after the fall of apartheid, government statistics show that black South Africans are still significantly poorer than their white counterparts."

Who is angry - the poor, the desperate? No.

"The most angry group of South Africans today is not unemployed people in the townships," he said. "The most angry group of South Africans, who also have the capacity to do something about their anger, are black middle-class South Africans. And they are angry precisely because, in their view, they have the qualifications that their parents and grandparents didn't have, they have some of the job opportunities that their grandparents and parents didn't have, and in their view, they encounter the same racial attitudes that their grandparents and parents encountered."

Anyone who has paid close attention to the defeat of Goodluck Jonathan in Nigeria in 2015, John Dramani Mahama in Ghana in 2016, and the disgrace of Yahya Abdul-Aziz Jemus Junkung Jammeh in Gambia, also in 2016, already gets the message.

The one thing voters across the world are, today, is angry. Without a doubt, it is the number one driver of electoral choices anywhere in the world, as we speak.

And that anger, fairly and squarely, is targeted at governments and politicians.

It is pulling down structures, powering populists, upturning systems and demolishing establishments.

It is the most powerful tool for citizens, and politicians who understand what truly matters for citizens.

Let those who have ears hear.

4

ESTABLISHMENTS MATTER

You probably don't hear a lot about Botswana, but you should.

Since its independence in 1966, it has had four presidents. All of them have respected the constitutional term limits, handing over power peacefully, right from the legendary Seretse Khama.

Khama handed over to Quett Masire, who handed over to Festus Mogae, who handed over power to Khama's son, Ian Khama; all of these done against the background of peace, respect for institutions and the strengthening of the economy and polity that had begun from its independence.

"Botswana, which shares a border with Zimbabwe, has for decades been mainland Africa's brightest star, a country that has gone from dust-bowl poverty to middle income status in a generation," TIME has reported of the country. "Where elections are peaceful, politicians retire voluntarily, civil society is vibrant and where natural resources (in Bostwana's case, diamonds) are not a curse or a spur to corruption and violent theft, but a blessing shared by all."

The Encyclopedia Britannica captures the quiet dignity that has attended the administrations and retirements of Botswana's leaders, through its entry on Mogae.

"In other respects Mogae continued the policies of his predecessor and successfully steered the BDP through the 1999 elections. He made himself internationally distinctive among African leaders by acknowledging the international scientific consensus surrounding the HIV/AIDS epidemic. President Mogae invited international assistance and, in a June 2001 speech before the UN General Assembly, described the epidemic as a national crisis that threatened the very survival of his people. Mogae was viewed as a shy but principled technocrat who did not shrink from the highest responsibilities. His background at the IMF and his criticism of the repressive regime of Robert Mugabe in Zimbabwe, however, left him open to being seen as too pro-Western.

"After relinquishing the presidency to Khama in April 2008, Mogae was elevated to the status of elder statesman. Later that year Mogae was the recipient of the Mo Ibrahim Prize for Achievement in African Leadership, which carried a $5 million award over 10 years, a $200,000 annual lifetime stipend thereafter, and a discretionary $200,000 sum to be awarded (per year, for a decade) to Mogae-designated "good causes." In the following years, Mogae continued to have an impact on politics but on a global scale as he took centre stage as a speaker or panelist at various international conferences, lending his expertise to a range of topics, notably discussions about achieving growth in Africa and halting the AIDS scourge affecting that continent."

The Botswana Democratic Party (first known as the Bechuanaland Democratic Party) has won a clear majority of the votes every election, not by the violent suppression of dissent or the delegitimisation of opposition, but by the steady maintenance of the legacy from Khama to Khama.

It is very difficult to bring down the ruling party, or to mount an opposition campaign in this environment. The citizens are not uniformly pleased, as all citizens of any free country cannot be, but they are certainly satisfied with the progress and stability of their country.

In essence, despite the fact of a stable establishment in this nation for 51 years, the citizens see no need to change the status quo or, as they must see it, to interrupt the steady growth that they have witnessed. They are absolutely fine with the establishment that they have.

This is after all the country where Masire, while he was still in office, chose instead to align with a movement to limit his own term in office. In 1997, constitutional amendments were approved that limited the Presidency to two five-year terms, while lowering the voting age from 21 to 18.

Mogae explained the imperative of this selflessness, in an interview.

"There is always the danger that if a leader stays in power for too long there is an 'immense psychological block' amongst citizens who 'don't know whether they can be led by anybody else', resulting in 'trouble and confusion'," he told ThisIsAfrica. "Just look at the likes of Malawi's Hastings Banda," he said, "or Zambia's Kenneth Kaunda. They ruled for a very very long time, and as a result when they left everything went seriously wrong.

"I am apprehensive about people who have done the right thing - like the president of Rwanda, like the president of Uganda. I am apprehensive that when you rule, you reach a peak of your performance and you then begin to decline, and after a while you begin to mistake your personal interest for the national interest, and there is a danger that you may end up betraying the very values for which you stood."

It calls to mind Senegal's Macky Sall, who of his own will proposed to cut his own term in office by two years. The 55-year old had in 2012 defeated the incumbent, Abdoulaye Wade, who wanted a third term in office, and then he decided to do more.

Sall said he was doing this to "strengthen democracy."

The constitutional reforms referendum was held in March 2016, and the constitution was changed, shortening the president's mandate from seven to five, approved by 62% of voters. Sall wanted the reforms to apply immediately, but voters insisted it should begin in 2019.

Interestingly, the reforms included other measures to significantly weaken the office of the president, including "constitutional recognition for the leader of the opposition, enhanced powers for local authorities and changes to rights on land ownership and natural resources."

You see, voters are not mad. They don't routinely embark on suicidal exercises to unseat establishments that act rationally and responsibly and that appear to be hearkening to their voices. There is an anti-establishment wave blowing across the world yes, but there are nations – democratic, free nations – where this wind cannot take root because the existing establishment works for the people.

So here is the crux: establishments matter.

If they act with humility and efficiency, citizens maintain them as the vehicle for ongoing change. If they act with arrogance and insularity, citizens send them packing, and replace them with alternatives – sometimes, any alternative.

Citizens – voters – are not crazy. They understand clearly the imperatives of democracy. They know that power corrupts and they get that democracies in their essence entrench power structures when people win elections. They know, essentially, that establishments are a byproduct of democracies.

Establishments are of course formal and informal custodians of power across crucial levers in society, working together to maintain what its leading lights consider the needed stability of that society. Democracy is simply the process of changing this balance and the composition of this establishment from time to time, in order to maintain a useful equilibrium of performance and accountability.

Citizens know this.

They know that when they go out to vote, and vote out an existing group of power brokers, they are replacing an old establishment with a new one.

The question is: what kind of establishment do they have and what kind of establishment do they want?

People who want power – for whatever reasons – have to have an understanding of the delicate balance between leader and led, between politician and voter, in a functioning democracy.

It's a ceding of power and control by a mass of people to a very small group. It's the handover of the boundaries that govern existence. In return, the people expect a posture of humility and deference; one that continues to locate legitimacy and authority in popularity.

There are those who accuse politicians of pandering. But pandering is essential to democracy. A representative sent by constituents to a legislature is not there of her own accord to join an elite club that prizes its own comity and relationships above the needs of the voter.

The politician isn't there as a free moral agent. She is there as a conduit for the desires and imperatives of the voting public. The moment she begins to lose sight of that fact, the balance of power has tilted unnaturally, and she has ceased to be an asset to the voter.

When a collection of public officials act in this way, they have become an establishment that has gone astray. In any functional democracy, citizens begin to harbor resentments against this set. Continuous resentment towards the crop ultimately leads to a movement of anger. Movements of anger well channeled lead to movements like #OccupyNigeria or #OccupyWallstreet or Brexit.

Usually, establishments that have failed are unprepared, which is natural. If they were prepared, the circumstances would not arise for their removal in the first place. Leaders who are effective know how to connect with their voters in a sustained way, creating a feedback loop that modifies behaviour or produces outcomes that makes both parties happy.

The key to maintaining this balance is humility; the humility of the elected to understand the source of their power, and to keep that source happy.

This humility is also the humility to explain yourself, the humility to understand that your role is not to demand the understanding of the voter, or take for granted the frame of engagement, but to steadily ensure that both voter and voted are on the same page. The burden to create and maintain that frame lies on the person contracted to do a job, and that person is the public office holder.

In the light of Brexit or Donald Trump's win, many have taken to the newspapers, to television or to social media, decrying, essentially, the stupidity of the voting public. Doing that shows a misunderstanding of the power dynamic.

If establishments have lost credibility with the electorate, and with it the power to convince, that is on them and not on the electorate. Citizens are very busy with everyday living, making ends meet and making society run efficiently. In doing that, they outsource decision making, consensus building and action engineering to their elected and appointed leaders.

To take them out of their daily lives and get them to commit to a course of action or a set of imperatives, the politician must understand what drives them, must connect with the issues that matter to them and must empathise with the evolution of their worldviews, actions and decisions. Any politician who is not so deeply connected with the citizen does not deserve to be rewarded with election or re-election. Any system that doesn't maintain this connection is malfunctioning and deserves to be replaced.

Establishments are not the problem.

They are inevitable, and in many cases – everywhere from the United Arab Emirates to Australia –are infinitely useful organs for social cohesion and financial prosperity.

Disconnected, self-involved establishments are the problem; those that forget the source of their power, legitimacy and imperative.

Wherever they emerge, citizens have the right, and the duty, to punish them. Sometimes in punishing them, they over-react and over-correct. But in all these examples, the essential right to punish a recalcitrant establishment should be inalienable.

If the establishments don't like it, then they need to behave themselves.

5

CANDIDATES MATTER, FIRST AND FOREMOST

There are plenty of buzzwords in politics these days: big data, psychological profiles, micro-targeting.

Of course, there have always been buzzwords in politics. Just like there have always been buzzwords in communication. There are always buzzwords in any venture that requires intense competition, the need for differentiation and the potential for endless value.

Politics ticks all of these boxes, so there will continue to be an evolution of the practices that enable superior competition, the skills required to stay on top of the trends and realities, and the language that will evolve to describe the potential and priorities.

There's even more to come in the field as the age of social media expands, as the tools and platforms we deploy to engage the world and to engage governance and politics multiply.

Wherever things evolve to however, the fundamental truth of politics does not change: politics is about voting for people that represent a particular vision.

"Governance is about channeling aspirations," a commenter on David Brook's New York Times piece 'The Trump Elite' noted in March 2017. "The aspirations of a people: what kind of society do we want to live in, how do we want to ensure the common welfare, how do we want to facilitate its growth and prosperity?"

The primary vehicle for articulating, advancing and representing this aspiration is the political leader. In a democracy, this is the politician. While popular aspiration is an imperative, human beings are best able to article the desires and aspirations of other human beings. Human beings understand the common themes that drive us, the common hopes that inspire us and the common actions that advance us.

That human being matters above all else in realising the common aspiration of the people.

The candidate thus becomes the most important part of the democratic process, only surpassed in importance by the citizens exercising their democratic rights themselves.

The right message without a host goes nowhere. People vote for people, people believe in people, people go to war for people. People inspire people to think, to act, to decide, to move, to come together, to progress.

All the messaging in the world, all the ideas in the world, all the great plans and purposes and visions in the world amount to nothing if they cannot find the candidate that embodies this, that expresses it and that symbolises it.

Yes, there are many factors that converge in electoral victory, and many of them rely on systems and institutions that go beyond candidates. There are demographics, party identification, the bread and butter issues important to the voter, and the ability to create a familiarity with voting blocs that some refer to as identity politics.

But all of these factors always need a variable to ignite them in a competitive race, especially when both parties have access to the same existing advantages that come from being smart and well-resourced. The crucial difference becomes: who is the person that can inspire people to believe, and to act?

It achieves two purposes: galvanising natural constituencies, and attracting opposing constituencies and swing voters.

In 2016, the candidacy of Ghana's Addo Dankwa Akufo-Addo was able to push the New Patriotic Party's strongholds of the Eastern region and Kumasi to come out en masse whilst Mahama's candidacy couldn't inspire the traditional Volta base of the National Democratic Congress to come out in matching numbers.

In 2008, Barack Obama inspired Americans from the political Right to vote for a man whose core beliefs were misaligned with theirs because he was a charismatic, inspiring figure who painted the picture of a future that was appealing. Bernie Sanders was a towering enough figure that he almost made socialism – a hitherto radioactive word - mainstream in American political discourse.

Donald Trump – despite rhetoric that was hostile to large swaths of Black and Latino voters – won a higher percentage of those voters than Mitt Romney or John McCain, because he managed to project a persona that connected with the primal aspirations of many voters. This primal person-to-person connection allowed him leapfrog over gaffes and flaws that would have taken down another man at another time.

Figure 4: Trump Counties where Obama Won

Candidates matter. Or, more to the point, candidacies matter (the distinction will be treated below).

In 2016, the so-called Obama Coalition didn't turn up for Hillary Clinton. The young voters, minority voters, and cross-carpeting voters that were expected, and that had showed up as an advantage for the Democratic Party in 2008 and 2012, chose to stay home.

The reason was simple: They were Obama voters. Their votes were principally tied to a man, a candidate that inspired them.

Democrats should have known. Two years earlier, after the democratic rout of the 2014 mid-term elections, the number crunchers at RealClearPolitics.com warned about the reality that was to come.

"No matter how you slice it, demographic changes in the midterm electorate account for a relatively small portion of the Democrats' problems in 2014," they had said. "The real difference between 2012 and 2014 isn't changes in the demographic makeup of the electorate. It is changes in the way that demographic groups voted. This, in turn, has everything to do with the president's job approval rating.

"On Election Day 2012, the president had a 49.9 percent job approval rating and a 47.4 percent disapproval rating. In 2014, by contrast, the president had a 42 percent job approval rating, and a 53.3 disapproval rating. Notably, this isn't ascribable to likely voter screens; the highest the president has been in polls of adults since June was 45 percent.

"This low job approval interacted with state partisanship more heavily than it did with state demographics. After all, Obama was popular enough in 2012 in places such as Montana and North Dakota to enable Democratic Senate victories. If Obama's job approval had been 54 percent in the overall 2014 electorate, rather than 44 percent (as exit polls indicated), the Republican purple state wins would not have occurred, and some of the red states would have elected blue senators.

"Of course, this should be intuitive. After all, several models based on "fundamentals" had suggested that Democrats were in trouble in these elections. Yet none of these models, to my understanding, include a variable distinguishing between Democratic performance in midterm elections and in presidential elections. If this were a substantial factor, the models would skew badly toward Democrats in midterms and toward Republicans in presidential elections.

"We might even go a step further and inquire if perhaps what is frequently being called the "presidential" electorate is really simply the "Obama" electorate, something political scientists like John Sides have questioned, and something that Democratic strategists are increasingly fretting about.

"Regardless, the Democrats' problem in 2014 was not simply the map, nor was it mostly a demographic/turnout issue. It was an unpopular Democratic president. If Hillary Clinton (or whoever) does not perform better among these groups in 2016 (and she/he might!), the best turnout machine in the world will not save her or him."

In November 2016, their calculations were proven right.

The Washington Post captured the Hillary Clinton problem in a post-election analysis titled 'How Voters Who Heavily Supported Obama Switched over to Trump'.

"Kenosha, south of Milwaukee and north of the Chicago suburbs where Hillary Clinton was raised, was telling of the threat that sneaked up on Democrats," it wrote. "The industrial economy had been replaced by tourism, but the county was growing. No one would have picked it for a travelogue of trade-racked America.

"And it had voted for Democrats. It voted for Barack Obama, twice. It voted against George W. Bush, twice, and for Bill Clinton, twice. It helped Michael Dukakis carry the state in 1988 and, four years earlier, gave Walter Mondale a five-percentage-point victory over Ronald Reagan. No Democrat had lost since 1972.

"Hillary Clinton lost it; in retrospect, the trend was obvious. In her 2008 loss to Barack Obama, Clinton lost Kenosha County by just three points, as she lost by 18 points statewide. In the 2016 Democratic primaries, Clinton lost the county to Sen. Bernie Sanders by 15 points — despite a closer result across the state. She carried heavily black Milwaukee County, and Sanders carried everything else."

The filmmaker and Democratic activist, Micheal Moore also blogged about this in a viral piece months to the election titled 'Why Trump will win'.

"Let's face it: Our biggest problem here isn't Trump – it's Hillary," he said. "She is hugely unpopular — nearly 70% of all voters think she is untrustworthy and dishonest. She represents the old way of politics, not really believing in anything other than what can get you elected. That's why she fights against gays getting married one moment, and the next she's officiating a gay marriage. Young women are among her biggest detractors, which has to hurt considering it's the sacrifices and the battles that Hillary and other women of her generation endured so that this younger generation would never have to be told by the Barbara Bushes of the world that they should just shut up and go bake some cookies. But the kids don't like her, and not a day goes by that a millennial doesn't tell me they aren't voting for her.

"No Democrat, and certainly no independent, is waking up on November 8th excited to run out and vote for Hillary the way they did the day Obama became president or when Bernie was on the primary ballot. The enthusiasm just isn't there. And because this election is going to come down to just one thing — who drags the most people out of the house and gets them to the polls — Trump right now is in the catbird seat."

Candidates make the crucial difference.

There is a reason the power brokers in the All Progressives Congress pulled all the stops to ensure the candidacy of Muhammadu Buhari in Nigeria's 2015 elections. There was no better symbol for the change message with a national profile that could overcome the institutional disadvantages for opposition candidates in a primitive democracy.

The legend of Buhari the Incorruptible and his unshakeable popularity in the North of Nigeria made it very easy to project upon him the aspirations of a people tired out by corruption and rampant insecurity. Running three times previously and consistently standing as the alternative to a People's Democratic Party behemoth that had only gotten more unpopular made it easy to present him as the change that Nigeria desperately needed.

Because of the strength of this candidacy, it was easy for him to overcome the deep misgivings about his candidacy – the imperfect record of his previous 1984 leadership, the questions of paper trail supporting his educational achievements, his vulnerability to charges of political incitement and the burden of belonging to the same establishment that he was now battling against.

Former Vice-President Atiku Abubakar, burdened by criticisms of corruption himself, could not have been that candidate. Former governor, Rabiu Kwankwaso having none of the nationally mythologised record that made Buhari magnetic could not have been that candidate. Senate President Bukola Saraki, symbol of a political and economic elite that the voting public viewed with deep suspicion, could not have been that candidate. At that time, in that context, for the battle being fought, Buhari's candidacy was one of the very few symbols that could seal the deal.

Without engaging fully the dimensions of the candidate and whether that candidate is the person for the moment and whether that candidate has the capacity to inspire loyalty, goodwill and passion, any other activities including the massive investment of resources, harvesting of data and distribution of messages will be ineffective.

In this case, it is important to note that a candidate and a candidacy can be two different things. A candidate is the human being herself, complete with flaws and weaknesses. The candidacy however, is the way that candidate is presented, consistent with the aspiration to be communicated, getting rid of any distractions and weaving personality into concrete narrative.

A man or woman is a composite of many parts, but not all of those parts are relevant to the establishment of political connection. The candidacy is the communication of the essential parts of that man or woman in ways that consistently reflect the ambitions and desires of the voters.

This means that it is possible to transform a weak candidate into a strong candidate and it is possible for a strong candidate to be mismanaged and misrepresented so that the candidate is misaligned with public communication imperatives.

The assignment of those who are responsible for winning the hearts and minds of the voting public is to find a candidate that is an easy sell to that public, or building a candidacy, block by block.

David Plouffe, who managed the Obama campaign understood this in his assessment post 2016 election.

"In Detroit, Mrs. Clinton received roughly 70,000 votes fewer than Mr. Obama did in 2012; she lost Michigan by just 12,000 votes," he wrote. "In Milwaukee County in Wisconsin, she received roughly 40,000 votes fewer than Mr. Obama did, and she lost the state by just 27,000. In Cuyahoga County, Ohio, turnout in majority African-American precincts was down 11 percent from four years ago.

"It's a reminder that presidential campaigns are driven in large part by personality, not party. Ronald Reagan, President Obama and now Mr. Trump all were able to create electoral coalitions unique to them."

Elections begin with candidacies. And often, they rise and fall on candidates.

If the essential candidacy is defective or inadequate, almost everything else is doomed to fail.

6

PERSUASION MATTERS

Politics is the art of persuasion. Period.

"Persuading people to support a particular candidate or party is an essential test of any political campaign," according to a 2015 Harvard Working Paper on 'Explaining Attitudes from Behavior: A Cognitive Dissonance Approach'.

No one who has worked in politics or pays close attention, however, needed Harvard to confirm this. The entire cycle of political activity is centered around persuading people, to believe in an idea, to act on that idea, to contribute towards the idea, to change their ideas, to change their choices even if they don't change their ideas, or to stay on the path of a particular idea.

This would appear to be common sense, except for the fact that over the past few years as big data has gone from trend to religion, people have begun to forget the fundamentals. Elections are about candidates with messages, and the purpose of the message is to persuade people to take a course of action.

Demographics may be destiny, but destiny can be diverted or truncated based on a politician's powers of persuasion.

It is the power to persuade that swung the entire Southwest that excitedly came out in 2011 to vote for Goodluck Jonathan to decide – in 2015 – to vote for the same Northern hegemony it was so offended by in 1999 that it rejected Olusegun Obasanjo.

The coalition Bola Ahmed Tinubu built and the appeal of Muhammadu Buhari against the background of perceived failings of Goodluck Jonathan, plus the series of images and symbols centered around the powerful message of actual change were enough to overcome every possible impediment that history, geography, and demography could have presented.

In 2012, the New Patriotic Party only won their traditional strongholds of Eastern and Ashanti regions and still got only 47.81% of the vote. But in 2016, when we worked for them, they were able to persuade four more regions to vote for their candidate with messages that were specifically targeted at their needs, resulting in about 53.80%of the vote.

The same is true in much of the world. The United States Democratic Party, buoyed going into the elections by what it termed demographic advantages from younger voters, Latino voters and African Americans learnt this lesson afresh in 2016.

"America's changing demography doesn't guarantee a progressive majority," the Daily Beast noted in post-election analysis. "Each nominee has to chart a unique course to the White House and build their own majority. This means that the art of political persuasion is still more important to winning presidential elections than the mechanics of mobilization."

Obama's candidacy in 2008 and his own powerful message of change was enough to persuade a huge swath of Americans post 9/11, to ignore the middle name 'Hussein' as well as years of racially charged history and his own thin resume.

The entire architecture of political action lies at the intersection of "social psychology, psychology, and behavioral economics about how humans act and how preferences are formed" and it assumes that even though normally humans are "rational actors" who will act in a way consistent to their beliefs, previous actions and world views, there is a force so powerful that it can lead both to a cognitive dissonance – where people fall out of step with their own supposed convictions, or act against their own self-interest, or adjust their political preferences.

That force is persuasion.

The human being is nothing if not a thinking being, and not just a thinking being, but a feeling being, a reacting being, a receptive being. It is that ability to change, to adapt, to reconcile, and to evolve that distinguishes us above everything else from other sentient beings. Our being is centered on our capacity to embrace new experiences, to accept new information and to process new knowledge.

Politics would be nothing and thus impossible without this reality. There would be no point to candidacies, elections, manifestos, referendum, politicking, conventions and the entire works if human beings didn't have the capacity to respond and to evolve.

And that means any politician who relies on the past to predict the future is defying the actual forces that determine human behavior.

Yes, humans are predictable and act in groups most of the time, usually based on an established pattern of needs, wants and actions. But the entire utility of politics lies on the fact that they can be spoken to, they can be carried along and they can be persuaded.

"What do you have to lose?" was the remarkably pointed argument Donald Trump used as he tried to get Black voters to overcome his offensive attack on Barack Obama's United States citizenship. And, despite the ridicule from a media dead certain that demographics were unshakeable, his message broke through. NBC exit polls from the election showed that he got "29 percent of the Hispanic vote on Tuesday compared to Romney's 27 percent in 2012. With blacks, exit polls show Trump claimed 8 percent of the vote to the previous Republican nominee's 6 percent."

This was a candidate routinely called a racist. But his message appeared to break through. Because, "the art of political persuasion matters more than the mechanics of mobilization."

Democrats had the better operation, according to all pre and post-election reports. A robust data operation, a fine-tuned Get Out the Voter machine, a flawless campaign, and an alignment of the stars that led to the only candidate in recent history to have the uniform endorsement of every mainstream national media outfit. And yet they lost, despite running a mobilisation machine that was, to all intent and purpose, well-functioning and well oiled.

This happened because Trump had a message that was deeply persuasive: he would shake things up in Washington.

According to the Daily Beast piece, "exit polls showed 63% of voters agreed (with Hillary Clinton) that Trump lacked the temperament to be President—but a fifth of them voted for him anyway. Evidently, their desire to shake up Washington outweighed their qualms about Trump's sociopathic personality and total lack of political experience."

The rest of the piece bears repeating:

"She fell back on 'experience,' while he at least offered restive voters a theory of big change, however implausible the details. And while she succeeded in deepening public doubts about Trump, she failed to engage anxious white working class voters in a conversation about their economic and cultural discontents.

"Even in this era of extreme polarization, presidential elections are two-sided affairs. Candidates must energize their core supporters and get them to the polls. But they also have to frame appeals to a growing cohort of independents and to soft partisans of the other party. No Democrat was going to convert blue-collar whites en masse, but they didn't need to. Empathetic but straight talk to these voters could have tempered their enthusiasm for Trump and hostility toward Democrats on the margins. In a contest decided by 100,000 votes in a few swing states, that might have been enough.

"Unlike Trump, Clinton offered a richly detailed policy agenda in her 250-page policy book, *Stronger Together*. Lacking overarching themes or vision, however, the book is a prosaic collection of programmatic promises to Democrats' target constituencies.

"Which brings us to Team Clinton's second and related strategic failure: A message and electoral strategy tailored narrowly to the demands of identity politics. The Clinton campaign bet heavily on recreating Obama's huge advantages with groups that are growing in the

U.S. electorate: minorities, millennials, single women and secular voters. Obama's success had convinced many Democrats they could count on this "Rising American majority" to maintain their lock on the Electoral College.

"Such demographic determinism, however, proved unavailing as Clinton won smaller margins among these groups than Obama. That was not a problem in overwhelmingly Democratic states on the two coasts but it was devastating in the more thinly blue rustbelt states of Wisconsin, Michigan and Pennsylvania. And Clinton's enthusiasm gap even extended to white voters, with whom she also underperformed Obama."

If people don't buy your message, political machines can't save you.

Nigeria's Goodluck Jonathan made that costly calculation in 2015. He counted on too many variables in a time of fundamental dissatisfaction, and at a time when the electoral commission – a creation of his – was determined to be impartial.

He relied on the People's Democratic Party juggernaut, he relied on the primitive power of ruling party fundraising, he relied on a history of winning elections from the ruling party, the unfailing power of incumbency and the control of all state actors including national media.

But he failed.

He failed because his candidacy and his message were unable to convince people in a time of an intense desire for change that he was the man for the moment.

Edward James Bernays, often called "the father of public relations" and with a keen scholarly interest in politics, propaganda and persuasion, identified three elements of successful persuasion – technique in delivery, spin in the interpretation and persistence in forcing mindsets.

Of course, the line between persuasion and manipulation – both on two sides of the art of engineering consent – can be thin. At what point is the language moving a person towards a willful course of action, and at what point is it overpowering the person's will? This invisible line is difficult to identity of course, the art of persuasion belonging in the realm of emotions and decision-making. But walking that fine line is where most successful politicking lies.

Now, persuasion depends on language. It is the conversion of the key message of a campaign, translating that into the symbols and language that connects with the voters that inspires those voters to take action.

"In a modern democratic society, politics is persuasion, and persuasion is conducted predominantly through language," Alan Partington writes in *Persuasion in Politics*. "Evaluative language is defined as the linguistic methods of persuading us of what is *good* or *bad* – in a democracy, one presumes, good or bad for us, the people."

This is a process of focusing on what the voter values, how the things that appeal to the voter appeal to the voter. Not you, the voter.

"This rule of salesmanship, as we demonstrated in a series of experiments detailed in a recent article in the journal Personality and Social Psychology Bulletin, also applies in political debate — i.e., you should frame your position in terms of the moral values of the person you're trying to convince," Robb Willer, a professor of sociology at Stanford, writes in the New York Times. "But when it comes to politics, this turns out to be hard to do. We found that people struggled to set aside their reasons for taking a political position and failed to consider how someone with different values might come to support that same position.

"To do it, you have to get into the heads of the people you'd like to persuade, think about what they care about and make arguments that embrace their principles."

It sounds easy. But it isn't at all easy – it starts from the process of the politician focusing on what citizens want rather than what the politician thinks they want, moving away from the frame of mind centered on self to one that springs from the active desires of people.

There are five identified rules for this.

The first is to understand the audience – to understand who can be persuaded and who cannot be, why they can be persuaded and on what terms they can be persuaded.

The second is to start from the place where you agree with them. "In talking to people, don't begin by discussing the things on which you differ," Dale Carnegie wrote in *How to Win Friends and Influence People*. "Begin by emphasizing—and keep on emphasizing—the things on which you agree. Keep on emphasizing, if possible, that you are both striving for the same end and that your only difference is one of method and not of purpose."

You start from that place of agreement and move them to a place of decision. "Our goal is not to change people's minds, it is to show them that they agree with us already," Bernie Horn has written on DailyKos. com. "We do this by using empathy and expressing our values."

The third is to deploy empathy. Ensure that you completely and totally understand what the audience is feeling. You don't preach at them, you don't talk at them, you channel them. They must feel like you have lived that experience, that you understand it, that you validate it. The fourth is to align with that understanding by projecting values that express this common aspiration – what do the voters want, and how does your candidacy hope to achieve that aspiration?

The fifth is to embrace the audience – tightly. Tell the story in the light of them and them alone. Not why this party deserves to win because of all it has done, but why this party will be the one to deliver for them. "It is hard to convince persuadable voters to support a policy that appears to benefit people other than themselves, their families and their friends. When faced with a proposed government policy, people look for themselves in the proposal. People want to know 'what the proposal will do for me and to me?'."

You can summarise this into three crucial points: start by agreeing with your audience (if you don't agree with them, that they need change for instance, how can they trust you to represent them effectively?), show them how they stand to benefit, and say all of this in their language and not your own, in a way that acknowledges that their lives don't revolve around you. They are busy living their lives – it's your job to explain to them why they should make choices that align with your imperatives. It's your job to make that case.

The candidate should not be the center of attention. The voter should be the center of her attention.

"Persuadable voters aren't like partisan activists," Horn added. "They don't pay much attention to politics, public policy or political news. They don't understand political ideologies. They don't care a lot who wins elections. In general, they're the citizens who are least interested in politics. After all, with America's highly polarized parties, anyone who pays attention has already taken a side. You need to accept persuadable voters as they are, not as you wish they were. They don't necessarily know what you know or believe what you believe. And yet, if you empathize with persuadable voters and use language they understand, you have the upper hand in any argument."

And as Africa's dictators and entrenched politicians suddenly have to contend with a changing landscape where they cannot rely on manipulation of electoral commissions, controlling the press and intimidating the public, this is a skill they will have to learn.

This is good news for the opposition or for upstarts. Because they have spent years having to do this the hard way, they have learnt what works for citizens, what drives them, and how to speak to them directly.

This is an advantage they can wield moving forward in races where they are out-raised and out-gunned.

There is an African electorate hungry for people who can powerfully make their case.

7

MESSAGING MATTERS
ABOVE ALL ELSE

The key to persuasion really is the message: What am I saying to people that will make them vote for me?

One of the dangers of this can be its simplicity. Everyone assumes they know what a message is: of course, to talk to anybody you need to have a message.

But a message is much more complex than that. Messaging – or what you can call effective messaging – is alignment of the purpose of your running (taking for granted that in an ideal world, no candidate should be running without a distinct purpose) with the mood and desires of the electorate.

This is where many candidates miss it. Because getting a message that resonates with audiences is not easy. So many people confuse messaging with issues i.e. 'If I do a list of solutions to the issues people are facing, then they will vote for me.'

'If I tell them that Northern Nigeria needs schools and I have built *Almajiri* schools. If I tell them that feeding is our most urgent imperative and I have invested in agriculture. If I tell them Igbos need airports and

I am the one that has built airports, with more airports to come' – this is how the Goodluck Jonathan campaign approached 2015; as a laundry list of issues and achievements.

Marshall, quoted previously, mentioned this same laundry list in Clinton's 250-page policy book, *Stronger Together* " which lacked a unifying theme and instead robotically targeted promises at various Democratic constituencies: "For labor, a hike in the minimum wage and opposition to the Transpacific Trade Agreement; pay equity for women; for young voters, free tuition at state colleges for middle class families and caps on student loan payments; criminal justice reform for African Americans; for Hispanics, a humane path to legalization for illegal immigrants; strong anti-discrimination measures for the LGTB community, and so on."

What it didn't have was an overarching consistent message. From the beginning Trump had 'Make America Great Again' (MAGA). It was so powerful in the primaries that it was transplanted to the general elections without missing a heartbeat. MAGA was a statement of American greatness, leveraging on the constant desire for a golden age of American perfection, and projecting himself as the singular person who understood that imperative and could make it a reality for the future.

Nigeria's All Progressives Congress (APC) had a constant message for almost three years and it was poignant and simple and lethally effective: it was "change".

Change was the idea that all that existed was uniformly and overwhelmingly bad, and the urgent imperative was to break it all down and give it to someone, anyone but the incumbent. You build such a large tent, and it is big enough to accommodate almost anybody. It wasn't just a message tailored for Muhammadu Buhari's candidacy, it was a message tied to everything and everyone who stood against what Goodluck Jonathan represented.

"For all his failings, we know what Buhari stands for," Peter Oshun wrote in February 2015. "We know he won't tolerate corruption and incompetence in whatever administration he presides over. Those whose tendencies are corrupt are removing themselves from his vicinity or from his party, or subtly adjusting their rhetoric or behaviour to comply with his mien. His very presence at the apex of the APC conveys the impression, not so accurate in reality, that the APC is a party of non-corrupt competent people. It has a galvanising effect in convincing all those who still believe that standards matter that their thankless efforts might not be in vain after all. That is the power of symbolism in leadership, the tacit message a personality can convey to millions just by being."

What was Jonathan's message though? Transformation, he said. But it really was at its core 'continuity'– the continuity of the transformation he insisted he had presided over as leader of the country. The problem was that this didn't jive with the prevailing mood of the nation – one that signified a certain rudderlessness and insecurity.

To make a case that this was transformation that should continue was jarring to a lot of people; to ask them to maintain the status quo without painting an active picture of how the future was going to be distinctly, significantly different, even worse.

It was incredibly easy for us as strategists to destroy that message: we simply took all of the things that had gone wrong in Nigeria, and planted simple messages across the highways, television spots and newspapers asking: "Is this transformation?"

Indeed, when we transplanted our work to Ghana, it was like a gift to see that John Dramani Mahama had taken up the same themes of transformation, obviously learning extremely little from the failed candidacy of Goodluck Jonathan. The same situations existed – the same tired electorate, the same narrative of corruption and the same desperate desire for a different candidate who would channel the dissatisfaction.

Effective messaging is the art of creating a simple, powerful response the prevailing desire of the electorate. Not what you want to say, not what you want to do, not what you think is important, but – what is your answer to the question the voter is asking today? What is your response to the popular aspiration?

When the voter goes to the polls, she is answering the question "who is the person who best answers the questions you ask of the world and of your country?"

"It is a narrative that explains why voters should favour you over your opponent(s)," the book, *Voicing Our Values: A Message Guide for Candidates* explains. "The idea is to frame the question you want voters to answer as they vote. 'Which candidate will protect me from crime?' or 'Which will stop the developers from ruining our neighborhood?' or 'Which will side with the middle class against the rich?'"

If voters are desperate for a change, the incumbent's answer shouldn't be 'no you don't need change, what you need is experience'. Far from that, the incumbent's answer should be 'this is why I am the change you represent. This is how exactly my experience translates into the actual, specific kind of change that you are looking for'.

"Whatever the theme, notice that all of them are about 'you' and 'your'," *Values* notes. "We ardent progressives like to talk about the common good, but that is not what average voters care about. Voters are focused on themselves, their families, and their own communities. Your theme has to be about how you are going to help them, personally. When you highlight issues, it should be to show how you will directly and indirectly improve the voters' quality of life. Parks will be cleaner; traffic problems will improve; government offices will serve citizens better; unwanted real estate development will be thwarted."

Answer their questions. Not yours.

In answering their questions, you have to keep it simple. Now, this is especially hard for legacy politicians or incumbents to do. They are so focused on all they think they have done that it is very difficult to cut out the fat and focus on the meat that the voter actually cares about. Yes, you have done all of these things, but while you are proud of them, do the voters care?

Focus on the voter. Focus on the one thing that galvanises voters above all else, keep the message simple (no campaign should be based on anything more than three major anchor-promises) and speak the language in a way that shows that you are focused on them, and only on them.

"(Trump's) nostalgic message clearly convinced enough people to secure him the presidency," an analysis on Mashable noted the day after the American elections. "Many have written about the improbability of being able to turn back time to the days when America led the world in manufacturing. The rise in automation, the need for skilled labor and the continuing increase in manufacturing output are just a few of the reasons cited that would keep jobs from returning.

"Still, it was a message that worked. It was simple and it resonated with voter concerns. By the end of the campaign, Clinton, along with the Obamas, was largely campaigning simply against Trump as a candidate and not forwarding a cohesive, straightforward message about what mattered most to swing state voters. Mere days before the election, reporters at CNN discussed the complicated and unclear economic message that Clinton used to woo voters. 'If you ask someone to describe in 30 seconds what Hillary Clinton's views on the economy is, she still hasn't gotten there,' Chief National Correspondent John King said."

Everything else flows from this. Every ad buy, every press release, every speech, every social media post should flow from this simple, consistent, citizen-driven central message. It is the anchor for persuasion.

"The risk in the (Clinton) campaign is, it doesn't fit easily on a bumper sticker," Alan Krueger, a Princeton economist and former chairman of President Obama's Council of Economic Advisers who advised Clinton, told The Washington Post.

It didn't help that the crux of her messaging 'Stronger Together' didn't come from answering the questions voters were asking but were a response to what she decided was Trump's divisive politics. It was perhaps weak enough that the de facto slogan of the campaign became #ImWithHer, which to be honest might have been a more effective emotional driver.

"The email was one of thousands released by WikiLeaks on Monday that provided a revealing glimpse into the inner workings of Mrs. Clinton's campaign," a New York Times story in October proved that messaging was at the core of the problem. "They show a candidacy that began expecting a coronation and was thrown badly off course by a misreading of the electorate and a struggle to define what she stood for.

"Stretching over nine years, but drawn mainly from the past two years, the correspondence captures in detail the campaign's extreme caution and difficulty in identifying a core rationale for her candidacy, and the noisy world of advisers, friends and family members trying to exert influence."

"This staggering fact underlines the perceived lack of enthusiasm with which Clinton's campaign entered Election Day. If she could have convinced less than a million more eligible voters — people who had formerly voted Democratic — to turn out to the polls for her, she would have won the election."

Nothing can replace messaging because it is the crux of persuasion. Technology enables not replaces.

"For four straight election cycles, Democrats have ignored research from the fields of cognitive linguistics and psychology that the most effective way to communicate with other humans is by telling emotional stories," Dave Gold has written in Politico. "Instead, the Democratic Party's affiliates and allied organizations in Washington have increasingly mandated "data-driven" campaigns instead of ones that are message-driven and data-informed. And over four straight cycles, Democrats have suffered historic losses.

"After the 2008 election, Democrats learned all the wrong lessons from President Obama's victory, ascribing his success to his having better data. He did have better data, and it helped, but I believe he won because he was the better candidate and had a better message, presented through better storytelling."

Campaigns who haven't figured out a message that answers the primal voter questions need to spend all their time focusing on it. If it doesn't resonate, it can't be sold. If it isn't organic, it can't be manufactured.

It's never about you, it's never about your candidate, it's never about what you think it should be about, and it's always about the voter.

It's always about what the voter wants answered, and how effective your answer is to that question. Period.

8

INSPIRATION ABSOLUTELY MATTERS

The one thing that 12 years of working with citizens at our media group, RED, has taught us is this: citizens always want, desperately, to be inspired.

People live in a world that is often depressing, where problems are often intractable and the media presents evidence daily – even when the data says otherwise – that everything is getting worse, everything can only get worse, and everyone is doing badly.

In the midst of all of this, people desperately want to believe in something bigger than themselves – something that speaks to their deepest desires for a world that works, and a country that helps them achieve those desires. They want a realm of possibility of a better place, and want to be led towards that place.

Countries are constantly on an Exodus journey.

In the minds of many citizens, where they are is unacceptable, even deplorable, there is grass greener on the other side, and all they need is a Moses to take them from this place of slavery into a Promised Land.

"We have a lot of crises in this country, but maybe the foundational one is the Telos Crisis, a crisis of purpose," David Brooks wrote recently in the New York Times. "Many people don't know what this country is here for, and what we are here for. If you don't know what your goal is, then every setback sends you into cynicism and selfishness."

Purpose, he said, is "the narrative that unites us around a common multigenerational project, that gives an overarching sense of meaning and purpose to our history."

"It should be possible to revive the Exodus template, to see Americans as a single people trekking through a landscape of broken institutions. What's needed is an act of imagination, somebody who can tell us what our goal is, and offer an ideal vision of what the country and the world should be."

Every nation has this narrative. For most African countries, this narrative often stems from colonial independence.

You can find this in Nigeria. Nigerians speak wistfully all the time about the times just after independence when the United States dollar was equivalent to the Nigerian naira and a honest day's work was equal to value and respect. You see it often in the wistfulness for the days of murdered leader, Murtala Mohammed and the organising vision he brought to his duty as Head of State, however brief.

And that narrative is what, principally, drove the myth of Muhammadu Buhari for the 20 years since he was last Nigeria's Head of State. Over that time, the brevity of his regime gave ways to nostalgia for what could have been. The symbols of discipline and responsibility that he evoked, inspired Nigerians to connect to a national narrative of possibilities, to a sense of cohesion and purpose.

It enabled him become a symbol; allowing a man who doesn't give the best speeches to suddenly become an inspiration machine, galvanising a nation to believe.

If politics is about persuading people, then the most effective way to persuade them is to inspire them.

Inspiration is like magic. It enables people leapfrog over their disagreements with you, to believe in your over-arching message. It inspires them to cross over and even abandon their worldviews and values to give you a chance.

Inspiration leads to passion, and in an election there is nothing more valuable than an army of passionate people; people who simply believe in something that they think is bigger than themselves; something that makes so much sense to them that they abandon self-interest for enlightened self-interest, or selflessness.

And that inspires people above everything else? Big visions.

No one is inspired by a laundry list of accomplishments, plans or promises. It is impossible to inspire people with detail, and for good reason. What inspires people is all of the important details tied into a giant vision that paints a picture of the future people want to see, or the future people need to see.

Bernie Sanders had this in the United States Democratic primary of 2016. A contributor on Quora.com simplified what made him electric.

"The guy is carrying the weight of the problems and suffering of the people he cares for," he wrote. "In case you noticed from your own life experience, the words of such people who have such burdens on their shoulders hold a strange weight as compared to the words of the people who live a comfortable life without any concern for their fellow men. The former makes you stop and listen, the latter sounds shallow and intangible. All this is amplified by being honest - someone saying what he means has power to pierce indifference.

"And he is saying all the right things, stuff which a lot of people are already consciously aware of, or stuff that people have subconsciously noticed. He is telling the right things that need to be told, about right things that need to be done, at the exact right time as they are necessary."

Herein lies the ultimate flaw of his opponent, the Hillary Clinton candidacy. The candidate and her message did not inspire.

"But millennial voters may not turn out to vote if Clinton fails to inspire them," the authors of *When Millenials Rule* wrote in July 2016. "The central argument behind the Clinton campaign is that she is qualified for office. The problem is that millennials want a candidate to inspire them, not win by default. Millennials won't just vote for Clinton because Trump is a bad candidate — she needs to convince them that voting for her will make them better off. Clinton's failure to do this — and her lack of a central message during the primary season — has already led to strong rebuke. Millennials gave Clinton less than 30 percent of their votes in key primaries and nearly precipitated her defeat."

And it is important to remember just how much Sanders inspired people. The IndyStar.com painted a powerful picture in April, 2016.

"Who cares if his policies seem fantastical in this era of broken government? Who cares if the bottom-line numbers show that it would take something equally fantastical to push him to the Democratic presidential nomination? And who cares if many people dismiss him as a socialistic joke? Who cares?

"I didn't see anyone who did Wednesday night in Bloomington as I watched Bernie Sanders lift up a mostly student crowd of about 3,000 on the Indiana University campus, and as I witnessed some things that have been missing from this year's political campaigns. Happiness. Joy. Inspiration. You know, little things like that.

"'Our job is to think big,' the Vermont senator told the raucous crowd. 'Our job is to think outside the status quo.' That's definitely what Sanders' overachieving campaign is doing. And even if you disagree with every bit of policy driving it, it's hard to argue against the benefit of a campaign that has made so many people believe that this country can still do big things, and that politicians can still drive important change. Even if you think there's a more qualified candidate in the race, as I do, you have to appreciate Sanders for pushing the debate forward on important issues and providing us with a needed reminder that all those reports about idealism's death were somewhat exaggerated.

"'He really tries to include everyone, and to make sure everyone has the same opportunities in life,' freshman Lauren Lad told me just before Sanders took the stage. 'Bernie really is a unique man'. In this so-called Year of the Angry Voter, a year that has been dominated by so much understandable dissatisfaction, Lad's words were refreshing, as was the jovial scene in Bloomington. Thousands of students lined up on a rainy night hours before Sanders' speech (most could not get into the modest-sized auditorium), cheering for a candidate who has made them believe in the art of the possible."

The art of the possible.

That's what inspiration does. It makes people believe in what is possible, even if it is not practicable.

That's what enabled Sanders raise a historic **$229.1** million from over two million small donors giving $27 on the average, without a cent from ubiquitous Political Action Committees. "Precisely because so many of his supporters are emotionally committed and haven't maxed out their donations," Fortune reported. "He has been able to continue reaping a big cash harvest—even when he notches poor results."

And on the flip side, this cost Clinton the election as filmmaker, Micheal Moore had predicted.

"Stop fretting about Bernie's supporters not voting for Clinton – we're voting for Clinton!" he explained in his viral July 2016 piece, 'Why Trump Will Win'. "The polls already show that more Sanders voters will vote for Hillary this year than the number of Hillary primary voters in '08 who then voted for Obama. This is not the problem. The fire alarm that should be going off is that while the average Bernie backer will drag him/herself to the polls that day to somewhat reluctantly vote for Hillary, it will be what's called a "depressed vote" – meaning the voter doesn't bring five people to vote with her. He doesn't volunteer 10 hours in the month leading up to the election. She never talks in an excited voice when asked why she's voting for Hillary. A depressed voter. Because, when you're young, you have zero tolerance for phonies and BS. Returning to the Clinton/Bush era for them is like suddenly having to pay for music, or using MySpace or carrying around one of those big-ass portable phones.

"They're not going to vote for Trump; some will vote third party, but many will just stay home. Hillary Clinton is going to have to do something to give them a reason to support her — and picking a moderate, bland-o, middle of the road old white guy as her running mate is not the kind of edgy move that tells millenials that their vote is important to Hillary. Having two women on the ticket – that was an exciting idea. But then Hillary got scared and has decided to play it safe. This is just one example of how she is killing the youth vote."

To those who claim inspiring candidates sell fantasies, it is important to say this, there is nothing essentially deceptive about inspiration.

History has shown that despite whatever challenges humans face, nothing inspires creativity and action, especially over the impossible, more than a people who are bound together by a common purpose that fires them up.

Inspiration is the most effective tool to sell an authentic message.

Goodluck Jonathan inspired in 2011. He was the symbol of breaking boundaries – a minority candidate who was not part of any of the cabals that had previously held Nigeria hostage. His emergence looked like luck and, in a superstitious country, spoke of the hand of the divine.

People felt they could get behind that. This was a blank slate upon which Nigerians could project hopes and dreams and possibilities.

If you're looking at the reason his candidacy failed to catch fire in 2015, it is because he stopped being inspirational. His story stopped inspiring. People went in search of new inspiration.

"When we are met with cynicism and doubt, and those who tell us that we can't," Barack Obama said in his 2008 victory speech. "We will respond with that timeless creed that sums up the spirit of a people: yes we can."

It is incredibly difficult to find any electorate across the world who will not be fired up by a sentiment so simple but so powerful, by a candidate with the credibility to communicate this message.

This can be a world of deep and trenchant impossibilities; elections offer citizens the opportunity to believe in something bigger than themselves. Apart from good governance itself, it is the most important gift that democracy presents.

9

AUTHENTICITY MATTERS

"Trump won not because the press failed but because he was selling something more valuable to voters than integrity—honesty and humanity," American media critic Jack Shafer wrote in a piece the day after the last United States presidential elections. "His cause was helped by the fact that his opponent was judged worse or equal on a couple of scores.

"However negative Trump is—and you don't need a refresher course on that, do you?—he was selling a positive vision about greatness and restoration to voters. He slung praise upon a constituency that was starved for the respect of a plain-speaking candidate, and they rolled over on their backs and grinned, tongues akimbo, as he scratched their bellies. For these people he conveyed dignity and the rescue of lost honor. He delivered their payback. He embodied their grievances."

In an age of social media, broken down walls, democratised communication and the rise of Human2Human as the primary means of connecting with people and selling products, authenticity has become the most prized quality in public communication.

The inversion of influence has led to consumers who demand authenticity – whether in detergent commercials or contestants for presidential office.

They want people who transparently think like humans, care about humans, talk like humans, listens to other humans or 'show their human'.

"Right in line with the personality, human brands aren't afraid to let their human show," a presentation by our sister company, Red Media Africa on brand communication in the 21st century has explained. "They laugh, giggle, sing, dance, talk, and may even get frustrated sometimes. They often let you see the people behind the avatars as they know they are their own best ambassador.

"No human being is perfect and no brand is perfect because it is made up and defined by humans. Human brands are humble. They make mistakes and they aren't afraid to own it. Consumers want to see that."

Politicians have become accustomed, like corporations over the years, to essentially, talking down on the consumer. They have forced, by repeated behaviour, public communication to require an unnaturalness that is pointed and overwhelming – not at all aligned to reality, or human behaviour.

As humanity has evolved and social experiences have made communication more intuitive and intimate however, this contrived state of affairs became unsustainable. Audiences began to react negatively to this state of affairs and to demand something that felt truer to them.

It started, as always, with consumer products, filtered upwards to luxury goods, and has inevitably affected politics – the ultimate art of selling that society has constructed.

"With exactly one year to go before America chooses its 45th president, voters left, right and center say they crave "authenticity" in their candidates," the Los Angeles Daily News reported in November 2015. "And though Americans disagree on exactly what the word means in a political context, nobody can deny that the notion of authenticity is having an unprecedented impact on the 2016 race for the White House.

"Fueled by anger at government, partisanship, big money in politics, the hunger for the "real deal" is driving the polls like never before.

Republican Ben Carson, a soft-spoken neurosurgeon who has never held public office but gets high marks from his supporters for his genuineness, is leading Democratic front-runner Hillary Clinton — a former secretary of state, U.S. senator and first lady who has been dinged for seeming cloistered, evasive and inauthentic — by 10 percentage points, a Quinnipiac University poll found this past week.

"Bernie Sanders, Clinton's Democratic rival, has drawn surprisingly big poll numbers, record crowds and millions in contributions with his unabashed democratic socialist populism. And Carson has only now caught up to Republican rival Donald Trump, the "authentic" billionaire who dominated the polls all summer despite often-outrageous, headline-grabbing statements."

Guess who won that election, and guess who started out his bid with just 20% name recognition, but ended up almost snatching the Democratic primary victory from the eight-years-ready Hillary Clinton.

Of course, people who possess authenticity or who are best able to simulate it have always gained the electoral advantage through the years, but the difference in this century, is that audiences now demand it as the price of entry.

What does authenticity mean, though?

The Times defined it as "saying what you mean without apparent handling or scripting and seeming not to care about the consequences."

That 'seeming not to care' clearly led to Trump's ultimate victory.

"Trump, meanwhile, is hailed as a paragon of "telling it like it is" even though his positions on drug legalization, abortion, taxes, gun control, health care, Social Security and Hillary Clinton have all changed dramatically in the past 15 years," the Times noted in a bit of shock.

In the first Democratic debate, former Maryland governor Martin O'Malley must have thought he looked competent and articulate, which is the kind of thing that political consultants have always aspired to remake candidates into. They called it "presidential".

But to observers, the paper noted, he came off "like one of the audio-animatronic robots at Disneyland — programmed and stilted." He came off as inauthentic.

This demand for authenticity isn't however just a question of how you appear to people, it's a sophisticated assessment of what people notice about how you live your life.

In Ghana, the key issue in the campaign was the economy, and associated with this was corruption. Fortunately, the candidate we worked for, Addo Dankwa Akufo-Addo and his running mate, Dr Mahamudu Bawumia had built careers on those two issues. As a former Deputy Governor of the Ghana Central Bank, he had the credibility and the ability to break down economic issues in a way that regular people understood. When the both of them spoke about corruption and fixing the economy, they had the credibility.

And so people believed them.

"What sets him apart most in my mind is his ability to maintain a position over time, If you go back and look at the things he was fighting for in the late '60s and early '70s, they're pretty much the things he's fighting for now," Vincent Casalaina, 69 – which proves this is not just a millennial desire – said to the Times about Sanders. "Those are issues that are core to his being, and it doesn't matter whether they're in vogue or out of vogue."

There are two major reasons for the authenticity movement.

One, as we have mentioned, is the extreme democracy of the social generation. This democracy has led to an abundance of experience, an abundance of interaction and the perception of options.

"In a democratised media space however – thank God! – consumers now have all kinds of alternatives from all kinds of angles, and so they will not take it anymore," the Red Media African presentation noted. "They no longer have any motivation to act unnaturally because they are so many options for so many things, attention spans are short, and everyone is struggling to gain their attention in a saturated market.

"They are violently demanding by their buying habits that corporations adapt to human behaviour. They must align with how people act, how they think, how they speak, how they actually love the things they love, and how they buy. Then they must interact with them in that true, honest way."

The second reason is that, after decades of the manipulations of modern campaigning, citizens have reached a saturation point where it is time for something new. People got bored, and then they get turned off.

"People are more sensitive this time around to the sense that candidates are going to say one thing and do another — they're done with that," said J. Ann Selzer, an American political pollster.

Of course, no one can truly say if a person is "authentic" or not; you can only really make judgements based on public appearances, and it is true that it is very possible for effective communication strategists working with talented candidates to project authenticity.

But what citizens have decided to do is to judge authenticity by a politician's record and then by a politician's vocabulary.

Because the former can present a complicated picture, the latter has become the important test in many democracies, especially in a time of populism, for determining who the public judges to be authentic.

"I don't care what his actual positions are," American billionaire Mark Cuban wrote about the public standard in a July 2015 piece about Trump. "I don't care if he says the wrong thing. He says what's on his mind. He gives honest answers rather than prepared answers. This is more important than anything any candidate has done in years."

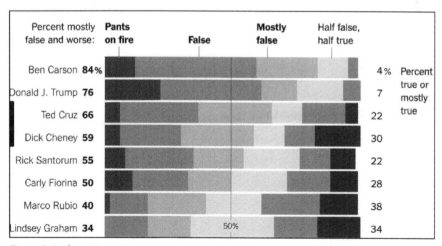

Figure 5: Authenticity matters

About Clinton? A FiveThirtyEight.com headline in September 2015 captured the problem: "No one knows whether Hillary Clinton is authentic."

To be sure, this is not a statement about appropriateness, because in fact, certain character types are more likely to be seen as inauthentic. If you're introverted, not a people person and predisposed to order and meticulousness, you are likely to be seen as too 'planned' and thus seen as inauthentic.

"Humans behave differently in private than they do in front of groups, and audiences expect different things when they know they're listening to a political speech, versus when they're meeting someone one on one," the site argues. "We make a dangerous mistake if we evaluate authenticity on the basis of how a person responds to the artificialities of the American campaign season."

A New York Times piece in October 2015 also makes this point: "The presumption of these claims is that politicians should reveal their true selves to us, and that those who don't have something to hide," it pointed out.

"An alternative explanation is that candidates who appear inauthentic trigger our suspicions about politicians — they don't seem to behave normally, which must mean they are up to something. But few people appear comfortable under bright lights during highly staged events; most of us would act just as awkwardly or unnaturally as Mrs. Clinton or Mr. Romney sometimes do. That behavior is likely to be a reflection of their performance skills, not a lack of authenticity.

"Conversely, we shouldn't assume that politicians who appear to be sincere are actually more genuine or revealing of their true selves," it pointed out. "Like the stars you see telling scripted anecdotes on talk shows, they're often just skilled at performing their public role. As the political scientist Richard Skinner has noted, the personas of popular presidents such as George Washington, Abraham Lincoln and John F. Kennedy were artificial constructions."

Unfortunately the media narrative about authenticity, coinciding with an audience enamoured with this imprecise metric have conspired to rob many candidates of almost certain victory. So it may not be an appropriate standard, but it is one that voters routinely use today.

In *The Politics of Authenticity in Presidential Campaigns*, Erica J Seifert captured how this hole swallowed America's Albert "Al" Gore Jr in 2000.

"The characterization of Al Gore as wooden was so widespread," she wrote. "And the campaigns attempt to dispel that image so well known, that when the candidate and his wife enjoyed a long and passionate kiss at the convention, the ensuing media frenzy focused only on its authenticity.

"Rather than examining the acceptance speech, the poll numbers or the post convention campaign trip, the media scrutinized the convention footage and demanded to know whether Gore's advisors had mandated a timed practice run with the candidate's wife."

"Once these narratives develop, candidates like Mrs. Clinton can get stuck in what I've called the authenticity doom loop — the same fate that plagued Mr. Gore and Mr. Romney," the Times piece noted. "In this phase, candidates are criticized for not being sufficiently authentic and urged to reveal their true selves. But any efforts to demonstrate authenticity prompt the news media to point out that the candidate is acting strategically and is therefore actually still inauthentic. This coverage in turn motivates further efforts to reveal the "real" person, and the pattern then repeats."

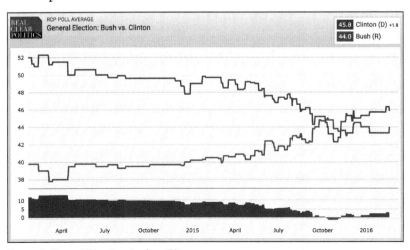

Figure 6: General Election: Bush vs Clinton

In the 2015 Nigerian elections, you had two candidates who could have this label tagged on them. Both Dr. Goodluck Jonathan and Muhammadu Buhari were neither natural public talents nor did they know how to charm a room.

Dr. Jonathan was distinctly uncomfortable in many public setting, turning to reticence or overcompensating with self-deprecating comments like telling CNN's Christiane Amanpour: "You know more than me."

On the same hand, Buhari is notably defensive in public, conditioned by a natural introversion to recoil from attention or uncomfortable conversation. This trait more than anything was the one reason for the campaign decision to avoid public debates. Putting a winning candidate who is an introvert in a situation that rewards extroversion can only lose him votes.

And that latter point conveys the strategy that campaigns must evolve in an environment that demands, in effect, the appearance of authenticity.

It is the job of campaigns to present their candidates and their visions in the best possible light by avoiding situations that emphasise the negative, amplifying situations that emphasise the positives, and understanding how to filter that to achieve consistency in a ravenous age of constant media attention and psychoanalyses.

The Jonathan campaign clearly didn't take this into account.

He was instead punished with many public rallies that forced him to go on the attack against his opponent; leading to optics that showed him evidently uncomfortable. To voters it came off as furtiveness – unhelpful imagery for a candidate dogged by a perception of corruption. It is impossible to judge his authenticity, but it is the case that the public judged him.

It is the reality of the new political environment. Those who wish to capture the public heart need to come to terms with it.

Politicians brought these problems on themselves, after all.

They brought the audience to this point by gaming the system and trying to manage perception with deception over the past few decades of public life, accelerated by the invention of electronic media. It will take a while for them to get themselves out of it.

In the interim, they have to find ways to communicate to the audience a sense that they are truthful, that they have integrity and that they will do what they say.

That is the essence of authenticity as a public demand, no matter how inverted certain talented candidates have made it.

Is this really that terrible?

In the balance of things, not really. This is not a net negative.

If anything, the natural foundation of communication has been restored. Those who want to reach, convince and convert audiences and consumers must align themselves with this new reality.

So think of it the way we do: at the end of the day, anything that forces politicians to behave more like human beings cannot in fact be a bad thing.

10

CORRUPTION MATTERS

"The corruption perception index by the Transparency International stated about 71 percent of people living in Ghana say corruption has increased over the last twelve months," Ghana's Citi FM wrote in 2016.

It was quoting the People and Corruption: Africa Survey 2015, part of the Global Corruption Barometer, from Transparency International and Afrobarometer. Beyond its report on Ghana, its conclusions of Sub-Saharan Africa as a whole surmise something that citizens are very familiar with.

"(The survey spoke) to 43,143 respondents across 28 countries in Sub-Saharan Africa between March 2014 and September 2015 to ask them about their experiences and perceptions of corruption in their country.

"The majority (58 per cent) of Africans in the surveyed countries, say corruption has increased over the past 12 months. In 18 out of 28 countries surveyed a large majority of people said their government is doing badly at fighting corruption."

An October 2016 State Department's Office of Investment Affairs' Investment Climate statement painted the stark picture for Ghana: "A few American firms have identified corruption as the main obstacle to foreign direct investment. Ghana's 2015 score and ranking on the Transparency International Global Corruption Perceptions Index slipped slightly from 2014, tying with Cuba for 56th place out of 167," it said. "In 2015, there were a number of corruption allegations involving government officials. Corruption in government institutions is pervasive. In fact, the judiciary is reeling from a major bribery scandal that was exposed in September 2015, resulting in 20 judges being fired and several others being suspended while the judiciary conducts internal inquiries into the allegations."

This was under the administration of Johm Dramani Mahama. It is no surprise that when the elections held in December, he lost to Addo Dankwa Akufo-Addo by a ratio of 54% of the vote to 44%, making him the first president in the country's history to lose a second term bid.

"In 2012, Transparency International again deemed Nigeria one of the most corrupt nations in the world (Uzochukwu 2013)," a piece 'Corruption in Nigeria: Review, Causes, Effects and Solutions' a 2016 piece by Uzochukwu Mike notes. "In that year, the country ranked 139th out of the 176 surveyed countries, making Nigeria the 37th most corrupt nation.

"In 2013, Nigeria ranked 144 out of 177 surveyed countries in terms of transparency. The score made Nigeria 33rd most corrupt country in the world that year. The result published by the organization also showed that Nigeria scored 25% out of 100 in terms of transparency. In the 2014 ranking, Nigeria is ranked 136 out 174 surveyed countries (Transparency International 2014). The result shows that there is an improvement, though things are still bad. Nigeria was the 38th most corrupt country in the world in 2014.

"In that year's survey, Nigeria seats at number 136 on the table with Guatemala, Kyrgyzstan, Lebanon, Myanmar, and Papua New Guinea. From calculation, it shows that Nigeria and the mentioned countries were ranked 40th most corrupt in 2016.

"Nigeria failed when it came to transparency in the country. By contrast, in 2013, Denmark and New Zealand scored highest at 91% each, meaning the countries are clean and have higher Confidence Intervals than Nigeria. In the other words, Nigeria is highly corrupt. What can we say about the $2.1 billion arms deal? The money which was budgeted for the purchase of arms in the fight against Boko Haram insurgency group in the country all of a sudden disappeared. Whether the fund developed legs and ran away is what the Federal Government of Nigeria could not explain to the citizenry.

"The stain of corruption did not spare anti-graft agencies as former Chairman of the Economic and Financial Crimes Commission, EFCC, Ibrahim Lamorde, was accused of fraudulently diverting over N1tn proceeds from corruption recovered by the agency (Adeyemi 2016). This is incredible as those who were appointed to fight corruption in the country are also found as the victim of the same problem they fight. That is to say, that trust is difficult in the country."

This was under the administration of Goodluck Jonathan. His image for supervising a corrupt government was so ingrained that one of the most lethal gaffes that Goodluck Jonathan was unable to escape from was when in a televised media interview, he tried to make a nuanced observation that "stealing is not corruption."

The attempt to delineate between simple acts of theft for which laws already exist to combat them compared to the complex nature of corrupt actions that sometimes navigate slippery terrains of intent, motive and interpretation got lost because the audience saw him as the wrong messenger for the right message. His image already tainted and weakened by a perceived softness towards corruption, anything he said was easily used against him.

It is no surprise that when the elections came, Goodluck Jonathan lost, 53.93% to 44.96%.

It is not that African voters haven't known that corruption has been squeezing the life out of them in the decades since many countries gained political independence. It is that, finally, across these countries, they have had enough.

The coincidence of flagrant corruption, by the same cycle of leaders – sometimes, literally the same cycle – without the cushion effect of development or economic progress, has conspired over time to produce desperate citizens looking for someone, anyone, who can break this vicious cycle.

The accumulated desperation has, more than anything else – more than the lack of a free press, the stifling of political dissent and the absence of leap-frog development – led citizens to organise, to coordinate and to begin to strongly demand a new political order and a different type of government.

This has coincided with an era of global democracy and citizen power that has made it infinitely easier for them to translate anger into action and frustration into decision.

It is not even the poverty alone that angers the citizenry, it is the impunity. They hear often of other forms of political and petty corrupting in the West or in Asia, where this is contemporaneous with development and growth for the peoples of those countries, but they look at their own realities and find they are cursed with a consumptive elite with no desire to replace, to build or to increase wealth.

The lack of imagination from their leaders has underscored the immorality of the corruption that the general citizenry has had to contend with, and they can't take it anymore.

This, more than anything else, is becoming the tipping point for the overthrow of incumbencies and establishments across much of the continent, from Gambia to Ghana, Nigeria to Kenya. Many of these leaders have the same narratives of corruption or the appearance of corruption, either by themselves culpable, or accommodating of the prevalence by their associates and benefactors. And so citizens across the continent are bound by a common cause and the sense of a common destiny.

As we see from Nigeria to Ghana, many of them connect with the capacity of their neighbours to cast away corrupt leaders, and gain inspiration to challenge their own status quo.

As establishments defined by corruption continue to collapse one after the other across the continent, other citizens in other nations will gain the courage to organise and to draw lines for their leaders.

Corruption is the easy enemy for many African nations. And it is just as well, because it is the biggest danger that failed leaders constitute to their own people.

11

THE ECONOMY, OF COURSE, MATTERS – BUT NOT JUST IN THE WAY YOU THINK

It's the stuff of global campaign lore – the classic Clinton campaign slogan: 'It's the economy, stupid'.

It is thrown around often that all political consideration by voters come down to the economy, and people act or react based on the amount of money in their pockets and the opportunities for wealth and growth that a nation provides.

American analysts and journalists, certainly seem to agree that the economy is the biggest driver of voting decisions, and have a library full of column inches post the 2016 elections that insist on this theory.

"Having served in the '92 Clinton campaign, and having been part of the economic dialogue with the Midwest in the industrial heartland in 1992 when we did very well, it's hard for me to understand how Hillary's campaign didn't really see the centrality of her leading with economic issues," Simon Rosenberg, founder of the New Democratic Network and veteran strategist for the Democratic Party said in a Politico.com piece titled 'How The Left Created Trump'.

"A Gallup poll assessing what Americans perceived as the "most important problem facing this country today" helps to explain the disillusionment of this once-faithful constituency: 'Economic problems' consistently took the No. 1 spot, while issues like 'lack of respect for each other' and 'unifying the country' appeared at the bottom of the list. Trump's campaign rhetoric and slogans were aimed directly at the former, while Clinton ("stronger together") chose the latter. Rosenberg says Clinton's misjudgment of voters' concerns is his greatest criticism of her campaign.

"While Clinton traveled the country insisting that 'America *is* great, because America is good,' Trump was busy cultivating a vision of economic prosperity—make America great *again*'—with the promise of 'beautiful' and 'tremendous' and 'big-league' change. Nowhere was the backlash from this act of liberal smugness more deeply felt than the Rust Belt states, in which counties like Kenosha, Wisconsin, broke more than 40 years of Democratic support in favor of Trump. The Democratic Party abandoned the economic issues that had locked that constituency into the party."

In 2012, President John Dramani Mahama polled 5,573,572 to Addo Dankwa Akufo-Addo's 5,263,286., a difference of 310,286. Four years after with the economy in sharp focus, and after being hit consistently on the issues, Mahama, who came across as very likeable in his first election as president, polled 4,701,162 to Akufo Addo's 5,697,093. A difference of 995,931 was a lot of ground to lose to someone he defeated four years before in Ghana.

So we know for a fact that the economy surely matters.

But the truth is that the economic argument is a bit deeper than just money in the pocket. Yes, that is a very important component of the drivers of many decisions at the polling booth, but it is a complex mix that incorporates many other realities of civic life.

The economy is often a proxy for something more fundamental: who holds the power in society?

It is a proxy for who holds the power to control the culture and the national agenda, to influence behavior and trends and whether those people deserve the economic power that they have gotten. Underlying most debates over the economy is a more sophisticated conversation about fairness, and opportunity and power.

And that's why economy is often tied to identity politics.

So people will supposedly vote against their economic interest if they feel the economy is being used to assault their values.

It is the same reason Nigeria's ethnic lines are a better predictor of electoral decisions than its class or economic lines. People in Northern Nigeria are more likely to gravitate towards a candidate from their part of the country irrespective of the amounts of money invested by another in their region, for the same reason that, despite allegations of corruption and a legacy of questionable returns, many in the South-East of Nigeria maintained their votes for a man with the Igbo name, Azikiwe.

So there are two levels to the economic debate.

The first level is that of basic economics – are governments handling the economy effectively in a way that people feel the effects in their lives? Are politicians communicating a message that reaches the economic hearts of the people?

Micheal Moore captured the crux of this argument in his 'Why Trump will Win' piece: "Trump is ahead of Hillary in the latest polls in Pennsylvania and tied with her in Ohio. *Tied?* How can the race be this close after everything Trump has said and done? Well maybe it's because he's said (correctly) that the Clintons' support of NAFTA helped to destroy the industrial states of the Upper Midwest. Trump is going to hammer Clinton on this and her support of TPP and other trade policies that have royally screwed the people of these four states. When Trump stood in the shadow of a Ford Motor factory during the Michigan primary, he threatened the corporation that if they did indeed go ahead with their planned closure of that factory and move it to Mexico, he would slap a 35% tariff on any Mexican-built cars shipped back to the United States. It was sweet, sweet music to the ears of the working class of Michigan, and when he tossed in his threat to Apple that he would force them to stop making their iPhones in China and build them here in America, well, hearts swooned and Trump walked away with a big victory that should have gone to the governor next-door, John Kasich.

"From Green Bay to Pittsburgh, this, my friends, is the middle of England – broken, depressed, struggling, the smokestacks strewn across the countryside with the carcass of what we use to call the Middle Class. Angry, embittered working (and nonworking) people who were lied to by the trickle-down of Reagan and abandoned by Democrats who still try to talk a good line but are really just looking forward to rub one out with a lobbyist from Goldman Sachs who'll write them a nice big check before leaving the room. What happened in the UK with Brexit is going to happen here. Elmer Gantry shows up looking like Boris Johnson and just says whatever shit he can make up to convince the masses that *this is their chance! To stick to ALL of them, all who wrecked their American Dream! And now The Outsider, Donald Trump, has arrived to clean house! You don't have to agree with him! You don't even have to like him! He is your personal Molotov cocktail to throw right into the center of the bastards who did this to you! SEND A MESSAGE! TRUMP IS YOUR MESSENGER!*

"And this is where the math comes in. In 2012, Mitt Romney lost by 64 electoral votes. Add up the electoral votes cast by Michigan, Ohio, Pennsylvania and Wisconsin. It's 64. All Trump needs to do to win is to carry, as he's expected to do, the swath of traditional red states from Idaho to Georgia (states that'll **never** vote for Hillary Clinton), and then he just needs these four rust belt states. He doesn't need Florida. He doesn't need Colorado or Virginia. Just Michigan, Ohio, Pennsylvania and Wisconsin. And that will put him over the top. This is how it will happen in November."

But there is the second level, and this is the gut level where voters make decisions not based on economics alone, but based on economic identity. In this case, economy is both about 'what's in my pocket?' and 'who has the money in society and is that person like me and is that person a person I approve of?'

Moore captured this in the same piece, calling it 'The Last Stand of the Angry White Man'.

"Our male-dominated, 240-year run of the USA is coming to an end," he wrote, paraphrasing the sentiments. "A woman is about to take over! How did this happen?! *On our watch!* There were warning signs, but we ignored them. Nixon, the gender traitor, imposing Title IX on us, the rule that said girls in school should get an equal chance at playing sports. Then they let them fly commercial jets. Before we knew it, Beyoncé stormed on the field at this year's Super Bowl (our game!) with an army of Black Women, fists raised, declaring that our domination was hereby terminated! Oh, the humanity!

"That's a small peek into the mind of the Endangered White Male. There is a sense that the power has slipped out of their hands, that their way of doing things is no longer how things are done. This monster, the "Feminazi," the thing that as Trump says, "bleeds through her eyes or wherever she bleeds," has conquered us — and now, after having had to endure eight years of a black man telling us what to do, we're supposed to just sit back and take eight years of a woman bossing us around? After that it'll be eight years of the gays in the White House! Then the transgenders! You can see where this is going. By then animals will have been granted human rights and a fuckin' hamster is going to be running the country. This has to stop!"

A New York Magazine piece the day after the election took this deeper by looking at the numbers.

"The simplest way for progressives to complete that task is to remember what we've always loathed about this place: That its wealth, power, and formal embrace of egalitarian values — its 'greatness', so to speak — was built on the backs of enslaved African-Americans and subjugated women of all ancestries," it said. Which is to say: The answer to how Trump won is racism and sexism. His victory was propelled by the sense of loss that dominant social groups feel when they see the lower castes climbing toward equality.

"While the polls underestimated the strength of Trump's support across-the-board, there were early indications that he was making inroads with white, non-college-educated voters, including those who backed Obama.

"The idea that this was an important development — one that Clinton should adjust her message to account for — was often met with fierce resistance by progressive commentators. There were justifiable complaints about a predominately white media's idealization of the light-skinned proletarian, with his hardhat and lunchbox — and the way this image erased the multiethnic, "pink collar" character of the rest of working-class America. There were justifiable fears that a political strategy composed to appeal to such voters would lead Democrats to compromise on racial justice — to sacrifice more Ricky Ray Rectors and welfare programs on the arc of "real America."

"Above all, there was a sense that any voter who would cast their lot with a soft-core white nationalist wasn't one worth trying to keep in a liberal coalition. The thing is: Trying to win over such voters doesn't feel as optional right now as it did a few hours ago. To be sure, progressives must strive to organise African-Americans, Latinos, single women, and millennials. And wherever Democrats have power over election laws, they much try to reform the voting process to increase these demographics' presence in the electorate.

"But there are a lot of older white people in this country. And if highly educated whites weren't willing to vote against their (narrow) economic interest in large enough numbers to produce an electoral-college majority — when *Donald Trump* was the GOP standard-bearer — Democrats can't rely on them to compensate for any extended erosion in the party's share of downscale whites."

This is remarkable.

It frames an economic argument against the light of identity politics. It is money as an expression of identity – who is winning and who is losing. Who deserves to win, and who deserve to lose; even if that money isn't coming directly into my pocket.

It frames economic matters as driving, essentially, a politics of resentment.

"I think they also wanted some sense of dignity, some sense of being heard," New York Times columnist David Brooks said in a post-election interview on PBS News Hour. "I mean, in some sense, there is something noble, in that that was people who felt marginalized, working-class voters, taking over their party from basically what had been a corporate party, and then asserting their will on the country, against groups of people who were more privileged than they are, both on the left and the right."

He then dug deeper as he advised "college-enlightened," "educated, enlightened" Americans not to look down on Trump voters as "those primitive hordes."

"Their culture, their life economically, socially, families breaking apart, drug use, it's going downhill," he said. "And I think the two things — one, we don't want to turn this into a children of light, children of darkness, where us college-enlightened people, educated, enlightened people are looking down at those primitive hordes. We do not want that."

According to Brooks, rapidly increasing technology has made life good for "people who are good at using words," but not "people who are not good at using words."

"We have had populist movements that often, often, often have this ugly racial element," he said. "But, often, there are warning signs of some deeper social and economic problem. And we have rapidly increasing technology, which is making life very good for people who are good at using words, and not so good for people who are not good at using words."

Again, remarkably, commentators from both sides of the aisle often noted that Clinton had the detailed, sensible plans to actually make life economically better for many of those voters, but still they felt she represented an economic interest that was aligned against them and so, in effect, they made an economic interest decision by voting against their economic interest, but in a way that affirms what they consider their (economic) identity.

To dig into deeper, a Washington Post piece on its Wonkblog on the day just before the elections was titled 'A new theory for why Trump voters are so angry'.

"There's been great thirst this election cycle for insight into the psychology of Trump voters. J.D. Vance's memoir "Hillbilly Elegy" offers a narrative about broken families and social decay. "There is a lack of agency here — a feeling that you have little control over your life and a willingness to blame everyone but yourself," Jeff Guo writes. "Sociologist Arlie Hochschild tells a tale of perceived betrayal. According to her research, white voters feel the American Dream is drifting out of reach for them, and they are angry because they believe minorities and immigrants have butted in line.

"(Kathy) Cramer's recent book, The Politics of Resentment offers a third perspective. Through her repeated interviews with the people of rural Wisconsin, she shows how politics have increasingly become a matter of personal identity. Just about all of her subjects felt a deep sense of bitterness toward elites and city dwellers; just about all of them felt tread on, disrespected and cheated out of what they felt they deserved.

"Cramer argues that this "rural consciousness" is key to understanding which political arguments ring true to her subjects. For instance, she says, most rural Wisconsinites supported the tea party's quest to shrink government not out of any belief in the virtues of small government but because they did not trust the government to help 'people like them.'"

"Support for less government among lower-income people is often derided as the opinions of people who have been duped," she writes. "Listening in on these conversations, it is hard to conclude that the people I studied believe what they do because they have been hoodwinked. Their views are rooted in identities and values, as well as in economic perceptions; and these things are all intertwined."

"Rural voters, of course, are not precisely the same as Trump voters, but Cramer's book offers an important way to think about politics in the era of Trump. Many have pointed out that American politics have become increasingly tribal; Cramer takes that idea a step further, showing how these tribal identities shape our perspectives on reality.

"It will not be enough, in the coming months, to say that Trump voters were simply angry. Cramer shows that there are nuances to political rage. To understand Trump's success, she argues, we have to understand how he tapped into people's sense of self."

The global globalisation debate is perhaps a way for the world to understand the argument that American voters just had around the economy that it's not really about the economy.

Common sense question: Who benefits when a Nigerian TV show – Big Brother Nigeria – is shot in South Africa in the name of international competitiveness? The profits of the company, Mnet - or the lives of the everyday Nigerian who would have benefited from the investment in world class studios, training and employment from that investment within the country's borders?

We know that globalisation is good. Of course.

We know that trade boosts economies, increasing exports and creating opportunities for businesses.

We know that it reduces the costs of products, because imported components and materials lower cost. We know that trade somehow opens markets abroad – as local producers can reach out and then employ more people. We know that this, somehow, also leads to improved competitiveness, because of the global market. And ultimately these pacts help countries undertake domestic policy reform that aligns to a global standard in exchange for globally agreed benefits – to the effect of lifting everybody up.

We know that protectionism is, as someone has described it, historically, a special-interest bonanza that delivers benefits to specific industries only at a disproportionate cost to the rest of the economy.

But, do we really know these things?

Well, we know all of the above because of what we have read and seen from people we should trust and respect. And that's how human civilisation makes leaps and bounds – people achieve expertise via domain knowledge of specific issues, thinking through the substance, consequence and future, and they share those ideas with the rest of us. Common sense demands that we agree, since we know no better ourselves.

This exchange of expertise – "you tell me what you know for sure, and I'll believe you because you have proof of study or experience" – is the basis on which modern economies and politics are sustained.

Unfortunately, citizens across the world are deciding that it shouldn't be so simple after all.

They see something completely different, at least in the short term. They see benefits to businesses, but not to people. They see privileged citizens enjoying the cost-savings but find no such benefits for themselves or their friends. They see median wage reducing because of pacts with low-wage countries. They see their jobs leaving because of trade deficits and the effects of 'global competitiveness'.

And those promised better and higher paying jobs? They see so few of them that it makes no sense at all.

What the experts say, and the reality they see in front of them every day are in such sharp conflict that every day from Nigeria to Britain, and from France to America, people have decided to revolt against the experts. They have become deeply suspicious of their consensus – especially where that consensus disproportionally benefits those same experts.

It is easy for those lucky to live amongst the elite to mouth the goodness of globalisation, even if – like me – they only know it because they trust the experts. After all, there is no immediate consequence. As a business person with open lines of client acquisition from across the world, whatever is happening has only been good for me.

But what if I were a South African with a job about to disappear? Or a trader in Kumasi whose life has only gotten worse as the one per cent accumulates the benefits of global markets? Yes, I wouldn't be so sanguine.

Then let's even investigate the legitimacy of elite consensus.

Anyone who has had a brush, for instance, with African Studies in the hallowed chambers of American colleges knows something for a fact – the elite academic consensus is a large dose of genteel misunderstanding.

The understanding of African politics is held hostage by 1970-80 paradigms of communist panic and Pan-African reflexes. Then there is the now-outdated understanding of African markets as one big whole. Yet any businessman on the ground knows that Nigeria is more connected as a market to Texas than it is to Togo.

Many people who know the reality of practice in various fields across the world know how often their common sense understanding hits the ceiling of elite consensus, one that is earnest, but earnestly disconnected.

So that consensus deserves respect because it is hard-won – but based on both its inherent fault-lines and the demands of common sense, shouldn't it be often explained and interrogated? Should it be so arrogant that it need no longer convince?

Should citizens simply take for granted that open and closed economies have some kind of moral undertone that is ultimately good for them, irrespective of what their eyes see and their ears hear?*

Trump's election became a wake-up call for much of America's economic elite.

"The election was a wakeup call about how much discontent there is from technological progress and globalization, that it's not just all a clear good thing," California Democratic Rep. Ro Rhanna said to Politico.com in 2017 just before he began a trip to Angry White Man territory in Kentucky. "And it's time for an industry that has played a role in shedding American jobs — by advancing artificial intelligence, among other things — to invest in helping communities like this one share in the upside. There's got to be greater empathy among those in Silicon Valley for some of the pain that has been caused."

It's about the economy yes, but for many people the economy is a symbol for what they consider a debate about fairness – whether they are right or not.

Whatever else is happening, in a time of debilitating income inequality, this much has to be true: citizens across the world deserve better.

Unless the global elite economic – and political – elite finds the humility to answer questions like these with the clarity and simplicity that popular consensus requires, the burning down of the system – from Nairobi to Paris – will continue.

And Donald Trump will be the least of the upheavals that the world will be forced to confront.

*This piece borrows substantially from a piece by one of the authors titled 'Globalisation is good, but care to explain why?'

12

MOBILISATION MATTERS, AND SO (BIG) DATA WILL MATTER

We've noted that "the art of political persuasion is still more important to winning presidential elections than the mechanics of mobilisation." But the primacy of the former doesn't invalidate the necessity of the latter.

If persuasion is the engine, mobilisation is the entire vehicle.

Mobilisation is the act of getting your natural voters – those who have already been persuaded – to actually vote, or connecting with the persuadable voters and bringing them over to your side, as well as getting them to actually physically vote.

This includes ensuring turnout, deploying canvassers, voter education, information gathering, party relations and the whole gamut of campaign management.

A Brookings Institute book *Why Voter Mobilisation Matters* captures the mechanics of mobilisation in one theoretical case study:

"Imagine that you are a Republican candidate running for local office. There are 8,000 registered voters, and Election Day is approaching. The 2,000 registered Republicans favor you 80 versus 20 percent, but ordinarily only half of them vote. The remaining 6,000 people in the electorate favor your opponent 67.5 versus 32.5 percent; one-third of them can be expected to vote. So, with 800 votes from registered Republicans and 650 from the rest of the electorate, you are in danger of losing 1,450 to 1,550.

"Thinking about how to win in this situation is really a matter of thinking about where to find at least 100 additional votes. All the factors that got you those 1,450 votes—your good looks, your record in office, and so forth—are important in shaping the eventual outcome of the election, but the strategic decisions from this point forward must focus on what you will do now to change the expected outcome.

"A GOTV (Get Out The Vote) strategy aims to transform nonvoters into voters. If you can identify the 2,100 abstainers who would vote for you, try to get at least 100 of them to the polls. Voter identification (ID) programs use brief polls to identify these potential supporters, who will later be targeted for mobilization.

"Voter ID programs require planning and money, however. A simpler approach is to focus GOTV attention solely on Republicans. Bear in mind that if you attempt to mobilize some of the 1,000 Republicans who otherwise would not vote, you will need to get at least 167 to the polls because you only gain sixty net votes for every 100 Republicans you mobilize.

"Conversely, a demobilization strategy strives to transform voters into non- voters. You could accomplish this by scaring or demoralizing some of the 1,550 people who would otherwise cast votes for your opponent. Finally, a persuasion strategy attempts to convert some of these 1,550 voters into your supporters."

In modern campaigning across Europe and North America, data has now become the key tool of mobilization – of finding, reaching and motivating voters to canvass and to vote.

"Movements in Artificial Intelligence have also considerably moved the boundaries of data operations, and psychographic profiles, psychometrics and emotional analysis are replacing gut and experience in "predict(ing) the personality and hidden political leanings" of voters are getting popular and driving microtargeting.

"But it is crucial that candidates don't put the cart before the horse, as is usually the trend when novelty goes mainstream.

"The natural order of successful political campaigns is usually candidate first, message second and mobilization last. More efficient would be message first, candidate second, and then mobilization next. But the reality is that candidates are not usually chosen by parties. This doesn't matter too much though; as long as there is understanding that the messaging is more important than the mobilization, then parties are generally on the right track.

"The Hillary Clinton campaign in the United States got this equation wrong and paid the price for it.

"Ada is a complex computer algorithm that the campaign was prepared to publicly unveil after the election as its invisible guiding hand," The Washington Post wrote in an article titled 'What did she miss?' "Named for a female 19th-century mathematician — Ada, Countess of Lovelace — the algorithm was said to play a role in virtually every strategic decision Clinton aides made, including where and when to deploy the candidate and her battalion of surrogates and where to air television ads — as well as when it was safe to stay dark.

"The campaign's deployment of other resources — including county-level campaign offices and the staging of high-profile concerts with stars like Jay Z and Beyoncé — was largely dependent on Ada's work, as well.

"While the Clinton campaign's reliance on analytics became well known, the particulars of Ada's work were kept under tight wraps, according to aides. The algorithm operated on a separate computer server than the rest of the Clinton operation as a security precaution, and only a few senior aides were able to access it.

"According to aides, a raft of polling numbers, public and private, were fed into the algorithm, as well as ground-level voter data meticulously collected by the campaign. Once early voting began, those numbers were factored in, too.

"What Ada did, based on all that data, aides said, was run 400,000 simulations a day of what the race against Trump might look like. A report that was spit out would give campaign manager Robby Mook and others a detailed picture of which battleground states were most likely to tip the race in one direction or another — and guide decisions about where to spend time and deploy resources.

"The use of analytics by campaigns was hardly unprecedented. But Clinton aides were convinced their work, which was far more sophisticated than anything employed by President Obama or GOP nominee Mitt Romney in 2012, gave them a big strategic advantage over Trump."

This all sounds complicated, appropriately complex and fitting with the global, important move towards big data and machine learning.

But she lost.

"Like much of the political establishment Ada appeared to underestimate the power of rural voters in Rust Belt states," the story noted. "Clearly, there were things neither she nor a human could foresee — like a pair of bombshell letters sent by the FBI about Clinton's email server.

Campaign operative, Dave Gold, in a Politico piece titled 'Data-driven Campaigns are Killing the Democratic Party', captured what exactly happened that converted a strength into a weakness.

"I appreciate the role that data can play in winning campaigns," he wrote. But I also know that data isn't a replacement for a message; it's a tool to focus and direct one.

"We Democrats have allowed microtargeting to become microthinking. Each cycle, we speak to fewer and fewer people and have less and less to say. We all know the results: the loss of 63 seats and control of the House, the loss of 11 seats and control of the Senate, the loss of 13 governorships, the loss of over 900 state legislative seats and control of 27 state legislative chambers.

"Yet despite losses on top of losses, we have continued to double down on data-driven campaigns at the expense of narrative framing and emotional storytelling.

"Years ago, my political mentor taught me the problem with this approach, using a memorable metaphor: issues are to a campaign message what ornaments are to a Christmas tree, he said. Ornaments make the tree more festive, but without the tree, you don't have a Christmas tree, no matter how many ornaments you have or how beautiful they are. Issues can advance the campaign's story, but without a narrative frame, your campaign doesn't have a message, no matter how many issue ads or position papers it puts forward.

"Storytelling has been the most effective form of communication throughout the entirety of human history. And that is unlikely to change, given that experts in neurophysiology affirm that the neural pathway for stories is central to the way the human brain functions ("The human mind is a story processor, not a logic processor," as social psychologist Jonathan Haidt wrote)."

What's the problem with a data-first strategy?

"The problem is that science, by definition, requires controlling for a single variable in a way that can be replicated by others, allowing over time for findings to be validated and a consensus to emerge. I believe that quantitative political science, at least as applied to the world of campaigns, is an oxymoron, as campaigns exist in a multivariate world."

"Like many people around the world, I expected a comfortable Hillary Clinton victory on Tuesday," wrote David Plouffe, manager for both winning Obama campaigns in the New York Times. "My confidence was not partisan spin. It was based on public data, voting history and some sense of the Clinton campaign's own models. I played with various state scenarios, and even in the most generous outcomes, could not get Donald J. Trump to 270 electoral votes.

"Still, the nagging worry about a lack of broad-based enthusiasm for Mrs. Clinton, which I noted often as someone familiar with the Obama coalition, proved to be justified. She had passionate supporters and volunteers, for sure. But for sporadic and potential first-time voters, the spark was not there."

The bottom-line is clear: effective campaigns should be "message driven" and then "data informed".

Nowhere is this more important than in African electoral settings where the mechanics are sadly still primitive, held back by sit-tight dictators, and democratic manipulators who have restricted the evolution of political parties, hamstrung the operations of electoral commissions, and dis-incentivised the pulling into the future of political operations.

In this case, and has been our experience, messaging can galvanise large swaths of voters based on basic assumptions – sometimes poll-tested, sometimes focus-grouped – about voter demography and psychography.

The time for elaborate data mining will come very soon, and serious minded social engineers are already mastering the dimensions of that field (and, more importantly, its applications to our social and cultural contexts) especially with the dominance of social media, but in many constituencies across the continent, the time has not yet come for this to immediately influence electoral outcomes, so that its utility lies in political parties having the foresight to build competitive advantages.

In the meantime though, mobilisation in our contexts depend on the traditional system of party identification and demographic cleavages - and for these traditional assumptions, messaging is still the winning formula.

In fact, the Brookings Institute book project used the Kansas State Board of Education election to illustrate how effective mobilization is an oxymoron without messaging that works. "*A personal approach to mobilizing voters is usually more successful than an impersonal approach,*" it noted, the italics its own for emphasis. "That is, the more personal the interaction between campaign and potential voter, the more it raises a person's chances of voting."

And personal interaction works on witnessing, the same way that religious canvassing works. If your message is not powerful, and your witness not passionate, enough to persuade or to inspire, then everything physical you do is worthless, and fails.

Mobilisation is crucial. Data across the world is now a necessity and Africa will follow suit.

But whatever happens with new inventions and innovations in social and political engineering, a powerful candidate with an effective message is still the deal closer in free and fair elections.

More importantly, this is squarely where Africa is, at this moment of its collective democratic evolution.

13

TECHNOLOGY DOESN'T MATTER AS MUCH AS IT WILL SOON

N o discussion about any institution or idea these days goes without an interrogation of the effects or intersection of technology. How technology can accelerate, can upgrade or can simplify systems and processes underlying the levers of society.

So inevitably, even though those involved in political engineering in Africa will laugh at the disconnectedness of the conversations on technology from on-the-ground realities, it is still necessary to discuss the global technology trends in the context of our political institutions.

It's important to note that we are isolating social media from technology as a theme. We will speak of social media in a separate chapter, not as a technology tool, but as a significant social experience, enabled by technology.

This is a difficult separation to make in a time of convergence, and so there will be inevitable slip ups, but the isolation is worthwhile to truly understand cause and effect.

Now, the truth about technology and politics is this: Apart from the proven narratives of social media being able to shine light into the darkness of electoral manipulation (and of this, it needs to be said that there is a dearth of quantitative or qualitative academic research data to isolate causation from correlation), there is no evidence, in Africa, that technology has led to any major social or political transformation.

The same can be said for the rest of the world, in fact.

"Although many people are anxious to understand how much influence old and new media had over the US presidential election," the guys at research institute, Data & Society say, "the reality is that we will never know comprehensively."

However it is still possible to have a qualitative discussion about the possible effects that technology and disintermediation have had on the quality and activity of political choice.

Five broad categories would be attention management, propaganda, popular media consumption, the limits of free speech, polarisation (or hyper-partisanship, accentuated by filter bubbles) and, of course, fake news.

Broadly, technology reflects in our society through its disruption of data and information, both the gathering and the flow of both, and how it affects the future of work, and opportunities.

We have dealt with data comprehensively in a preceding chapter, however it may be important to recall that the essential disruption is in how data is aggregated and mined, and how it is used to develop psychometrics that determine societal and voter behavior. To use one simple example: how an aggregation of 'likes' across all technology-enabled social tools can help give insight into consumer behavior that is both conscious and unconscious.

The unconscious parameters cut close to the ethical lines around privacy. And different countries have responded to these challenges in different ways.

"At stake are not merely bragging rights, but also an emerging science that many believe could reshape American politics and commerce," a New York Times piece notes. "Big data companies already know your age, income, favorite cereal and when you last voted. But the company that can perfect psychological targeting could offer far more potent tools:

the ability to manipulate behavior by understanding how someone thinks and what he or she fears."

"You can do things that you would not have dreamt of before," says Alexander Polonsky, chief data scientist at Bloom, a consulting firm that offers "emotion analysis" of social networks and has worked with the center-right Republican Party in France.

In the light of the supposed successes of these tools in the United Kingdom's Brexit campaign, the government has now stepped in to understand the trend at least, through its privacy watchdog, the Information Commissioners Office (ICO).

"(The ICO) is launching an inquiry into how voters' personal data is being captured and exploited in political campaigns, cited as a key factor in both the Brexit and Trump victories last year," the Guardian reports. "It comes as privacy campaigners, lawyers, politicians and technology experts express fears that electoral laws are not keeping up with the pace of technological change.

"We have concerns about use of personal data. We are conducting a wide assessment of the data-protection risks arising from the use of data analytics, including for political purposes, and will be contacting a range of organisations," an ICO spokeswoman confirmed. "We intend to publicise our findings later this year."

In a recent story, Buzzfeed revealed how the Leave campaign paid £625,000 to a student, Darren Grimes, "which he then used to hire AggregateIQ to produce a targeted pro-leave Facebook ad campaign - apparently with spectacular results."

The campaign director of Vote Leave campaign, Dominic Cummings, confirmed this: "Without a doubt, the Vote Leave campaign owes a great deal of its success to the work of AggregateIQ. We couldn't have done it without them."

"A rapid convergence in the data mining, algorithmic and granular analytics capabilities of companies like Cambridge Analytica and Facebook is creating powerful, unregulated and opaque 'intelligence platforms'," says Dr Simon Moores, visiting lecturer in the applied sciences and computing department at Canterbury Christ Church University. "In turn, these can have enormous influence to affect what we learn, how we feel, and how we vote. The algorithms they may produce are frequently hidden from scrutiny and we see only the results of any insights they might choose to publish."

Bloomberg has reported Europe's discomfort with the huge technology capacities of global networks. "U.S. technology giants from Google Inc. to Facebook Inc. are too big to be left in the hands of individual national privacy watchdogs, according to the European Union's top data protection official," it says. "With U.S. companies such as Facebook, Apple Inc., and LinkedIn Corp. having Ireland as their main European base for data-protection purposes, policing privacy violations already resembles a battle between David and Goliath for thinly staffed agencies in some of the EU's smallest nations."

So, one issue is privacy.

Another issue is not with technology itself, but with its effects – especially on what many now call "the future of work"; how technology accelerates change while dislodging the conventional idea of opportunities, probably creating new jobs while certainly destroying old ones.

The 2017 gathering of the global elite at the World Economic Forum in Davos captured the current state of affairs in this regard excellently, and the tension between old and new as well as how this drives and affects political decision and calculation.

"Many of the world's current and future problems identified by the event's agenda had their roots in the rapid pace of technological change," the Telegraph reports. "In his valedictory appearance as the United States Secretary of State, John Kerry said the politicians who are stoking a populist backlash against globalisation have identified the wrong cause for many of the anxieties building among their electorates."

"Trade is not to blame for job losses." The real problem, according to Kerry, is automation.

Attendees contended with the statistic that about four out of every five job losses in the US has been the result of galloping technology – with the next frontier being artificial intelligence.

Of course, technology innovators are sensitive to the implicit criticism. "Artificial intelligence is about the augmentation of people not the replacement of people," said Ginni Rometty, the chief executive of IBM.

But, essentially, the more citizens hear about technology, the more suspicion it creates – about the concentration of power in the hands of unaccountable corporates, and the concentration of wealth in the hands of a few as a continuing sacrifice to widening income inequality, while decimating the expansion of opportunities for those left behind. These were dominant, decisive themes in the 2016 American elections and British referendum.

"Technology has changed everything," says Meg Whitman, United States politician and chief executive of Hewlett Packard Enterprises. "It can be a huge force for good in areas such as climate change, agriculture, food, and medicine but it has also meant changes for jobs. We need to manage technological change better.

"We need to understand how we got here. There is a distrust of institutions and the changes brought about by technological change…it is a far bigger cause of job losses than globalisation."

The British Prime Minister, Theresa May has in fact sounded an alarm beyond the specifics of elections management or decimation of jobs to the massive social engineering capacities of technology tools and the companies that incubate them, which is the third issue. She attacked technology giants who have refused to cooperate with nations across a broad range of areas with a focus on terrorism.

It mirrors the thesis of Duke University's Professor Mary Cummins. That these companies are essentially "corporate states" that have become "shadowy forces of globalization" operating, as the Telegraph says it, at levels that few understand and until now have avoided serious examination.

The newspaper notes that the technology of these companies are so sophisticated that they move beyond social media into matters of national security, even beyond the comprehensions of the British M16, America's Central Intelligence Agency or Germany's Federal Intelligence Service.

Citizens of the world are routinely affected by these far-reaching consequences of technology advancement. But these trends are not accelerated yet in Africa. Much of the continent remains resolutely offline despite premature celebrations, poverty still significantly limits access, and economies have not been radically improved for that matter.

Save for social media and financial services, many African economies are not yet significantly affected by the truly transformative effects of the technology much of the world is already familiar with. And it certainly hasn't affected the way our political parties do business, the way our governments are organised and operated and the way that cultural conversations and debates are resolved.

But this is inevitable in the immediate future, and the indications are already here.

"But possibly more significant than the online campaigning was the use of biometric machines to identify voters, which prevented the ballot-box stuffing and multiple voting that characterised past polls," Reuters reported after Nigeria's 2015 elections.

"The card reader played a constructive role in deterring individuals who, in the past, have tampered with the electoral process either through ballot stuffing or tampering with the election results," said Dr Christopher Fomunyoh, of the National Democratic Institute for International Affairs.

"As a result," Reuters said. "This election was judged Nigeria's freest and fairest election yet."

Those who are engaging the future of nation building though across Africa need to begin to engage the inevitable questions that will arise when the disruptions finally come – for our economy and for our politics.

As at today, we are woefully unprepared. Which means that when the future comes, citizens will react with panic and confusion. Whoever answers their questions effectively when it comes will own the political power that ensues from the revolution of minds and action.

14

DEMOGRAPHICS ALWAYS MATTER

You've heard it, if you pay attention to the backend of political competition – demographics is destiny.

It is true.

Let's move away from politics a little. Everything we know about the way the world works today predicts that demographic forces will shape the future of the world.

In America, Hispanics have gone from four per cent of the population to 18 in the last 50 years. 23.7 million Hispanics are eligible to vote presently. According to the New York Times, "so-called minorities, the Census Bureau projects, will constitute a majority of American children under 18 by 2023 and of working-age Americans by 2039. For the first time, both the number and the proportion of non-Hispanic whites, who now account for 66 percent of the population, will decline."

In Europe, immigration has brought significant social transformation. There were approximately 43 million Muslims living in Europe in 2010. But Pew Research estimates that the number will be more than 70 million by 2050, which will be over ten per cent of the continent's population. The refugee crisis leads to significant changes in demography.

"While the political fallout from the flow of Muslim migrants is just

What is the World's dominant political ideology?

For every country, political ideology has been graduated on a scale from Far-Left to Far-Right.

The resulting GeoMap shows clear concentrations of left-leaning countries in South America and Southern Africa, whereas Europe has a concentration of Centre-Right parties.

Unclassified: a country with a political ideology that cannot be defined. 47 out of 197 countries are considered to be unclassified.

Ideology Classification	Ideology Score	Number Ruled		Ideology Score
Far-Left	-3	X 1,521,133,622	= -4,563,400,866	
Left-Wing	-2	X 253,787,982	= -507,575,964	
Centre-Left to Left-Wing	-1.5	X 76,892,368	= -115,338,552	
Centre-Left	-1	X 2,579,670,216	= -2,579,670,216	
Centrist to Centre-Left	-0.5	X 140,909,414	= -70,454,707	
Centrist	0	X 209,184,796	= 0	
Centrist to Centre-Right	0.5	X 4,469,905	= 2,234,950	
Centre-Right	1	X 770,858,550	= 770,858,550	
Centre-Right to Right Wing	1.5	X 230,469,839	= 345,704,759	
Right Wing	2	X 270,447,095	= 540,894,190	
Far Right	3	X 117,525,571	= 352,576,713	

6,235,349,353 ← ÷ ← -5,824,171,144

The world's ideology score is -0.934, meaning that the world is firmly in the "Centre-Left" ideology state.

Sources: Wikipedia, CIA, CIDOB, ZPC, Election Resources on the Internet, UN
Notes: Southern Sudan and Kosovo not included, Taiwan included as an individual country, European Principalities not included

Figure 7: What is the world's dominant political ideology?

beginning in Germany," TIME surmises. "It's well underway in France, where Marine Le Pen and her party, the Front National, have capitalized on rising anti-Muslim sentiment to boost their popularity to 27 percent. Far-right politicians across the continent are reading from a similar script. The arrival of so many Muslims will play an outsized role in European politics for years to come."

China is on track to becoming the world's largest population of old people. "In 15 years, the country will have more than 400 million people over the age of 60. By 2050, its working-age population will have declined by 200+ million people."

Africa, of course, has its own peculiar demographic problems – some have called it a demographic burden. At no point in recorded history has our world been so demographically lopsided, with old people concentrated in rich countries and the young in not-so-rich countries, Somini Sengupta, United Nations correspondent for the New York Times writes in the piece 'The World Has a Problem: Too Many Young People': "Much has been made of the challenges of aging societies. But it's the youth bulge that stands to put greater pressure on the global economy, sow political unrest, spur mass migration and have profound consequences for everything from marriage to Internet access to the growth of cities.

"The parable of our time might well be: Mind your young, or they will trouble you in your old age."

In March 2017, blogger, Marcus Roberts actually wrote these words in a blogpost: "In early 2015 we wrote a post about Turkey's declining fertility rates. What worried some in the Turkish government was that the Kurdish minority continued to have large numbers of children and could become a majority in a few decades if current trends continued. Despite some demographers doubting the possibility of a Kurdish majority, the Turkish Prime Minister called on Turks to do their patriotic duty and have more children so that the "disaster" of a Kurdish majority will not occur."

You get the picture across the world.

Since politics largely comes down to decisions about the allocation of resources across nations, the first place where these trends will immediately disrupt behaviours, apart from consumer products, is governance.

The United Kingdom's Brexit vote, as all major votes across the world, famously broke along demographic lines.

"Those aged over 60 were the most likely group to want to leave the EU, according to the polls before the vote," the UK Telegraph reported. "The East coast areas that scored the highest anti-EU votes are also the areas with the highest pensioner populace. According to the polls, university graduates were the most likely people to want to remain in the EU - while those with a GCSE or equivalent as their highest qualification were more likely to back Brexit. This was a pattern that was reflected in the results - with the Brexit vote correlating with areas with high shares of people with no education.

"Considering how the Leave campaign adopted immigration as one of its key arguments, claiming that the current level of net migration is too high, it is unsurprising that the Remain campaign resonated more strongly with Britain's immigrant population. London, where immigration is massively higher than the rest of the country, voted overwhelmingly to Remain - by 60 percent to 40. But it's the areas in the South East and the East Midlands, where immigration has made a bigger impact only recently, that Ukip and now the Leave campaign have most resonated with."

America's elections also broke heavily amongst demographic lines. Racial minorities continue to break sharply for the Democratic party, older – and a sizeable number of young - white men broke strongly for Donald Trump, and when it came to the intersection between, for instance, female, gay and black, that went almost exclusively to the Democratic party.

To understand strongly how these party identification-driven demographics hold, despite a woman at the top of the ticket, the Democratic Party held on to its historic share of the female vote 54% of women backed Clinton compared to 42% for Trump. In 2012, for Barack Obama, it was an almost identical 55-44 ratio. According to Pew Research, "Trump won white voters by a margin almost identical to that of Mitt Romney, who lost the popular vote to Barack Obama in 2012."

Demographic destiny is thus the logical idea that "that population trends and distributions determine the future of a country, region or even the entire world. For example, if the human population increases too fast or too slowly, or if there are too many young or old people, then certain outcomes are likely to follow, such as economic boom or bust, political unrest or mass migration."

And this just makes perfect sense. Despite the danger of stereotypes, the fact is that people act mostly as a collective, defined as they have by location, gender, biology, class and education. The more your experiences cohere with others, the more you are likely to act in tandem in them. And the more they diverge, the more difference in action and decision you are likely to find. That's basically how humans are made. We are defined by what we know and what we have gone through.

It's just common sense, cause and effect for demographics to largely define the ways that we live and the ways that we behave and the futures that we co-create.

Hence, destiny. But that doesn't mean of course that destiny cannot be thwarted or re-directed.

Nowhere is this more apparent than in the shocking American elections. For years, writers had argued that Democrats had structural advantages that gave them large advantages for the future – millennials, minorities for instance. As FiveThirtyEight.com noted post elections, that just wasn't true. "Trump was able to win, in large part, because he won over a lot of northern white voters without a college degree — in states like Wisconsin, Michigan and Pennsylvania, for example. Many of these voters had cast ballots for Obama twice. Trump's more populist message likely helped him outperform recent GOP nominees with these voters."

The two reasons for this are simple, human beings evolve. A 26-year old today voting for marijuana legalisation will become a 42 year old middle-aged American in a few years, with a daughter and the kind of age-driven sensibilities that replace data with anxiety – he suddenly doesn't want marijuana readily available where his daughter can see it.

Human beings change their minds. That means that, despite the demographic assumptions, a human being is open to being persuaded, which is the entire function of politics as an institution. People become convinced by ideas, emotions, realities, images that don't come naturally to them. Without this, political activity would be moot.

The same South-West that went for Goodluck Jonathan massively in 2011 swung totally, and completely, for Muhammadu Buhari in 2015. Nothing significant changed in that period in any of the demographics. A 24-year-old Yoruba woman in 2011 was only a 28-year-old Yoruba woman in 2015. Nothing dramatic happened. She was just persuaded differently.

What led the Democratic Party to lose its natural margin advantage with union voters in its so-called Rust Belt states? Someone had a more compelling message and candidacy, according to a Forbes analysis.

"Clinton's support for climate change legislation, a lower priority among the electorate than other concerns, was seen as necessary to shore up support from greens threatening to attack her from the left," it explained. "Yet the issue never caught on the heartland, which tends to see climate change mitigation as injurious to them.

"This may have proven a major miscalculation, as the energy economy is also tied closely to manufacturing. Besides climate change, the heartland had many reasons to fear a continuation of Obama policies, particularly related to regulation and global trade, which seems to have been a big factor in Trump's upset win in normally moderate to liberal Wisconsin.

"Trump either won, or closely contested all the traditional manufacturing states – Ohio, Wisconsin, Indiana, Iowa and even Michigan, where union voters did not support Clinton as they had Obama and where trade was also a big issue. Trump did consistently better than Romney in all these states, even though Romney was a native of Michigan. Perhaps the most significant turnaround was in Ohio, which Obama won with barely 51% of the vote in 2012. This year Trump reversed this loss and won by over seven points. Agricultural states, reeling from the decline of commodity prices, not surprisingly, also went for the New Yorker."

In fact, in the entire 2016 American elections, demographic trends were all over the map, confusing pollsters who had main assumptions based on what they considered steady trends.

"Class has been a bigger factor in this election than in any election since the New Deal era," Forbes noted. "Trump's insurgency rode largely on middle- and working-class fears about globalization, immigration and the cultural arrogance of the "progressive" cultural elite.

"Trump owes his election to what one writer has called "the leftover people." These may be "deplorables" to the pundits but their grievances are real – their incomes and their lifespans have been decreasing. They have noticed, as Thomas Frank has written, that the Democrats have gone "from being the party of Decatur to the party of Martha's Vineyard."

"Many of these voters were once Democrats, and feel they have been betrayed. And they include a large swath of the middle class, whose fury explains much of what happened tonight. Trump has connected better with these voters than Romney, who won those making between $50,000 and $90,000 by a narrow 52 percent margin. Early analysis of this year's election shows Trump doing better among these kind of voters.

At the same time, however, affluent voters – those making $100,000 and above – seem to have tilted over to the Democrats this year. This is the first time the "rich" have gone against the GOP since the 1964 Goldwater debacle. Obama did better among the wealthy, winning eight of the 10 richest counties in 2012. In virtually all these counties, Clinton did even better."

The lesson is a simple one really: demographics matter. People act in unconscious collectivity, and you can always spot trends based on the commonality of experiences between people.

The issue is, you can predict that a bloc will act together, but you cannot predict *how* that bloc will act. You can predict there will be a collectivity to their decisions, but you cannot predict what those decisions will be.

As always, the message and the candidate are the key to influencing how a demographic will act now and in the future. And demographics describe human beings, and human beings are always persuadable.

15

PSYCHOGRAPHICS WILL MATTER AS MUCH AS DEMOGRAPHICS

D emographics are usually distinguished by their focus on the physical – location, gender, race, class.

But, in a world where intersectionality has become a buzz word, and social media has truly broken down traditional boundaries, it is important to understand that people's interior lives may sometimes stand in stark difference to what you see in the physical.

A young 19-year-old university student in Iganmu who is hooked on Twitter, and exposed to enough American cultural influencers may have more in common, and make decisions more in tandem, with a 20-year old in Illinois than he would with a 20-year-old high-school graduate living in the very same flat with him.

Nowhere is this more pronounced, for instance, than in Nigeria's evolving attitude towards homosexuality.

A focus group organised by a sister company recently investigated the attitudes of 26 young people aged 15 – 19 in a private Nigerian university, and the question was: "How many of you are fine with having a best friend who is gay?" 17 of the students raised their hands.

An educated guess can be made that their parents would certainly be shocked by these responses, and would sharply disagree, irrespective of similarities in location, ethnicity, race, even gender.

These young people belong to a different psychographic than their parents and even than their neigbours who don't participate actively in the same global millennial community with shifting attitudes towards sexual and gender identity.

Educated women in Nigeria who are feminist would identify more in terms of values, worldviews, choices and one would assume even purchase decisions with British feminists than they would with Nigerian female traditionalists. Nigerians who belong to the thriving Yaba technology community, incubated via online tech forums, Twitter and co-creation spaces are more likely to have completely different views about business, capital, investment and opportunity than other members of their demographic who are exposed solely to businesses in agriculture locally.

The lesson is that, in a rapidly changing African space – changing fast as much to technology and its social consequences, as it is by global cultural shifts in establishment and identity politics, it can be very dangerous to make assumptions about people as we move into the future based on the typical trend lines that African politicians and governments always have.

The future is more global, more cosmopolitan, more diverse and more intersectional. Inevitably, as surely as women's rights are steadily expanding even in Saudi Arabia, attitudes about governance, culture, religion and sex are rapidly changing the more educated and more connected Africa's population gets.

The lesson is that, in the immediate future, demographic decisions have to be made contemporaneously with psychographic decisions. Potential voters are to be analysed based not only on who they are as far as the eyes can see, but what they think, how they think and what experiences define their life's values.

"Marketers are used to thinking and speaking in *demographics*, since slicing a market up by age, gender, ethnicity and other broad variables can help to understand the differences and commonalities among customers," a March 2016 Harvard Business Review article notes. "Think 'our target audience is 14- to 34-year-olds' or 'we are launching a campaign aimed at urban Latinos.' But *psychographics*, which measure customers' attitudes and interests rather than "objective" demographic criteria, can provide deep insight that complements what we learn from demographics."

There is a massive opportunity for future-focused players in the space, not just politicians, but even activists, advocates, donors and multilateral bodies to take advantage of this schisms and chasms that exist even within a geographic or cultural space to drive the ideas and attitudes that can create social and political change.

A generation more conscious of diversity, equity and equality is more open to messaging that drives these imperatives and is more likely to take action when their vision of the world doesn't cohere with their local realities. Because they often have a frame of reference that is both global and essentially activist, they are transformed in their thinking and their attitudes.

Old-time politicians unaware of these significant changes in behavior stick with the old lines and old realities and old concepts of rational action, but they are usually – in Africa's leadership context –woefully unprepared for the future, especially a future driven by independent political choice expressed by free and fair elections.

It is easy for dictators to force uniformity and conformity by limiting press freedom, attacking cultural expression, delegitimising social media, restricting travel where they can and imposing a reign of poverty, both of body and soul. In that terrain, they have all the advantage.

However, as they bow to global pressure for democracy and inclusive capitalism, the ground will slowly but inevitably shift under them. Open societies make it incredibly difficult to control thought and to manipulate action. Once societies get more open, the field of play is leveled, and human beings can begin to rise to full potential.

That is the reason Africa's leaders from the old guard are desperately working to limit access to social media under the pretext of nationalism or national security. Under the complex assault of a psychographic confidence, Africa's usually comfortable leaders are finally running scared.

"The Internet has made these kinds of psychographic differences much more apparent and relevant to both consumers and marketers alike," says the HBR article above. "It also makes it easier to find like-minded souls, so people spend more and more time engaging with people who share their particular interests and attitudes, even if they're from a different community or country: those online tribes help to consolidate psychographic differences, and lead people to identify more and more with their communities of interest or value rather than their geographic or demographic community."

It was barely two years ago after all that Nigeria's energised youth popularly took massive advantage of social media and the internet to dislodge a 16-year monopoly of the previous ruling party and delivered electoral change that the former is yet to recover from. The three-year strong #BringBackOurGirls campaign has barely 50 people at its weekly sit-outs this year, but continues its tradition of rattling obtuse governments by a devastatingly effective use of Twitter and other social media.

In Ghana last year, social media is credited for the historic movement that unseated the ruling National Democratic Congress and installing its new president after three unsuccessful attempts.

Then, of course, according to observers, it was the rise and influence of social media that overwhelmed its 20-year dictator, Yahya Jammeh and ushered him out of office in January 2017 under a thick cloud of disgrace and powerlessness. It will be remembered that he had shut down the internet in the country on the eve of its December 2016 elections.

So Africa's leaders have reason to be scared. And the gasps of a dying establishment are seen in the desperate attempts to limit expression, dampen enthusiasm and battle connectivity.

But they will fail.

Try as they might and succeed in the interim as they may, recent history will show that there is no force on earth that can stop a hashtag whose time has time.

Ensconced by the safety of life-presidencies, self-affirming political corruption and access to unlimited resources, they have been unaware of the revolution that has occurred under their noses – as citizens inside and outside the country can link arms with neighbours to make life difficult for their leaders, to organise above and under the radar and to strategise with tools that the old order cannot understand.

It would be wise for them to learn from Jammeh. But it would be too much to expect that an elite set used to maintaining and transferring power within its ranks would easily relinquish that power to the will of an angry, frustrated, organised citizenry.

Luckily, they are set to confront, in a series of elections and other actions across the continent in the immediate future, a resolute, determined and well organised youth population, supported by a continental aspiration and strengthened by mobile technology.

"Until recently, however, it was a lot harder to get psychographics than demographics, and even if you had psychographic data, it wasn't always obvious how to make it actionable," says the same HBR piece. "The internet has changed the relative importance of demographics and psychographics to marketers in three key ways: by making psychographics more actionable, by making psychographic differences more important, and by making psychographic insight easier to access."

Africa is going to change whether its leaders like it or not.

Because, yes, you can close down the internet, but you most certainly cannot close down the fortitude of a people who have, quite simply, had enough.

16

OF COURSE, YOUTH MATTER

When it comes to Africa's political space, the most talked about phenomenon by the rest of the world is the huge potential of the youth population. It has been talked up so much it has become cliché.

What that means is that the capacity of this population in the interim is overstated, its potential becoming the stuff of myth rather than strategy, and sufficient detail isn't available country to country to create easy pathways for converting trends into action.

So a headline like 'Bill Gates Thinks Africa's Youth are Vital for Driving Innovation', can induce eye rolling amongst the highly educated in that group. After all, youth drives innovation in just about every accessible nation in the world. The statement is so broad and anodyne that it doesn't capture any specific actionable reality. It's more likely to lull the demographic to sleep than to inspire it to action.

And there is the fact that we are not even certain that this demographic bulge is a positive indicator of anything.

"There's work to be done: between 2000 and 2008 Africa created 73 million jobs, but only 16 million for young people," GE noted in a recent piece. "Surely, this would be a challenge for any economy, but the charge stands even taller for a regional labor market that is already struggling to absorb workers into formal employment.

"Currently, an overwhelming majority of workers are either self-employed or work unpaid for their families. And the need for job creation is particularly crucial for Africa's youth—they comprise around 60 percent of Africa's unemployed, compared to a 44 percent global average.

"But while Africa's potential labor force is hefty and growing, big parts of the workforce remain unskilled, and there is a need for more colleges and technical schools to generate those skills. According to the World Bank, about two-thirds of all young workers in the sub-Saharan labor market—95 million people—lack the basic skills needed to be competitive. What's more, unemployment rates for graduates are often high."

Still, the fundamental truth of the narrative remains: Africa's youth population is a massive advantage for the future, if harnessed.

"Between now and 2050, over half of the global population growth will take place in Africa, with the continent adding 1.3 billion people, compared with Asia's 0.9 billion," a Quartz Africa piece notes. "Thus, by 2050, Africa's share of the global population will reach 25%, as Asia's share falls to 54%. Sub-Sahara Africa's population boom is one of the main reasons for optimism about the continent's economic growth potential."

There are two fields of play where this advantage is of strategic importance: entrepreneurship and political participation.

It is important that we have used the phrase 'political participation' rather than the term 'politics' which can often be synonym for political office.

The fact is there are considerable roadblocks to young people running for political office, as Jideonwo has noted in an article also for Quartz.

"Another reason is pragmatism," he wrote. "Our current political leaders have the massive networks, resources and name recall that win elections. As the next generation has just come into its own over the past half-decade (in Nigeria, real youth participation in elections as a bloc began in 2011) it has only now begun to build the street savvy that can win elections or hijack political systems. Until this happens, there is little choice."

Where the huge potential of the largely unemployed population can be as it steadily builds its capacity in the interim - and this is a hugely crucial necessity - is as an active citizenry.

The historic election upsets in Nigeria, Ghana and Gambia, for instance, make it clear the massive influence that young people can have in the process. But there needs to be a systematic follow through that leads this mass into a sustained civil society that keeps governments on their toes, and continues to practically modify behavior on a day to day basis.

When youth show up, they make a considerable difference. The tragedy however is that, even though this is an attractive storyline for international media desperate for local comparisons to Western models, Africa's young are not showing up as much as they can, or ought to.

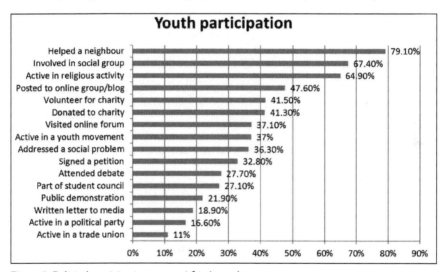

Figure 8: Political participation among Africa's youth

A 2011 paper by Danielle Resnick and Daniela Casale, 'The Political Participation of Africa's Youth: Turnout, Partisanship and Protest' which combined country-level variables for 19 of Africa's more democratic countries with individual-level public opinion data from Afrobarometer survey data found that Africa's youth tend to vote less and express a lower level of partisanship (attachment to a particular party) than older citizens.

Even worse, it reports, "Africa's youth are not more likely to protest than older citizens: claims that disillusioned African youth will foment instability do not yet appear warranted in many of the region's electoral democracies. Findings also raise the questions of whether the electoral process is a legitimate means of conveying young people's concerns and whether political parties are accurately representing younger citizens' interests."

It made four other conclusions. The first three should worry you:

+ Unlike older voters, the youth tend to vote less the longer an incumbent party has been in office.
+ Poor incumbent performance on job creation increases the likelihood of the youth expressing either no partisanship or an affinity with the opposition. Dissatisfaction with government's handling of job creation also has the largest substantive impact for the youth group with respect to their support for the opposition. For the non-youth group, dissatisfaction with a broader range of issues is associated with partisanship.
+ The likelihood of Africa's youth being involved in protests is not significantly different to their older counterparts. This suggests that while they are less engaged in elections and party politics, they are not channelling discontent into extra-institutional participation.

The fourth however gives cause for hope. "Higher levels of education and economic deprivation, as well as lack of satisfaction with democracy, increase the likelihood that the youth will protest," it said.

Considering that this is a 2011 paper, we are happy to report that things have considerably changed since then, only not at a fast enough rate to create a wave of transformation that can lift the continent effectively. If anything, many of these changes only began in 2015, with Nigeria's elections inspiring a continent's youth to believe in possibilities.

These trends need to be isolated, they need to be interrogated and conclusions reached, by massive investment in youth capacity to truly open societies and shake up political systems and establishments.

Cute anecdotes of young people using gaming to touch 600 people in Abuja, or participatory video to address local governments in Nairobi, or a couple of infographics getting a few hundred retweets in Accra are the kind of low-expectations games that have kept Africa's youth from truly achieving the potential of political reform.

Campaigns to create youth parties might be quixotic considering that youth is not a permanent state like gender, race or sexuality and campaigns to lower voting ages have been timid, often seeking to triangulate with the same establishments that they hope to defeat.

For the youth capacity in politics to match the potential we have seen in entrepreneurship from iROKO TV in Nigeria to m-KOPA Solar in Kenya, there needs to be an equally massive investment, not just in easy social entrepreneurship activities, but in hard-core political engineering.

Young people with the capacity to build movements, capture the attention of the masses and direct mainstream action should be given the resources to create the kind of large scale political change that truly changes the establishments – and beyond just national elections.

The youth have actual capacity to, like Nigeria and Ghana, change election outcomes. But because the attention of a global community focuses solely on presidential elections, these changes have not cascaded down to regional, state and local government elections.

Youth have the capacity to enact large-scale constitutional reform, to initiate election recall mechanisms and to activate massive national judicial battles that force public officials to behave or step aside. It is possible to create country-to-country youth-led national movements that are actively involved in the processes of political and social engineering that handicap corrupt governments and tip the balance of power to the hands of citizens, who will now learn to deploy that power in ways that remake their nations and ignite their capacity to transform themselves.

That is the true potential of Africa's youth, to get actual political results that shake up systems and upset comfortable establishments.

But we need commissioned, major transformative research that unlocks the potential of the sleeping population, understanding the attitudes that drive non-participation in universities, cynicism in new voters and limited post-election action generally, and in understanding the population across class, gender, education and other boundaries, we will then be able to activate drivers that will ensure the large-scale engagement of numbers.

There is nothing politicians fear more than numbers. But presently they don't really fear the numbers of the youth. The international community, focused as it is on the future, is more attuned – sadly – to the actual economic and political potential of the youth of these nations, than their own political and economic leaders.

What's worth doing at all however is worth doing well. There is an entire generation of African doers with the strategy and capacity to lead actual revolutions that change political outcomes and modify political behavior.

If politics is what ultimately changes lives, then there is no time as now to really drive that innovation that Bill Gates spoke about, in the most meaningful, sustainable way for Africa's much celebrated youth bulge.

17

POLITICAL PARTIES WILL CONTINUE TO MATTER FOR A VERY LONG TIME

There is really no difference at the end of the day, in character and substance, between Nigeria's People's Democratic Party (PDP) and its All Progressives Congress (APC).

Without distinct, identifiable ideologies, both are simply effective vehicles for political competition, ensuring that voters have robust alternatives that force political power brokers to perform in expectation of polling booth reward. The candidates are the ideology that voters must associate with both parties.

Personalities often make the difference.

Which is just as well, seeing as in the world's strongest democracy, it has become apparent that parties can be the problem rather than the solution. And the two strongest movements last year in American politics happened in spite of the political parties, the reason many players in that space have begun to loathe the parties.

They have a point. By their nature, political parties are self-reinforcing institutions. Created as a tool to express political will of citizens, they have become, naturally, a self-perpetuating organ that can too easily forget the purpose for which it was created and then focus on strengthening their own real and perceived power rather than focus on channeling the aspirations of the people it should be primarily concerned with.

This means, in simpler terms, that rather than search for what makes people hopeful or angry and organising around that, political parties these days often organise to benefit the leaders of the parties and the things they consider to be priorities.

They become essentially about the consolidation of power, which leads them, for instance, to seek and find politicians who they assume can raise money and win elections, rather than those who express the party's ideals and are more likely to pass its agenda.

The second problem is that parties inexorably become slaves to agenda despite the constant state of flux in which the world operates in reality. So they establish orthodoxy, say about free markets or sexual liberties, and build a consensus around those, but then forget to adapt and innovate and react to the world as it moves, clinging to the safe and familiar when voter needs and human desires have, naturally, advanced forward, as they have throughout history.

They focus on themselves rather than the citizen. This is the essential reason why parties, in free and fair democracies, often lose power. Because, in terms that business people will understand, they forget to disrupt themselves.

It thus becomes important for citizens to rotate power amongst the parties to ensure a re-focus on what matters.

"Most periods of so-called permanent majorities in American history are not as clear-cut as they first appear. Not since the demise of the Whigs has an election destroyed a major American party," RealClearPolitics wrote in 2009 after the Obama Revolution. "Instead, the party that seems to have been reduced to permanent minority status is usually just a few cycles away from having a significant share of power.

"Second, the American public clearly has use for a two-party system. Why else would it keep returning the minority party to power? Many ideologies like to think that their side has a monopoly on the Good and the Right, but the broad middle of this country is non-ideological, and we can always count on it to elevate the minority party when the majority is not governing to its satisfaction."

Bernie Sanders captured this in post-election tweets last year.

"We can't be a party which cozies up to Wall Street, raises money from billionaires & stands with working families. We've got to pick a side," he tweeted on 10th November. "The Democratic Party has to be focused on grassroots America and not wealthy people attending cocktail parties. Millions of people are willing to put in 20 bucks, 30 bucks, 50 bucks, if there's a Democratic Party to believe in."

It is the reason the Sanders and Trump movements were essentially hostile takeovers of their respective parties. The voters didn't follow the neat lines of what it meant to be conservative or progressive. Indeed, for the first time in America's history, socialism stopped being a dirty word because Sanders made it so. But it wasn't really Sanders. It was the sense from these voters that political parties and the ideologies they sprout had stopped serving them.

"A recent Reason-Rupe survey found that a majority of Americans under 30 have a more favorable view of socialism than of capitalism. Gallup finds that almost 70 percent of young Americans are ready to vote for a "socialist" president," author Anis Shivani wrote in July 2016. "So it has come as no surprise that 70 to 80 percent of young Americans have been voting for Bernie Sanders, the self-declared democratic socialist. "Some pundits have been eager to denounce such surveys as momentary aberrations, stemming from the economic crash, or due to lack of knowledge on the part of millennials about the authoritarianism they say is the inevitable result of socialism. They were too young to have been around for Stalin and Mao, they didn't experience the Cold War, they don't know to be grateful to capitalism for saving them from global tyranny. The critics dismiss the millennials' political leanings by repeating Margaret Thatcher and Ronald Reagan's mantra, "There is no alternative" (TINA), which prompted the extreme form of capitalism we now know as neoliberalism.

"But millennials, in the most positive turn of events since the economic collapse, intuitively understand better. Circumstances not of their choosing have forced them to think outside the capitalist paradigm, which reduces human beings to figures of sales and productivity, and to consider if in their immediate lives, and in the organization of larger collectivities, there might not be more cooperative, nonviolent, mutually beneficial arrangements with better measures of human happiness than GDP growth or other statistics that benefit the financial class."

The takeover of the Democratic Party occasioned by the former Independent who only identified as a Democrat in order to participate in its primaries continues even today.

"It is absolutely imperative that we see a major transformation of the Democratic Party," Sanders told the Wall Street Journal in a post-election interview. "(The party has) to do what has to be done in this country, to bring new energy, new blood."

RawStory.com captured the drama: "Vermont Sen. Bernie Sanders may have lost the 2016 Democratic nomination, but the fiery politician and his large contingent of supporters don't appear to have given up the fight in 2017 and beyond. The progressive, self-described 'Democratic socialist' still has many loyalists who they are fighting along different battle lines: by running for local city and county government offices in an attempt to thwart President Donald Trump's conservative policies.

"A tough challenge awaits Sanders' supporters in the short term after his failed bid for the White House. Trump starkly opposes several of the former Democratic candidate's key policies, including climate change reform, supporting immigration nationwide and regulating local and national economies. But a new wave of liberal activism nationwide in the Democratic party's base has helped numerous Sanders supporters win low-level posts in blue areas like California, signaling a long-term fundamental shift that could shift the party further to the left."

"For now, the strategy of Mr. Sanders's followers is to infiltrate and transform the Democratic Party's power structure, starting with the lowest-level state and county committee posts that typically draw scant attention," the Journal notes. ""From where I come from in the Bernie movement, people believe that there are permanent obstacles to change," said Larry Cohen, the board chairman of Our Revolution, the political organisation that grew from the 2016 Sanders presidential campaign.

"The broader goal is not only to pull the party to the left on policy, but also to fundamentally alter how it operates by eschewing corporate donors, shifting resources from television advertising to neighborhood organizing and stripping power from longtime party elders—including the "superdelegates" who can tip presidential primary contests—ahead of the 2020 election."

The same reality was reflected in the Republican party where Trump's chief strategist, Stephen Bannon effectively kicked into gear a long-term campaign to fundamentally restructure the way the Republican party does business.

"We don't really believe there is a functional conservative party in this country and we certainly don't think the Republican Party is that," he said, at a 2013 event. "We tend to look at this imperial city of Washington, this boomtown, as they have two groups, or two parties, that represent the insiders' commercial party, and that is a collection of insider deals, insider transactions and a budding aristocracy that has made this the wealthiest city in the country."

"Bannon is radically anti-conservative, with no apparent regard for custom or continuity or prudence or the need to fear and restrain populist passions," a 2016 piece in the Atlantic on 'The Radical Anti-Conservatism of Stephen Bannon' noted. "But the Trumpist movement divided the Tea Party (and) stripped the principles that motivate limited government conservatives from the core of the Republican Party."

A May 2016 Politico piece on the future of parties explains what's going on: "On left and right, it feels as though a new era is beginning," it notes. "And a new era *is* beginning, but not in the way most people think. Though this election feels like the beginning of a partisan realignment, it's actually the end of one. The partisan coalitions that defined the Democratic and Republican parties for decades in the middle of the twentieth century broke apart long ago; over the past half century, their component voting blocs — ideological, demographic, economic, geographic, cultural — have reshuffled. The reassembling of new Democratic and Republican coalitions is nearly finished.

"What we're seeing this year is the beginning of a policy realignment, when those new partisan coalitions decide which ideas and beliefs they stand for — when, in essence, the party platforms catch up to the shift in party voters that has already happened. The type of conservatism long championed by the Republican Party was destined to fall as soon as a candidate came along who could rally its voters without being beholden to its donors, experts and pundits. The future is being built before our eyes, with far-reaching consequences for every facet of American politics. The 2016 race is a sign that American politics is changing in profound and lasting ways; by the 2020s and 2030s, partisan platforms will have changed drastically."

As a Huffington Post headline noted: "The hostile takeover of the GOP is now complete."

So we know that people are deeply dissatisfied with political parties, and beyond the United States.

But that is not the complete story.

Despite the takeover, political parties continue to be essential and are likely to remain essential for a very long time.

In fact, the term 'takeover' in itself is significantly telling of the imperative to maintain the structure while altering its operations.

Humans beings organise, and we gravitate towards organisation; mostly because the alternative is either chaos or anarchy. We can't function if we don't organise.

After Addo Dankwa Akufo-Addo won the elections, one of the authors walked into a store and one of the sales girls was telling a colleague "I am happy, my party is now in power". She had a sense of personal ownership of a political operation.

The power of the party in Ghana, as with many democracies, cannot be overemphasised. A candidate who becomes the nominee of any of the two major parties instantly inherits a passionate base of followers who identify with him/her.

In fact someone on the campaign famously told Williams that there are a lot of people in the country who will vote for a pair of slippers if the pair is put on a ballot box. Many families have a party they vote for in an election.

"Infact if the candidacy is problematic like Mahama," he told us. "The best you can hope for with many of those party's natural voters is for the people in that region to stay away from the ballot box as we saw in the Volta region."

Parties are fundamentally organisations of political belief or identity. People who want politics to be defined and expressed in a particular way that presumably benefits them will organise around that priority, or join organisations that prize that priority.

"The Republican Party throughout our history has been a party whose core constituency has been those who are considered, by themselves and by others, to be typical Americans," RealClearPolitics notes in another piece. "In the 19th century, that meant white Northern Protestants. Today, it means white married Christians. Yet such people, however typical, have never made up a majority in our culturally and regionally diverse nation.

"The Democratic Party throughout our history has been the party whose core constituencies have been those who are considered, by themselves and by others, to be something other than typical Americans. In the 19th century, that meant white Southerners and big city Catholics. Today, it means blacks and singles and seculars and those with postgraduate degrees. Such people, while atypical, potentially make up a majority."

It is an understanding of the power of these organisations as expressions, even if imperfect, of popular will that pushed Sanders and Trump to make the wise decisions to run under the banner of established parties rather than waste resources on third party runs. That's what led Sanders to affect real change in how the Democrats do business, and Trump to win the election and actually get the chance to change the country.

Political parties matter. Strong political parties matter.

Muhammadu Buhari needed the APC to have been created for him to win.

As far back as April 2007, Jideonwo had, in colourful language, spoken of the imperatives that finally brought about the coalition together.

"If all these candidates really did care about Nigeria or about 'their people', and keep saying PDP is the evil to be removed, then they should be ready to put biases aside and then work together for this 'common good' of dislodging the PDP," he wrote. "It is extremely, abundantly, completely, utterly stupid to match into these elections, after all the money spent, doomed to fail - when together they (and us) stand to benefit more.

"If Atiku, Ojukwu, Pat Utomi, and Kalu align with Buhari, THEN they well win this election. Kalu will come with Abia votes, Ojukwu will bring all the Igbo votes, Pat Utomi will bring that of all educated youth (operative word: educated) especially students, and Atiku will bring Lagos, Adamawa and Edo at least. Joined to Buhari's ANPP states, the core north, and those here and there who love his sound policies and clean record, he will beat Yar'adua. Any other way, these suckers lose!"

In 2014, it finally happened. Utomi, Atiku and Buhari came together to form a political alternative to the ruling People's Democratic Party.

Indeed, watching that party come together was the witnessing of a masterstroke in political engineering by its controversial national leader, Bola Ahmed Tinubu. It first required a steady but voracious weakening of the ruling party, the wooing of its unappreciated and disaffected members, and then the conscientious building of buy-in or goodwill across the country's power blocs symbolised by the dramatic landing of private jets at the homes of Nigeria's ex-leaders over a one year period.

Eventually, three political blocs were collapsed into one mega-party, including Tinubu's Action Congress, Atiku's multi-decade People's Democratic Movement, and Buhari's Congress for Progressive Change.

Despite the fact that the party has 'Progressives' in its name, it is not to be confused with the West's idea of progressive, even if it makes public aspiration to that ideal. The party is, essentially a look-alike of the ruling party right down to its leading lights and candidates that were a transplant from the PDP.

However what it did was provide an alternative, a necessity in any truly competitive democracy. That alternative became centered around personalities, but it was a crucial step towards rebalancing the axis of power in favor of voters; ensuring, at the very least, a contest for the affections and validation of citizens.

The collective capacity of a people to punish a failed government is one that has become a powerful motivation for a frustrated generation. Since rebuilding our nations will ultimately be a long-term march, then a change in government represents an important step in making revolution happen.

In any case, it is not unusual that parties become primarily vehicles for personalities.

"Parties are not static," as RealClearPolitics notes. "Instead, they're collections of individuals whose personal aspirations translate into a collective goal: the acquisition of political power. That goal forces party agents to rethink and refashion their message when they are in the minority. They select issue positions and emphasis in pursuit of an electoral majority. If those selections fail, they try again. Sooner or later, they succeed. That's why we know slogans like the 'Full Dinner Pail', the 'New Deal', the 'New Frontier", the 'New Democrats', the 'Contract with America', 'Compassionate Conservatism', the 'Change We Can Believe In' and so on. These are all the product of strategic actors within the parties fashioning new messages to appeal to the electorate in pursuit of a majority.

"In short, presidential elections have unique *and* stable qualities to them. The (political) parties (through their) electoral bases generally offer the stability, but the candidate's personalities, their messages, and the issues of the day make each one unique."

Again, it bears repeating, that they serve a crucial societal purpose: the certainty of competition.

So, will they continue to matter? For a while yes, alongside many entrenched social institutions across religion, economy, and academia because they are built to be durable and thus successfully resistant to change. But the way that they will express themselves will change. The way they do business will have to adapt to the fierce individualism of the 21st century, the barrier-breaking commonality of the social generation, and the incipient, insistent demands from the global upheaval in people power dynamics.

Ultimately, these drip-drip attacks on the institution are likely to give way to a new form of institution, a new form of political organisation that expresses the common will. That change is very likely to come. Political parties after all, are only about 400 years old.

"The ancient Greeks, who were pioneers in developing democracy, had no organised political parties in the modern sense," the *New Book of Knowledge* reminds us. "The senate of the ancient Romans had two groups that represented people with different interests — the Patricians and the Plebeians. The Patricians represented noble families. The Plebeians represented the wealthy merchants and the middle class. Although these two groups often mingled, at times they voted as factions, or parties, on particular issues that were important to the groups they represented.

"For many centuries after the fall of Rome (A.D. 476), the people of Europe had little voice in politics. Thus there were no true political parties — only factions that supported one noble family or another. Political parties developed as representative assemblies gained power. In England, this change began after what was called the Popish Plot of 1678."

Parties were created by humans to solve specific problems. They can be recreated or replaced by humans if they cease to solve those problems.

It is almost certain that it will take a while for anything to replace the party as a primary political institution. But the only thing certain in the future is not that political parties will continue to exist, but that political will will continue to be expressed, and citizens find the best human organisation to communicate that will. So, parties will have to change.

To paraphrase the Politico piece, "The old political system is crumbling and a new political order is being born."

18

POLITICAL INSTINCTS MATTER

In 2015, when we worked on the Muhammadu Buhari elections, the budget for voter insight was very thin.

So as we sought to deploy campaign ads in a particular section of the country, we went to the Director General of the campaign with a budget for conducting a series of focus groups and to commission another poll to gain insight into post-convention reactions, tracking any possible bounces.

The DG repeated a now-familiar refrain: no money.

This was particularly frustrating because we had created two distinct scenarios that we were very invested in, and also whatever broad narrative options emerged from the data gathering. One included a pet project for a tour of historically significant emotional touch points for a generation of voters in that area.

But the DG had no money to undertake this exercise, and more than that, he didn't think it mattered. "Those voters will never vote for the candidate," he explained dismissively. "When we find some money, let's focus on driving voter turnout in the areas where we have already measured deep support."

Nigeria has a corollary to America's Electoral College system, and so it worried us slightly that we had to calculate and assume the loss of over four states. But we had learned something in the course of our work, armed as were by strategy documents, position papers, situation reports, interim memos, voter data, and campaign material: we had learnt to listen with humility to a politician who had been working across Nigeria for at least 15 active years.

He had been in meetings at the highest levels, he had engaged in combat with intractable forces, he had actually visited many of the parts of the country that we were just now touring as part of the campaign and he understood instinctively, from years of directly canvassing voters, the attitudes that at least defined the past behaviour of voters, if not the future.

There was plenty to be learned, and plenty of resources to be saved by listening to a man whose political instincts were sharply fine-tuned by experience, by insight, and by interaction.

We encountered the same advantage in Ghana 2016. Our candidate, Addo Dankwa Akufo-Addo believed that in these elections instead of touring media houses and giving interviews he was better off connecting with the voters directly by going to those places repeatedly and giving the messages to them.

Because we had learnt to listen, we had an extended conversation to understand the premises of his thinking based on his experience from the last elections, and we went off on our own to brainstorm over the pros and cons. Crucial to our conclusion was the fact that international media would ensure free and fair elections, but would not move the needle with the bulk of the persuadable electoral. We decided that it made ample sense. So we re-arranged the press strategy - moving the major interviews to just a few days to the elections.

Political instincts matter because they bring the benefit of experience, patterns and history. And human beings are nothing if not creatures of habit.

Unfortunately, many young people who seek hostile takeovers of political systems or seek to make significant inroads via the hacking of political establishments often despise the knowledge that experience brings.

Much of that drives the conversations about creating youth parties, which is essentially code for disregarding the structures, behaviours and imperatives of the past and creating out of whole cloth a new system and platform that caters to what they imagine are a communal need for all young people.

This thinking is faulty and problematic, to say the least.

First, the problems with Africa's politics are problems of form not of essence. That means that essentially there is nothing wrong with political affiliations, party identity and the entire ebb and flow of political transaction. It is also natural for voters to form relationships with the power structures that presently exist. There is no urgent need to change the system of political parties and political relationships that exist.

What needs to be changed is the form in which they exist and the substance by which they are expressed. This can principally mean that we need to change the kind of people that hold the levers of powers within these structures and the kinds of ideas that power their actions. The bathwater, not the baby.

One of the most celebrated and effective political offices holders in Nigeria's recent history has been Peter Obi, the former governor of Anambra. Legend holds that he ran for office after witnessing a lynching at a popular market in the state. He immediately began to print posters and fliers announcing his candidacy, even before he was officially registered in a political party. He also had never voted in an election until then.

But, disruptor though he was, the very next thing he did was find a political party – the All Progressives Grand Alliance - that was prepared to accept him and his vision. This wasn't even a hostile takeover, this was a symbiosis. The party needed a candidate with the resources and moxie to win elections, and he needed an organised, legacy platform to actualise his ambitions. He transformed the party and remade it in his own image and so delivered victory for himself and for it.

To do this he focused on the important battles, and the important battles were governance battles. He did not need to create a new party, or waste time fighting for new political structures; he simply won the war of persuasion internally and converted the party into a vehicle for his vision.

He left the state one of Nigeria's most successful governors in recent history, with massive investments in education including technology upgrades, advancement in teaching methods and infrastructure, significantly – actually, massively – cutting waste in government spending, accumulated savings (for the first time in a long while)in the state reserves, massive overhaul of five government hospitals and laboratories, rebuilding more than 900 kilometers of roads and bridges and, crucially, paying all debts (over N37 billion) for salaries and pensions the state owed since 1999.

He did this by combining what he had with what already worked. "The parties' electoral bases generally offer the stability, but the candidate's personalities, their messages, and the issues of the day make each one unique," RealClearPolitics.com explains the dynamic.

The state of Lagos offers another textbook study of this important balance. While it may remain in that murky terrain of rumours, our interaction with numerous sources in the All Progressives Congress confirms that there was, at the least, friction between the national leader of the party, Bola Ahmed Tinubu and his former chief of staff-turned-governor, Babatunde Fashola.

The partnership between the two rested on Tinubu managing the politics of the state and administering the relationships that maintained peace and equilibrium, while Fashola focused on consolidating the gains made under his predecessor.

Often though, when there was a contest of wills between the both with the latter seeking to establish political authority, it led to a distraction from governance, as there were no political relationships for the governor to build upon and no blocs to rely on. The ensuring political drama, involving the beginnings of legislative maneuvers, briefly destabilised the focus for him. A quick reconciliation restored the balance, and he finished out his term in peace.

Towards the end of course, he did try to mount one last stand, favouring his own governorship candidate Olasupo Sashore, who was his

attorney general and commission for justice over the Tinubu pick, Akin-
wunmi Ambode, who was his accountant general.

For those who could make conclusions based on the series of events,
he however hadn't taken the time to develop political instincts and to the
hard work of building coalitions that can deliver political victory. Politics
is a network of relationships or, at the least the knowledge to take advantage of existing relationship networks. Success was far from certain
in this venture.

There were 5,700 delegates from 20 local government areas to vote
for the 13 candidates for the gubernatorial primaries of the APC. By the
time the elections were done, Ambode had won in a landslide – 3,735
votes to Sashore's miserly 121, less than one percent of the victor's share.

Revolutions always suffer from the temptation to believe the old can
completely be annihilated, and the new cut from whole cloth. Save for
genocides and witch-hunts however, this is almost as impossible as it is
unnecessary.

As the oft-talked about Chinese revolution and Malaysia miracle
have taught the world, often what governance needs is new attitudes that
replace traditional conventions, expressed by strong relationships and
sustained by strong institutions. To do this, there are legacies of the past
that need to be leveraged to build bridges into the future.

Humans have always advanced through evolution, through the ne-
gotiation of old and new giving birth to fresh. The substance and power
of the new however often decides how effective or sustainable they will
be.

There is a reason after all why Bernie Sanders actively courted superdelegates in the American elections, Donald Trump arm-twisted House
Speaker Paul Ryan for his support, and Barack Obama climbed on the
back of Illinois Senate President, Emil Jones Jr. (often called his 'political
godfather') "who helped Obama master the intricacies of the Legislature"
and "tapped Obama to take the lead on high-profile legislative initiatives
that he now boasts about in his presidential campaign," in addition to
needing the platform of the 2004 Democratic National Convention to
launch his unlikely career and presidency.

For those who want to transform their African nations, especially in a cultural context that is heavy on order, ageism and hierarchy, they may want to learn from Africa's most successful technology start-ups, that there are massive benefits to looking at the past as a signpost to the future. Case in point, what Nigeria's iROKO TV did with basic un-sophisticated Nollywood formats.

A new generation should wake up and pay attention.

The crucial skill for action and decision may come from the Serenity Prayer: the good sense "to accept the things I cannot change, courage to change the things I can, and **wisdom to know the difference."**

19

IDEOLOGY SIMPLY DOESN'T MATTER YET

There is a sense in which much of the developed world is in a post-ideological phase.

Certainly, America has to admit that it is. The Republican Party after all voted for a candidate who believes differently from all of its orthodoxy on social issues, and is wobbly on its traditional tenets on the economy.

"Trump is a pragmatic conservative, par excellence," UC-Berkeley professor George Lakoff wrote in a piece predicting his success. "And he knows that there are a lot of Republican voters who are like him in their pragmatism. There is a reason that he likes Planned Parenthood. There are plenty of young, unmarried (or even married) pragmatic conservatives, who may need what Planned Parenthood has to offer — cheaply and confidentially.

"Similarly, young or middle-aged pragmatic conservatives want to maximize their own wealth. They don't want to be saddled with the financial burden of caring for their parents. Social Security and Medicare relieve them of most of those responsibilities. That is why Trump wants to keep Social Security and Medicare."

The Atlantic summarised his distinction: "(This) is an Ivy League grad who has spent most of his life in Manhattan, where he is chauffeured around in limousines. He frequently brags to strangers about his massive personal wealth. In public statements, he has advocated government healthcare, a woman's right to an abortion, an assault weapons ban, and paying off the national debt by forcing rich people to forfeit 14.25 percent of their total wealth. When the man married his third wife, he invited Bill and Hillary Clinton to the wedding, and he has given many thousands to their political campaigns and their foundation. He's donated many thousands more that helped elect Democrats to the Senate and the House. And George W. Bush was 'maybe the worst president in the history of this country,' the man said in 2008."

"Trump comes to the presidency with no coherent ideology," Ben Shapiro wrote in the National Review in November 2016. "The most accurate appraisal of Trump actually came courtesy of President Barack Obama this week: "I also think that he is coming to this office with fewer set hard-and-fast policy prescriptions than a lot of other presidents might be arriving with. I don't think he is ideological. I think ultimately, he's pragmatic in that way. And that can serve him well."

Shapiro then takes his time, to put simply the reason why ideology should matter.

"Philosophy matters," he said. "It's long been a leftist trope that the president who governs best simply does what works'. That sentiment goes back to Woodrow Wilson, who stated in his first inaugural address in 1913 that he wouldn't govern based on a set philosophy, but rather based on "the facts as they are. . . . Step by step we shall make [our economic system] what it should be in the spirit of those who question their own wisdom and seek counsel and knowledge." Decisions would be made based on "our time and the need of our people." Wilson, of course, was no pragmatist. He was a progressive. Pragmatism is a progressive philosophy. There is no clear consensus on 'what works.' That's because pragmatism is a progressive philosophy.

"This is why elections matter, and why political ideology matters. It's an empty conceit of arrogant politicians that they alone can determine, based on expert reading of facts, the best solution; they can't. How we view facts — our worldview — determines our action. There is no dispassionate problem-solver. There are only people who believe certain things about the world and masquerade as dispassionate problem-solvers."

In an interview with Salon.com, fascism scholar Robert Paxton captured what many consider the essence of Trump: "It's a little risky to guess about whether somebody is or is not sincere. I'm quite sure he has a number of feelings about things, which have to do mostly, I think, with getting his own way. I think he surely feels very strongly about the things that favor his enterprises. If he has convictions, I think they're mainly related to his self-interest."

So he might as well be a contemporary African leader.

To be sure, Africa's democracy was founded on strong, vehement political ideologies. In the euphoria of political independence in the 50s and 60s, many African leaders came to office armed with East/West paradigms of ideology and had vigorous debates and consensuses around socialism, communism and capitalism, for instance.

For many of these leaders' ideologies were the most potent framework for the development of their nations, even if development is a vague and relational term.

"One fundamental assumption embraced by leaders in these countries is that they cannot achieve this worthwhile goal if they still lean heavily on the ideology of their colonial masters," said a 2012 paper 'Nkrumah and the Triple Heritage Thesis and Development in Africana Societies' published in the International Journal of Business, Humanities and Technology. "However, the starting point and the ingredients of this ideology differed from one leader to another. Thus while some believe that such ideology should be rooted in the traditional culture of these societies, others believe that the traditional culture alone cannot constitute a viable basis for such ideology given the fact that the traditional culture has become anachronistic and therefore it could not ground an ideology for development of the modern African state."

Communism became an effective weapon to attack the West and

either colonialism or apartheid, a record that the book *Communism in Sub-Saharan Africa: A Reappraisal* comprehensively delineates. A Communist Party was founded in South Africa in 1921.

Communists were very quick to label leaders like Ghana's Kwame Nkrumah and Liberia's William V. S. Tubman as "lackeys of imperialism."

Many Africans came to be more enamoured of socialism as a more equitable system for distribution of wealth. According to the 1964 book *African Socialism* by William H. Friedland and Carl G. Rosberg Jr., "Julius Nyerere of Tanzania, Modibo Keita of Mali, Léopold Senghor of Senegal, Kwame Nkrumah of Ghana and Sékou Touré of Guinea, were the main architects of African Socialism.

"As many African countries gained independence during the 1960s, some of these newly formed governments rejected the ideas of capitalism in favour of a more afrocentric economic model. Advocates of African socialism claimed that it was not the opposite of capitalism nor a response to it, but something completely different. (As an interesting side note, African billionaire entrepreneur, Tony O. Elumelu is these days often found pushing a new capitalism he calls 'Africapitalism).

"Common principles of various versions of African socialism were: social development guided by a large public sector, incorporating the African identity and what it means to be African, and the avoidance of the development of social classes within society."

Senghor claimed that "Africa's social background of tribal community life not only makes socialism natural to Africa but excludes the validity of the theory of class struggle."

To take a specific example, see the following excerpts from 'An Ideology for Africa', published by Foreign Affairs in 1969:"At the end of January 1967, the Tanganyika African National Union (TANU), the ruling party on the mainland of Tanzania, announced the Arusha Declaration, named for the town in the northern part of the country where the Declaration was first promulgated," recalls 'An Ideology for Africa', published in Foreign Affairs. "Supplemented by subsequent formulations throughout 1967, it has become something of a milestone, for it enunciated an ideology and articulated policies especially designed for the needs and conditions of an African country.

"According to Arusha, TANU stands committed to policies of socialism and self-reliance. Socialism is understood as a social situation which excludes exploitation of one man by another or of one class over another. The major means of production are to be under the control and ownership of the workers and peasants through the agency of the government and through cooperatives. Self-reliance means that development as a whole must be achieved through reliance on Tanzanian resources (which are chiefly agricultural) rather than through dependence upon foreign aid in capital development and technical assistance. This should enable Tanzania to remain independent in making and carrying out foreign policy. The Declaration also sharpens the definition of political commitment for both members and leaders of TANU who will be instrumental in carrying out this policy."

Nigeria also had its own strong ideological foundations – famous of which are Aminu Kano's and Obafemi Awolowo's via their parties the People's Redemption Party and the Action Group.

Awolowo's ideology is routinely referred to as a social democratic political philosophy, "which encompasses welfare programs among which are free education, free medical services, integrated rural development and full employment with which he painstakingly administered the old Western Region from 1952-1959," according to blogger Odusote Olukayo.

He expressed this most urgently through a desire for federalism. In his book *Path to Nigerian Freedom*, Olukayo writes: "He advocated federalism as the only basis for equitable national integration and as head of the Action Group, he was at the forefront of demanding for a federal constitution, which was introduced in the 1954 Lyttleton Constitution, following primarily the model proposed by the Western Region delegation led by him."

According to the Nkrumah paper referenced above, Awolowo's socialism "takes traditional African society as a point of departure and argues that the traditional African past along with its contents cannot be brought into existence as other theorists of African socialism were apt to suggest. This unique nature of the thesis as an ideology of development for African societies is its insistence that the traditional and the modern have to work in a complimentary/synthetic relationship with one another. After all, the African person is now both a product of the traditional and modern. Insofar as all development efforts are geared toward realizing human welfare the (metaphysical/existential) realities of the person have to be put into consideration."

The pillar of Awolowo's policies was 'welfarism' (what many called Awoism), at least as far as reading of his book *Case for Ideological Orientation* will uncover. "His welfarism was based on the premise that programmes, policies, decisions and/or rules should be evaluated on the basis of their consequences on the governed with the masses occupying the majority."

According to Olukoya, "Welfarism is the view that the morally significant consequences are impacts on human thus he propounded ideas that had human face."

It is no surprise therefore that, at least in public lore, Awolowo's leadership of Nigeria's Western Region, is seen as a model and a benchmark for good governance.

Unfortunately, as 'Ideology and Development in Africa', written by Crawford Young in Foreign Affairs affirms, in the decades that followed, none of the varied ideologies adopted by the leaders resulted in significant sustenance or growth in the economy, "human dignity, self-reliance, participation and societal capacity". Success, he noted, could not be tied to any particular ideology (in the very rare case that there was success).

It became a free for all as the years went by. Eventually, many of Africa's political parties stopped any active pretenses to political philosophies in substance, effectively becoming vehicles solely for the capture and retention of political power.

Of course, there are documents that make the appropriate noises about ideology, with the useful insertion of random terms. Parties like the African National Congress continue, in public, a rich tradition of a time when Africa was run on vigorous ideas, but in terms of a coherent

architecture built on well-interrogated philosophies, contemporary African societies have largely not referred to ideologies to lead. Instead, we
have built nations around people, sometimes to acclaim as with Rwanda's
Paul Kagame, or sometimes to global opprobrium as with Zimbabwe's
Robert Mugabe.

Let's look at Nigeria's ruling All Progressives Congress (APC) for
instance. Trying to condense its ideology into a coherent summary, this
is all Leonard Shilgba, a professor at the Federal University, Otuoke –
despite being sympathetic to the party – could come up with: "What
is the ideology of the All Progressives Congress? The All Progressives
Congress believes in public participation in, and where necessary, control
of the major means of production, distribution and exchange. We believe
the country should not exist for only the rich; but the poor must have a
fair shake. For instance, in public electricity supply, the APC would not
do what the PDP-led national government has done, which is to sell off
public electricity assets at a pittance to a few beneficiaries of the government of the rich, and then turn into apologists for the buyers who
obviously were not prepared enough. The APC government would not
contemplate selling of public-owned refineries to cronies of the government who are already pre-determined while making outrageous claims in
the name of fuel subsidy."

Capturing the shallowness of its offering, the APC manifesto actually says this: "We refuse to accept that we are not capable of forging a
much better society. We can do that; but first, we must create a political
arrangement that is fairly predictable—an arrangement that agrees with
our party laws."

In essence, the manifesto of the party was not based on a coherent
set of well thought-out ideas, but basically functioned as a response to
the operational deficiencies of the ruling People's Democratic Party.
They had replaced philosophy with housekeeping.

To find some coherence, one of the only useful sources is its Wikipedia page, which was most likely edited by a sympathizer outside of the
country considering the party leadership doesn't also own the Twitter
account of its name.

"The APC is generally considered to be a center-left political party that favors controlled market or regulated market economic policies, and a strong and active role for government regulation," it says, tellingly without attribution. "A substantial number of its political leaders are followers of or politicians who subscribe to the social democratic political philosophy of Obafemi Awolowo and the socialist and anti-class views of Aminu Kano."

But if the APC believes in controlled markets, then its administration in the essentially socialist economies – or at least politics – of states from Kano to Osun don't know that yet.

The editor of the page finally admits this body of contradictions in the very last paragraph: "Its social policy is a combination of social nationalism. Despite the parties' domination by pro-devolution politicians like Atiku Abubakar, Bola Tinubu and Chief Bisi Akande, the party's presidential bearer and the CPC wing is less inclined to federalism and this basic tension creates sorts of ideological strange bed fellows, accommodated in context of a desire to win and combine forces in the 2015 election cycle."

And that "basic tension" has become the lot of many African political parties, and African political systems. Politics has ceased to be a competition between ideas, but a competition between power brokers. It has become power for its own sake.

Citizens understand this instinctively, even where they cannot spell the word ideology, and this is why it has become very difficult to maintain fealty to parties for an extended period of time.

When the Communist Party of China keeps the loyalty of its people for 96 years, there is a reason, obviously for that. Since the 1978 economic reforms, GDP growth has averaged 9.9% annually and "more than 620 million people (have been lifted) out of internationally defined poverty – accounting for the entire world reduction of the numbers in such poverty."

And it all comes down, according to many sympathetic observers of Chinese politics, to an ideology-driven "economic policy (that) is extremely coherent and robust and can be readily understood in the Marxist framework utilised by its creator, Deng Xiaoping,"

What have the ideologies of Africa's nation builders done for them in comparison?

Africa's citizens therefore cannot be blamed for going to polls to vote candidates without a coherent set of ideologies. They often have no choice. They often have to swing for the fences and hope that the candidates that appeal more to them are capable of implementing the policies that they put on offer.

Caught essentially between power blocs, voters often find themselves choosing the best of the two options, as a kind of placeholder until Africa's democracies have matured to a place where competition provides innovation and innovation leads to substance.

In the meantime, the only ideology that works for many voters across the countries is "What works for now? Who is mostly to get things to work together for me and my family?"

It's a tragedy. But at least now many African countries have the luxury of choice.

Democracy is, at the very least, a useful starting point.

20

MONEY DOESN'T MATTER AS MUCH AS YOU THINK IT DOES

By the time the elections for US president held on 8th November 2016, the Democratic Party Candidate had raised $1,191,700,000 and she had spent $1,184.100,000. The Republican Party candidate, on the other hand, had raised $646,9000,000 and spent $616,500,000. In essence, the Democratic Party candidate raised and spent almost double the Republican candidate.

By the time the evening of the elections were over however, the Democratic candidate had lost the Electoral Vote 304 – 227.

What happened? One candidate focused too much on money, and the other understood that money doesn't matter all that much.

By the time the elections held, Hillary Clinton had attended at least 350 fundraisers, even using her birthday as an opportunity to raise funds. Her opponent was significantly behind, preferring to spend his time holding major rallies that fired up his supporters. In fact, he stopped holding fundraisers much earlier than Clinton.

Her campaign gave keen insight into why this was so. Asked by journalists why there were still furiously fundraising even two weeks to the

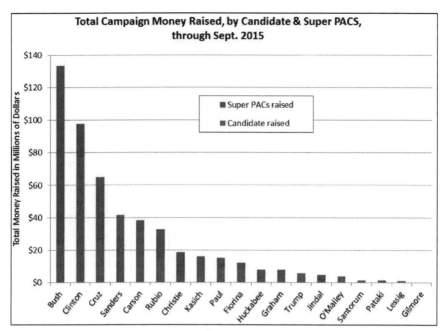

Figure 9: Total Campaign Money Raised by Candidates & Super PACS, through Sept. 2015

elections, her Communications Director Jennifer Palmieri told reporters, "We need resources to run out the campaign."

Well, it turned out, not so much.

It isn't that money doesn't matter at all, or a lot. Of course it does.

To use an unrelated discipline to explain how money works in politics, we should dive into human resources. The author of *Drive*, a book about what truly motivates people in the workplace, Daniel Pink talks about the utility of money in the book, and explained further in an interview on America's NPR.

"I mean, money does matter," he said. "First of all, the standard remuneration has to be fair and standard industry. You begin with that. If you're not - if people are being paid unfairly, if they feel like they're being treated poorly, if they're not - if they don't have enough money to support their family, you're not going to have motivation. You're not going to have this third, intrinsic drive. So you've got to pay people enough.

"But in many ways, money works more - past a certain level, money works more as a de-motivator than as a motivator. And in many ways, again, it's very counterintuitive. The science shows that the best way to use money is to take the issue of money off the people. Pay people enough so that money isn't an issue, and they can focus on doing great work."

Indeed, you could use this as the story of modern campaigning and its relationship with money: money matters, you have to have enough money to be able to do the things that you need to so that you don't worry about money. But after a particular point, money becomes a distraction, it lulls you into a false sense of comfort, removes the focus from what truly matters to how much you can raise and how much you can spend, and that is time not spent on doing great work.

After a certain baseline, money stops being any indicator of how well a political candidacy will go.

There was a time during the 2016 campaign in Ghana when National Democratic Party candidate and incumbent president, John Dramini Mahama had surrogates take out airtime across all the major media channels to talk about what he had done as president, and our ads were routinely swallowed by the opponent's frequency. Accra was full of Mahama billboards while our campaign for Addo Dankwa Akufo-Addo decided not to spend money on billboards. The Mahama campaign song *Onaapo* was so ubiquitous it was the most popular song in the country.

Our campaign knew it couldn't match the Mahama campaign in terms of media spend so it was decided that it needed to reach the people with a targeted campaign. The tripods of this strategy were rallies, Facebook and Whatsapp. While we cannot delve into detail on the latter strategy, suffice to say that deployment of Whatsapp for dissemination of messages evened the massive advantage the Mahama campaign had in terms of media spend.

In fact, the Mahama campaign seemed to be focused more on spending than on persuading. At some point, a popular Nigerian comedian, Nkem Owoh, was flown into the country for a campaign ad.

We knew immediately that this was a misstep.

First, elections are fiercely proprietary. Citizens resist any effort to be seen as influenced by people outside their countries. Elections are the most nationalistic of any activities globally apart from perhaps sports. Even consultants form neighbouring countries working on a campaign must be exceedingly carefully not to be seen to appropriate the will of the people. To bring a Nigerian to a Ghanaian election simply because they watch Nigerian movies appears the kind of misstep that happens when there is a bit too much money. It also reminds people, in an election where the candidate is accused of corruption, that there is waste in the government.

In Nigeria 2015, the People's Democratic Party's (PDP) Goodluck Jonathan campaign was also plagued with the same problem, dramatically outspending its well-funded, but drastically out-raised and out-spent rival from the All Progressives Congress (APC).

While there is no so proof and it's incredibly hard to believe the numbers, the Nigerian newspaper Punch alleged that the president spent at least $10,000,000,000 on his campaign.

"The president is not happy. They all went on property and car shopping. This was the most expensive election in history of this country, yet there was no result," Punch claimed to have been told by a Presidency source at the time. "The sad part was that even after the president lost on March 28, more money was given to all of them to make up for the dismal outing by winning their states during the April 11 elections. But that turned out to be a bad decision because apart from losing the governorship election, we didn't perform well in the other elections."

The president denied the allegations, but it is significant that this became the prevailing narrative before and immediately after the elections. It even became a scandal; with reports of officials fighting over monies, including the famous case in Ogun state in March 2015 where, in the bid to escape from angry coordinators demanding their share of monies, the South West Secretary of the party, Pegba Otemolu, got into an accident.

The scandal continued after the elections, with a slew of government officials from Jonathan's director of communication to ex-governors and ministers becoming embroiled in a wide-ranging investigation over campaign spend. At least one case is presently in court, brought by the nation's anti-corruption commission.

It is proof, again, that beyond a baseline, money in a campaign becomes a distraction. At the very least, it attracts an overdose of two sets of people: those who are not passionate about the candidate but only seek their share of slush funds, and those who will no longer be imaginative or creative because they have put their trust in money.

The candidate thus begins to experience diminishing returns.

Campaigns are expensive, but they are not a matter of expense alone. Without money you cannot run, but money won't buy you votes. Except of course you're able to rig the elections.

"One of the observations currently being made about the 2016 presidential elections involves the ineffectiveness of money as a campaign resource," a February 2016 post in the Huffington Post, by Professors of Public Policy and Political Science, Kirby Goidel and Keith Gaddie noted. "Jeb Bush and his affiliated Super PACs have raised over $150 million to barely register as a blip in the national polls or in the Iowa caucuses. There may be previous candidates who have won fewer votes with more resources and organizational support, but it is hard to think of them. While it is possible that Jeb will emerge Lazarus-like in New Hampshire or South Carolina or beyond, it seems increasingly unlikely. In this campaign cycle, voters don't seem inclined to buy what he is selling no matter how hard he is peddling it. The lesson for campaign finance is relatively straightforward, money can't fix a weak campaign or a struggling candidate. For at least some observers of the campaign, such anecdotes serve as evidence that money matters far less than we imagine."

The authors then make the crucial summary: "The campaign so far, however, is fairly consistent with what we understand about the effects of money on the electoral process. That is, money is a necessary but not a sufficient condition for winning an election. Candidates who can't raise money necessarily lose, but raising (or spending) the most money is no guarantee of victory. How the money is spent, the effectiveness of candidate messaging, and the overall political mood set boundaries around the effectiveness of campaign spending in any given electoral context."

The Director-General of the APC Presidential Campaign, Rotimi Amaechi made a statement about our work in the Nigerian elections at a public event in Lagos: "What (StateCraft Inc) did [was] make us look like we were battling the PDP dollar for dollar," he said. "Meanwhile, we had no money."

The Clinton campaign can further demonstrate how money can become a blinder through one key metric – advertising spend.

"Strategic decisions can make all the difference in a close race. Clinton lost the White House (despite winning the popular vote) to Republican Donald Trump on the strength of about 100,000 votes in Michigan, Wisconsin and Pennsylvania," the Washington Post noted on 12th November. That is the definition of a close race. But a review of Democrats' advertising decisions at the end of the race suggests Clinton and her allies weren't playing to win a close one. They were playing for a blowout. And it cost them.

"Clinton and the groups backing her aired three times as many ads as Trump and his supporters over the course of the general election, according to data from the Wesleyan Media Project. Despite that advantage, the Democrats left several key states essentially unprotected on the airwaves as the race came to a close."

What was happening? "What (the) maps show are that Trump and the Republicans were focused on a narrower path to the White House, focusing their ad dollars on a map that would net them, in a very best-case scenario, 332 electoral votes," according to the Post.

There you have it.

And therein lies the good news about money in politics.

"From the standpoint of democratic theory, this is mostly (though not entirely) good news: as in the corporate world, unlimited campaign spending can't make voters buy into candidates or ideas they don't want," the Post added.

All the recent African elections that have been won as election upsets – Somalia, Nigeria, Ghana, South Africa (municipal elections) – have been won by candidates who had significantly less resource than their incumbent opponents.

This is a fact: "Voters aren't malleable balls of clay who can easily be molded by candidates with unlimited resources."

And that should be something that gives the general populace some comfort.

21

CIVIL SOCIETY MATTERS

In January 2017, the government of Cameroon orchestrated an internet blackout in the small West African nation.

It was a panicked response to months of national protests, which came to a head in January when protesters stayed at home in a strike against what they called government marginalisation.

"Protests in Bamenda, Cameroon's third largest city, which started after school teachers embarked on an indefinite strike this week, have roots in the peculiar bilingual colonial history of the central African country," Quartz Africa reported at the time. "The Bamenda protests, which turned violent, were staged by aggrieved English-speaking Cameroonian youth, part of a building uprising against what is seen as the neglect of people of the southwest and northwest regions of Cameroon—former British colonies. Protesters mounted barricades and burned tires along major streets, and armed security forces responded with teargas and live bullets. One person is reported dead and many others have sustained injuries."

We will come back to this shortly.

In the same month, weeks before he finally threw in the towel and left his country on exile, the former Gambian dictator Yahya Jammeh fielded a plea from its new president, Adama Barrow: for him to end his crackdown on activists.

"Over the past few days, security officers claiming to be acting on orders from 'the top' have arrested and detained an unknown number of activists wearing t-shirts with the slogan Gambia Has Decided," a local media platform reported. "The officers have also shut down three private radio stations, Teranga FM, AfriRadio and Hilltop Radio without giving any reason.

"And as the crackdown continues and more activists going into hiding, Mr Barrow said he does not want to inherit a country where media freedom is fettered and human rights violated with impunity. He called on Mr Jammeh to uphold and protect the fundamental rights of the citizens."

The activists would have been familiar with the tactics. While protests had been rare in Jammeh's 23 years of maximum rule, in the past year the pace accelerated with demonstrations taking over the capital and scattered across the country.

"A Gambian opposition leader and another 18 people have been sentenced to three years in jail after being arrested for taking part in a pro-democracy protest in April that the government deemed as illegal," the International Business Times reported in July 2016. "Ousainou Darboe, leader of the United Democratic Party (UDP), and the other defendants were found guilty of participating in the unauthorised protest which occurred near the capital Banjul.

"Protesters had taken to the streets to call for electoral reforms and the resignation of Gambian President, Yahya Jammeh, who has been in power since 1994. Authorities claimed the protest was illegal as demonstrators had failed to obtain permission from the police."

Jammeh's Wikipedia entry detailed the terror: "Newspaper reports list dozens of individuals who have disappeared after being picked up by men in plain-clothes, and others who have languished under indefinite detention for months or years without charge or trial. The regional Economic Community of West African States (ECOWAS) court ordered the Gambia government to produce one journalist who was disappeared.

In April 2016, at least 50 people were arrested during a demonstration, and there were fears that Solo Sandeng, an opposition politician, died alongside two others while being held in detention. In July 2016, a Gambian opposition leader and another 18 people were sentenced to three years in jail for participation in the April demonstration. A Gambian diplomat publicly denied that Solo Sandeng had died in custody."

Leading up to the elections, he banned public protests under the pretext, as usual of national security. "Our election system is fraud-proof, rig-proof, you cannot rig our elections," he declared. "There is no reason that anybody should demonstrate. (Demonstrations) are the loopholes that are used to destabilise African governments."

And after his once-in-a-generation loss on 1st December 16, he was first shocked into conceding the election, but by the 9th he was soon back in form – jailing, harassing, and intimidating.

Thankfully, it was too late.

On 21st January, after the world reached a resolute consensus against him, riding on the back of a fed-up citizenry and an awake civil society, he had no choice but to give in and ship out.

"The effect of social media, including Facebook and WhatsApp, also helped close the gap between the opposing candidates' media presences, as mainstream outlets were dominated by the incumbent's information and propaganda during the campaign," said a WorldPolicy.org piece. "For example, the Gambia Youth and Women's Forum, a public Facebook group with 55,000 members, was very active leading up to the election. It regularly posted about and debated current issues, endorsing the opposition coalition and rallying voters."

The same thing happened in Ghana, where a generally less aggressive, but no less resolute civil society decided to steadily chip away at the support and moral authority of a president the country no longer wanted.

"Ghana's failed economic trajectory of market liberalisation has trapped the country in a cycle of export dependency based on primary commodities while destroying the domestic industry," a 2014 piece in Pambazuka News had warned. "A crash in living standards fuelled by high inflation has hit the poorest hardest. Now a new spirit of activism has emerged as a result of this crisis."

That spirit of activism fired up a citizenry that converted anger and frustration to action in its elections on 7th December 2016.

Nigeria is, of course, one of the biggest examples of this phenomenon.

Over the four years that Goodluck Jonathan was president a series of public protests defined his time in government, most against corruption and waste; the biggest being the historic #OccupyNigeria protests that, despite the hijacked narrative, became the single most important protest that signaled the falling out of the favour of that government with the general public.

Up until then, the president was viewed as a benevolent, harmless accident of political calculation. By the time the tanks rolled into Lagos to forcefully remove citizens from the Ojota hub and other small hubs of protests in the commercial capital, they had squashed any widespread goodwill that the citizen felt towards the man they voted for in a landslide less than a year before.

Other protests followed soon, including the National Immigration Service scam protests and even for small matters like the renaming of the University of Lagos.

By the time the lethally-effective #BringBackOurGirls protests that lasted throughout the last year of his presidency hit him, he was already so severely weakened that this was the last straw for a disgusted citizenry.

The president had become a protest-magnet and the image of an unpopular administration had stuck. Many observers of popular agitation in Nigeria would certainly agree that between the #OccupyNigeria and #BringBackOurGirls protests became the two most important public events that signaled the beginning of the end.

You can see the same trends today in Kenya. And you can see the same trends in South Africa, where for the first time in recent history, its 2016 elections were marked with protests and underlined by violence.

The chain of causation is now apparent and validated. First the people get angry, then civil society mounts a stand, then international consensus supports popular will, then a candidate with guts and gumption arises, and by the date of elections, change is ready to take effect.

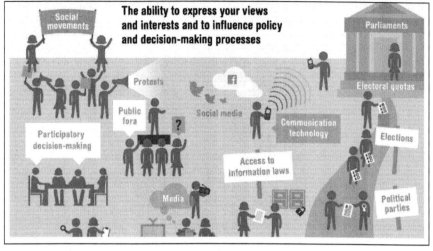

Figure 10: Political Voice

"South African universities have been affected by the biggest student protests to hit the country since apartheid ended in 1994," the BBC reported in October 2016. "South Africa's president has warned that the protests, which have caused about $44m (£34m) in damage to property in the last few weeks, could threaten to sabotage the country's entire higher education system.

"The proposed fee increases are not exceptional in comparison to usual annual increases, which are often between around 7% and 14%."

But. "Correspondents say the protests show growing disillusionment with the governing African National Congress (ANC), which took power after 1994, over high levels of poverty, unemployment and corruption in government.

"While there have been protests about fees at individual universities in previous years, the national scale of these protests over the last 12 months has been unprecedented."

Unprecedented.

In the years before a major national election.

Remember when we said we would come back to the Cameroon situation?

Well, "it has been nearly five months since political protests erupted in the English-speaking regions of Cameroon," Quartz reported again in March. "And there seems no end in sight. The government has launched a crackdown on what it sees as agitations.

"In a bid to stifle protest organisers, the government shut down the Internet in the Anglophone-speaking regions more than two months ago. The shutdown sparked the #BringBackOurInternet campaign from within Cameroon and has ended up bringing more unwanted global attention to Biya's recalcitrant government."

It all sounds deeply, almost reassuringly, familiar.

"Biya, who has been in power for 34 years, is facing increasing pressure even as the 84-year looks likely to run for office again in 2018. The government had likely calculated that the protests would peter out after a few weeks as they have in the past but instead tensions have been mounting since October."

If 2018 comes, and a ruthless 35-year dictator is brought crashing down by a determined citizenry, be sure to remember those who stood firm and resolute, and who are primarily responsible for ultimately bringing him down.

It's the classic death by a thousand cuts.

22

ELECTORAL COMMISSIONS
ARE INCREASINGLY BEGINNING
TO MATTER

D o you know who the real individual hero of the Gambian Revolution in 2016 most likely was?

"The first we heard from this good man was on 28 November when
he boldly expressed his disappointment at the Economic Committee of
West African States (ECOWAS) boycott of the Gambian elections,
which held on the 1st of this month," YNaija.com said in post-election
analysis on 17 December 2016. "The ECOWAS had complained about
the political field being un-level and as such refused observer status.

"But the elections organised by Gambia's Independent Electoral
Commission under the chairmanship of Mr. Alieu Mamar Njai still held
and it was largely peaceful and fair. It returned the coalition's candidate,
Adama Barrow as the winner.

"It was a successful election for all on all accounts especially as President Yahya Jammeh – a man who became President as a result of a coup
22 years ago and had once promised that he'd rule the country for a billion years if God willed – had called the President-elect to congratulate

him. That is until President Jammeh started to deny the elections last Friday.

"President Jammeh has already taken over the offices of the Independent Electoral Commission—the IEC election house, denying access to IEC workers, including Chairman Alieu Mamar Njai. His armed guards have also taken over the building."

But Njai – a Jammeh appointee – was having none of it.

"Nothing can change the outcome of the elections," he said. "Adama Barrow is the winner. The results have been certified and signed by all the political contenders. It has circulated around the world. The soldiers taking over the election house will not change the outcome of the election.

"Even if the place caught on fire, or set on fire, that will not change the status quo."

And with that definite statement, even in the face of physical intimidation, in a country where opposition to the government have routinely found themselves dead or arrested, Njai sealed the faith of Gambia's dictator, denying him any shade of credibility under which to sit.

The president, of course, came for him.

"The man who oversaw the last presidential elections in the Gambia has reportedly fled the country following death threats on his life," Africanews.com reported in January 2017. "Local media portals say his family confirmed that he was no longer in the Gambia but would also not disclose his location.

"Alieu Momar Njai, Chairman of the Independent Electoral Commission (IEC) had earlier vowed to defend the validity of the results he declared on December 2 last year. He was forced out of his office by security officials on December 13. Momar Njai has previously been defiant after President Yahya Jammeh questioned the validity of the election result, which he lost to opposition coalition candidate, Adama Barrow. Njai said the ruling party was likely to lose any poll petition arising from the elections."

Nigeria didn't suffer from a brutal dictator in 2015 (if anything, one of Jonathan's more enduring legacies was building a consistently fair electoral commission), but it shared a common thread with the Gambian story.

Professor Attahiru Muhammadu Jega – a former Vice-Chancellor, former president of the Academic Staff Union of Universities and activist who stood against the military government of Ibrahim Babangida –, the 4th chairman of the Independent National Electoral Commission (INEC), achieved legendary status in Nigeria's media for the integrity and calm with which he conducted Nigeria's general elections.

At several points, there were severe defaults in logistics and operations, ballot boxes arriving late, results collated inefficiently and mixed security reports leading to postponement of elections. But throughout the process the public maintained an overwhelming faith in his integrity, and his capacity.

"(Jega) faced fierce criticism from both the opposition and the ruling party," a Vanguard article just before the elections noted. "Nonetheless, most experts believe Jega will seek to declare an accurate result as quickly as possible, regardless of any political interference he may face."

On 31st March, after a widely praised electoral process, he justified that faith by announcing results that fundamentally changed the political trajectory of Nigeria and restored widespread faith in elections, in people power and in the nation's ability to achieve its destiny.

The status quo of course didn't let this go without a fight.

"On March 31, during the collation of results of the presidential election at the International Conference, some officials of the Peoples Democratic Party, led by Godsday Orubebe (then a federal minister), disrupted the exercise, accusing the former INEC boss of bias," Premium Times reported. "When it was obvious that the candidate of the PDP, former President Goodluck Jonathan, was losing, Mr. Orubebe dramatically seized the microphone for minutes insisting that Mr. Jega was biased against the PDP, hence, should suspend announcement of result.

"He accused Mr. Jega of promptly attending to complaints from the then opposition party, the All Progressive Congress, while disregarding those from the PDP."

But, more than the sore loser games, it was the reaction of Jega that struck national and international observers.

"As Mr. Orubebe fumed and cursed, interrupting the collation of results," the newspaper noted, "Mr. Jega maintained an unusual calm. He patiently educated the then minister on the methods and processes of filing complaints."

Asked about the lack of fear in doing his job, Jega told the newspaper in no uncertain terms: "Anybody who is afraid for his life will not do this kind of job. As you know, they say, 'Death is a necessary end. It comes when it will come.'"

And then he made the more crucial point: that INEC had transformed to a strong institution, "firmly rooted and can survive individuals; such that individuals can come and go but the organisation remains. I feel satisfied that a lot has happened in INEC and whoever comes will find it easier than we found it when we came, and will be able to continue to add value to what exists."

Electoral commissions matter, but perhaps they don't matter as much as the people who lead the commissions, since it takes a strong man first to build strong institutions.

Nigeria 2015 and Gambia 2016 would not have happened without men who stood up to be counted in the course of their jobs.

Insurgent campaigns hoping to dislodge years of misrule, an intransigent establishment and stubborn incumbencies have to pay attention to the records and character of the men and women who chair the electoral commissions, and to the potential and fault lines of the commissions.

Kenya, set to hold elections in 2017, understands this imperative.

"Failure to fix the problems exposed by the last two elections risks precipitating a repeat of the 2008 post-election chaos which brought the country to the brink of civil war. It is not terrorism but a bungled election that is the most serious national security threat Kenya faces today," The Star newspaper noted 17 months to the elections.

"With its credibility having been dealt severe blows following the controversies surrounding the 2013 election as well as with the "Chickengate" scandal, the Independent Electoral and Boundaries Commission (IEBC) faces an uphill task in convincing Kenyans of its neutrality and integrity.

"The Chickengate scam, in which IEBC commissioners, including Chairman Isaack Hassan, who served in the defunct Interim Independent Electoral Commission were implicated in taking bribes (code named "chicken") for the award of tenders to a UK firm, has inevitably cast a dark shadow over the IEBC itself. While investigations by the UK's Serious Fraud Office were completed and convictions and jail sentences secured last year, locally they have just begun and those involved still remain in office.

"The IEBC's credibility problem is already having serious consequences. Nyukuri notes that the poor turnout characterising the on-going voter registration effort is an indicator of an apathetic electorate. By next week, the commission should be winding up the first phase of registration that targets 4 million new voters. However, by last week, the Commission had registered less than 13 per cent of that number.

"If elections are stolen, the rights of the people are violated. If the status quo remains, what indication is there that they will come back again when people buy their way to the positions of leadership?"

In 2017, civil society, opposition parties and the press have loudly pointed out their issues with the body's selection of chairman and commissioners in the 9-member panel.

The importance of this in developing democracies cannot be over-emphasised. The burden of proof in these instances lies on the bodies and the authorities that appointed them to both be fair and be seen as fair.

The duty of all other players, local and international, is to continue to hold their feet to the fire.

They must put pressure on the government to make a widely popular selection that distinguishes itself by its track record of impartiality and integrity. And they must keep the commission on its toes by holding it to deliberately high standards, and highlighting every failing with evidence and detail.

In a free and fair election, where people are already tired of the status quo, if the person who sits atop this crucial position can be trusted, credible and firm, then half of the battle is already won. And it is the crucial half of the battle.

Figure 11: A United Kingdom Electoral Commission advert on voter registration.

23

INTERNATIONAL CONSENSUS MATTERS

How influential are young influencers – that educated, connected set that is the toast of endless international media articles about how social media is sweeping through Africa's elections and how connectedness and technology are driving social upheaval?

The truth is, not in the way that it is told.

There are not enough of people in that demographic to actually influence outcomes on the ground in any political context. There are far less than five million Nigerians on Twitter, and though no data sets exist, based on conversation tracking an educated guess can be made that those who vote amongst them are less than 50% (in Lagos, where much of Nigeria's Twitter users live, voter turnout was a mere 29%).

In a country where over 28 million voted in the 2015 presidential elections, that's not enough to influence outcomes. There is also a lack of anecdotal evidence for the repeated assumption that this particular psychographic has the economic or social influence to affect the way their immediate communities vote.

But there is one key metric by which the available evidence appears to suggest that this demographic is powerful and it creates some sort of virtuous cycle: international media.

In a type of self-fulfilling prophecy, the international media elevates the influence of this constituency, and they leverage this elevated status to actually influence outcomes.

This is how it happens.

Perceptions of Nigerian politics and politicians are often filtered to an international audience by the community of foreign journalists and reporters – not more than 50 at any time – spread across from the Associated Press to the Financial Times.

These reporters, because they are human beings alone in a new country and with teams small enough to constitute only of that reporter in many cases, have to form relationships, build networks and, quite simply, make friends. They often make friends of people who have a similar frame of reference, and are part of a global citizenry – in short, young Nigerians on Twitter.

Now these young Nigerians are increasingly well informed, well-sourced due to the loose lips of many of our leaders, and well-connected at least on a superficial level by building strong public relationships with public officials and other key figures from government who engage on social media. Above all else, they are influential because they are followed by a mass of young people that is easily verifiable.

Foreign media work through parallels from their own societies – so social influence is often seen as crucial because of the corollary in the West, and because Twitter is now a crucial echo chamber for elite media players in America as well as the definite source for elite consensus, the same is assumed for countries that they report on. It's only natural.

Therefore this Twitter-influencer psychographic becomes a very easy draw and source for building perspectives and opinions about Nigeria's politics and governance. Their consensus becomes the Nigerian consensus, and because they too are Nigerian citizens, sharing their thoughts and ideas, it may be an incomplete story, but it is certainly not a false story.

These young influencers may not be able to actually hurt politicians by affecting the number of votes they get (there is, again, a paucity of quantitative data to establish causation, though they are usually the drivers of major national action like protests), but they are able to hurt them by assaulting their image – and they are able to do this effectively by defining the conversation about these politicians on social media.

In turn the social media conversation is tracked and analysed by international media, and then presented to the global audience as representative either of the youth population, or sometimes of the general population.

Therefore whatever the consensus of young connected people on social media it becomes the consensus that the world sees. That is the biggest power that this audience has.

It is from this cohort that the world hears exaggerated tales of the huge impact of social media on elections, that the world hears of hashtags that provided food on people's tables, and isolated cases of technology-driven businesses became the narrative of transformative economics across the continent.

It is that power that they have used to help build coalitions against past Nigerian presidents, successfully tarring Olusegun Obasanjo as corrupt and Goodluck Jonathan as clueless.

February 2013 brought a powerful example of this.

"Nigerians, disgruntled by President Goodluck Jonathan's last CNN interview claim of improved electricity, seized on Sunday's U.S. Super bowl power outage, to issue a fierce rebuttal, stirring intense debate on social media on Monday and Tuesday," Premium Times reported at the time. "CNN's Christiane Amanpour, who interviewed the president a fortnight ago, said she received torrents of tweets from Nigerians after President Jonathan said during the interview that electricity had tremendously improved."

It became such a huge deal that Amanpour had to respond.

"Pres. Goodluck Jonathan's comments to me about power probs sparked so many tweets that CNN set up an Open Mic in Lagos," she tweeted. "Our OPEN MIC report has every-day Nigerians telling us about the power situation in their country.

"Received so many tweets from #Nigeria about #SuperBowl power outage that we decided to include them in the show tonight on."

The Portland Communications report on 'How Africa tweets' in 2016 emphasised: "Hashtags about the Nigerian presidential elections and strife in Burundi were among some of the most popular and wide-spread across Africa."

Considering that international consensus stems from both media reports and perspectives from undercover and visible operatives of foreign governments in the country, and that many of the perspectives are formed by easily available opinion, which is what social media creates, this power to direct public opinion internationally becomes immensely powerful.

It has pulled down governments across the continent.

It also helps that Africa's perennially insecure leaders are easy to bully by an international audience, and begin to modify behaviours mostly only when the international media has had enough. It's an inside joke that if you want to hear the truth from many African leaders, put them in front of an international microphone. Then, they lose their natural reticence.

Famously, the Nigerian government only began to move with visible speed on the matter of the missing Chibok girls when global public opinion turned sharply against it and the global spotlight put unrelenting pressure on the government's actions.

This weakening of the Jonathan image and mandate ultimately supported the cascade of events that led to his sack.

Gambia also provides another case study on two levels. One was the international opinion consensus, and the other was the African governance consensus.

"In Gambia, Barrow's upset turned the tiny country—population 1.8 million—into an unlikely international news story, as the world watched to see whether the president would step down," Newsweek reported in March 2017. "A week after he conceded, Jammeh rejected the election results and requested a fresh vote. Thousands of Gambians fled the country after the regional bloc Economic Community of West African States warned that it might intervene if Jammeh did not back down; Barrow left for Senegal in mid-January for safety and had to be sworn in on January 19 as Gambia's new president in an inauguration ceremony in Dakar."

President Barrow agrees: "Of course we welcome (international) support because it was something that Gambians needed, it was something that has taken five decades before it happened, for the first time in the history of this country."

In addition to international media attention just immediately before and after the elections, human rights organisations constantly knocked the Gambian leader down over an extended period of years for his crackdown on civil liberties.

Then there was the fact that international consensus, especially in Africa, is trending strongly and firmly towards democracy. African leaders are even now willing to publicly criticise sit-tight dictators.

"But Sall believes that he and other African leaders have a responsibility to ensure Jammeh's exit without damage to his country and Senegal will definitely play a decisive role in that direction," Nigeria's Olusegun Adeniyi had reported from a conversation with the Senegalese president, Macky Sall in January 2017.

He also recalled examples of other times African international consensus has held sway: When in 2012 President Amadou Toumani Touré was toppled by a bunch of military adventurers led by Captain Amadou Sanogo, a Nigeria-led ECOWAS initiative moved quickly to force out Sanogo who was granted all the benefits of a former leader, an allowance, a house, transportation and security as well as immunity of sorts while the negotiations also led to the resignation of Touré. A one-year transitional arrangement led by Dioncounda Traore was also put in place to lead Mali for one year.

"At that period, Nigeria was meant to send in a contingent of troops to create a buffer between the interim administration and the polarized Malian military. Unfortunately, because those troops were not on ground, mobs loyal to Sanogo invaded the presidential palace to give interim President Traore, 72 years in age at the time, the beating of his life after which they looted the Malian seat of government with images of that barbarism beamed to the world."

Ellen Johnson Sirleaf has been on the record remarking on African leaders who have refused to leave office even under democracies, and Botswana's Felix Mogae has specifically warned about the dangers of Paul Kagame perpetuating himself in office.

Of course Nigeria's Muhammadu Buhari – himself a former military dictator, which shows how far the pendulum has swung – led African leaders from Liberia, Senegal, Ghana and others first to plead with Jammeh to choose peace, and then when that failed, to move against him, sending troops from the Economic Community of West African States in.

"By evening, the troops had not yet appeared in Banjul, the Gambian capital, according to residents, but news of their deployment had spread," the Washington Post reported on 19 January. "Gambians poured into the streets in support of the Senegalese forces and Jammeh's ouster."

By the next day, he had agreed to step down.

"That a regional bloc is willing to go beyond mere rhetoric, and defend the will and democratic aspirations of an entire people, speaks volumes and will undoubtedly resonate well beyond the Gambia," said Jeffrey Smith, founding director of Washington-based Vanguard Africa, a nonprofit organisation that has worked closely with the Gambian opposition.

To be very clear, none of these narratives were an accident of history. In our work with our clients in the public domain and those not in the public domain, we have been careful to build international goodwill and to facilitate international consensus. Most times, this can be easy because citizens are already angry; the imperative is then to ventilate a strategy that connects this to global imperatives and narratives to weaken intransigent leaders.

Gambia was equally the result of a complex interplay of civil society, governmental and media forces intent on creating a new story for Gambia. This was a deliberate, strategic effort on the parts of certain local and international key players to ensure that Jammeh had to go.

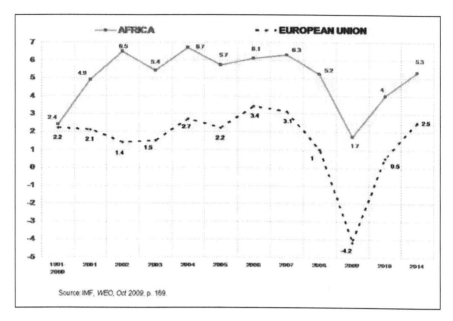

Figure 12: Africa does not support world economic growth 1991 – 2014 (in GDP, annual change)

The lesson is simple: popular will needs thinkers and builders who are able to set the irrevocable course for noise to transform into voice, and for aspiration to evolve into action.

The engineering of international consensus has become a crucial part of this important mix, for Africa's growing democratic culture. It can be the icing on top of a nation-wide cake.

24

SERIOUSLY, JOY REALLY MATTERS

It might sound touchy-feely, but this is actually a fact of winning operations in free and fair democracies: joyful campaigns matter.

Let's look at the facts.

"The final three weeks should have been an anxious but happy time for a Hillary Clinton team on the cusp of making history," Politico.com wrote in October 2016. "Her odds of victory, according to most prediction experts, sit north of 80 percent, and she has solidified modest but durable leads over Donald Trump in most battleground states.

"But Clinton's final sprint has become a joyless, nail-gnawing slog through Trump Tower's moat of mudslinging — and the day-to-day worries of WikiLeaks' dump of internal emails from campaign chairman John Podesta's hacked account is taking a toll."

If you want to understand how a campaign that was poised for success, snatched defeat from the jaws of victory, it is important to pay close attention to the last three weeks of that campaign for the American presidency.

"The Candidate Having the Most Fun Usually Wins," a headline on PolitalWire.com reported in January 2016 as it warned of an impending Trump victory.

"As a lark, I put a question I had never asked before on a survey and we tracked it: 'Which campaign is having the most fun?'" Republican strategist Alex Castellanos had written in a piece for CNN about a campaign he won for Panama's Ricardo Martinelli. "It was ours... Doubts about his lack of governing experience were overcome by his buoyant strength and self-assurance. We won.

"Which returns us to a reflection that should scare all of us in Washington's GOP establishment, as noted in an interview conducted by Chuck Todd of Meet the Press. Donald Trump is having a lot of fun, isn't he? More than anyone else."

Indeed this theme of joylessness permeated the entire Clinton campaign from start. Even victory, where it came, had the appearance of hard-slug; the campaign routinely in a state of panic, depression or under attack. Even when she was winning, it could feel like she was losing.

"Hillary Clinton's joyless victory," another Politico headline noted after her Kentucky primary win.

She was avoiding rallies, she was avoiding interviews, her rallies were reported – rightly or wrongly – to lack the energy of a fired up base. That was the narrative as she moved close to the election.

Trump on the other hand? "Republican presidential nominee Donald Trump is "finding joy" in the campaign trail and will soon start delivering strong-policy messages, his new campaign manager said today," a news report noted at the same time Hillary's narrative was undergirded by depression.

"Trump is finding joy in the campaign trail, which is very important," his campaign manager, Kellyanne Conway, told reporters. "You want a candidate who is having fun because the people, the thousands and thousands, overflow crowds show up at his rallies or his speeches, they're there to connect.

"They're there because I think typical politicians like Hillary Clinton erect campaigns, but Donald Trump has built a movement, and people feel included in that movement. People have travelled with him recently for the first time, including elected officials, are really struck by the energy, by the crowds, by the enthusiasm."

And she was absolutely right.

The thing is that movements, including angry movements (in fact, especially angry movements) are often powered by joy. Ask yourself why two-decade-oppressed Gambians poured into the streets in joy after Yahya Jammeh was uprooted.

The joy is that their anger is about to bear fruit; that their efforts are about to lead to change. Citizens are always excited when their aspirations are about to produce results. Democracy is powered on the back of citizen aspiration, and successful citizen aspiration produces excitement and joy.

Routinely, press narratives spoke of Trump rallies as filled with "laughter" and "cheer" and voters "having a really good time."

"Having no idea on what kind of crowd or attended mood to expect we were overwhelmed by the positive and electric energy," blogger, Peter Kizenko wrote in October 2016. "It was like attending a street party. The majority of these people had never had real political fire but were also drawn to attend. They felt like they were being a part of something much bigger. Trump rallies were initially portrayed as creating divisiveness and anger. It is the opposite. This felt like a Woodstock Peace and Love movement. People were in a great mood seeing the groundswell of support. There was no rage, only a true feeling that this country was on its way to healing."

Of course joy comes from a lot of things. Joy comes from a well-executed campaign; joy comes from an atmosphere of validation, strong poll numbers, well-resourced operations and an atmosphere of possibilities. That is true. But the fact also is that campaigns must keep their wits about them even when things are going wrong. And like plenty of ventures, it is precisely at that moment that things are going wrong, that it must hold itself firm.

Hear what Conway told CNN when her campaign was down in the polls: "I think it helps us to be a little bit behind, and we are. It lights a fire under us and it reminds us what we need to do to get this done."

The Barack Obama 2008 campaign was also a masterclass in this, as the New Yorker's Ryan Lizza noted in October 2015.

After a burst of excitement when Obama announced his candidacy, in February, 2007, his campaign flagged over the summer. He was down in the polls, his donors were complaining, and, hard as it is to believe now, he was even losing to Clinton among African-Americans.

"'A lot of our supporters nationally were very concerned that we weren't moving in the national polls,' Larry Grisolano, one of Obama's top campaign strategists, told me.

"Dan Pfeiffer, then the campaign's deputy communications director, told me, 'It's crazy to think now, but the big narrative was whether Obama was tough enough to take on Clinton and whether he was black enough to win the African-American vote. That's an actual debate we had in America. You could see the political world placing its bets on Hillary.'

"'We were trailing in national polls by a wide margin, the pundits were pouncing, and donors were panicking,' David Axelrod, who was Obama's top strategist and later became a senior White House adviser, told me.

"How did the Obama team turn it around? The conventional wisdom is that he inspired voters with an uplifting message and out-organised Clinton in Iowa and elsewhere."

Whatever happens, whatever else is going on, campaigns must not lose their joy.

Campaigns have a vibe, and that vibe is reflected through their events, their press clippings, their memos; it creates an entire atmosphere around it, because after all elections are emotional more than intellectual affairs. The talk is about 'passion' and 'history' and 'inspiration' and 'people power' and 'excitement', all of which are emotive considerations.

Without firing up people's emotions, even in the most level-headed democracies, people cannot be motivated to believe and to wake up in the morning to vote.

"No Democrat, and certainly no independent, is waking up on November 8th excited to run out and vote for Hillary the way they did the day Obama became president or when Bernie was on the primary ballot," activist and filmmaker, Micheal Moore famously wrote in his pre-election memo 'Why Trump Will Win'. "The enthusiasm just isn't there.

And because this election is going to come down to just one thing — who drags the most people out of the house and gets them to the polls — Trump right now is in the catbird seat."

John Ellis "Jeb" Bush understood this distinctly when he began his campaign, putting joy – literally – at the centre of his strategy.

Unfortunately his campaign was unable to build or protect that which he knew he needed.

"But catching fire is his bigger problem," Frank Bruni wrote in the New York Times in August of the same year. "He can't do it. In a bloated field of bellicose candidates, he's a whisper, a blur, starved of momentum, bereft of urgency and apt to make news because he stumbles, not because he soars. *Can* he soar? Or even sprint?"

He found it incredibly difficult, also, to keep these wits about him when Trump pounced. "Jeb Bush sets aside his 'joyful tortoise' persona to go after Donald Trump," the Los Angeles Times noted in a headline, September of the very same year.

"Bush once said he would only enter the 2016 race if he could campaign 'joyfully'," Buzzfeed reported in a June 2015 story. "Now that he's running, he seems miserable.

"The fundamentally oppositional nature of Bush's campaign is illustrated by his decision last week to swap out his perennially cheerful campaign manager, David Kochel, for the younger, more sharp-elbowed Danny Diaz, a master of rapid response and opposition research whom Bush touted as a "grinder." His campaign is now reportedly planning to use its well-stocked war chest to launch an aggressive assault this summer aimed at knocking off the other top-tier candidates in the field."

And then he lost.

The Goodluck Jonathan campaigns in 2011 versus 2015 are a crucial case in point for this imperative.

In 2011, his campaign was the joyful one, without a doubt – the breath of fresh air. Muhammadu Buhari was angry, for sure, and so were his supporters. Anger was the defining emotion. But joy was completely missing. The energy of purpose was completely missing. It looked and felt like what it was – a joyless campaign.

Jonathan was having fun, his wife was having fun, and the electorate – for the most part – was infected by an excitement. The theme song of that election was the TY Bello song, *The Future is Here*. He created the sense of a movement, of. . . yes, change. You could feel it in the way he was leading a movement towards something seismic in Nigeria's political history.

2015 was another story, however. This time, he was defined almost solely by bitterness. His campaign rallies focused on attacking Buhari. There was the controversial *The Real Buhari* documentary on the Africa Independent Television that got nationwide opprobrium and became the matter of a court case, and there was the infamous Governor Ayodele Fayose-sponsored ads on the cover of national newspapers.

The atmosphere of bitterness turned the campaign into a farce.

"We are constrained to urge him to prove to the Nigerian people that he really is as fit as a fiddle, as the spokesman of his PCO has said, by taking a brisk walk or even jogging around the perimeter of the stadium before any of his rallies," the Campaign Director of Media and Publicity said at a news conference. "If he can do that, it will go a long way to allay the fears of many."

This was based on a legitimate concern – the health of the candidate – but the tone of the campaign subjected its request to nationwide ridicule. And this tone, this negative energy, contributed to the factors that doomed the campaign.

Sure, politics is a contact sport and so negative campaigning can be avoidable in a necessary contest of contrasts, but there is a difference between negative campaigning drawing from a positive core and one based on negativity as overriding strategy.

"Emboldened by a New York Times poll that showed voters disapproving of McCain for fighting too negative a campaign, they concluded that every time McCain threw a punch, the person he hurt was himself," Jonathan Freedland wrote in a prescient piece in the Guardian in 2008. "By contrast, the Democrats reckoned that every time Obama remained cool and unruffled, bringing the subject back to jobs or healthcare, he looked presidential - and conveyed that he cared about the voters above all.

"That was the Democrats' hope, and the instant polling suggested they were right: viewers gave the debate to Obama by whopping margins, some more than 30 points. These days the overtly negative attack backfires."

In the case of Nigeria's 2015 election, the joylessness of the Jonathan campaign bled from the joylessness of the last year of his presidency, underlined as it was by its dramatic misstep in the matter of the kidnapped Chibok girls, but starting long before that.

"Jonathan's relations with party members at times resembled a football coach antagonising his star players into leaving for rival teams," Max Siollun wrote in a post-election piece in the Guardian explaining the historic loss. "His tendency to fall out with colleagues simultaneously weakened his party and strengthened the opposition. He quarrelled with one after another; leading several of them to leave the party in frustration and join the opposition All Progressives Congress (APC). The alliance between these and the opposition shoved Jonathan out of power."

Replacing the positive influences in his 2011 campaign led by the genius of late presidential adviser, Oronto Douglas – who managed to build a national coalition that captured the popular imagination – with old-time players who only understood smears and attacks robbed him of the inspirational quality that had once defined his image and his messaging.

The joy missing and electricity gone, the candidate became a shadow of himself, and his supporters found themselves in disarray, surrogates and officials descending into public battles over money, over strategy and over legacy.

In contrast, his opponent, despite the postponement of elections maintained a determined joy, and refused to betray any signs of distress, despite resources running out in those crucial final weeks.

"Change may be postponed," campaign copy that we deployed on the day immediately after the postponement was announced, declared with some strut. "But it cannot be denied."

This should be a cardinal rule for political strategists: it is crucial to find the passion and the excitement in the campaign operations, to ensure the candidate maintains perspective through a state of clarity and confidence that comes from joy.

That energy and passion filters through it to its supporters, to its surrogates, and to its events – that interconnectivity of excitement and passion routinely brings clarity, brings perspective and brings motivation, especially in the last days of a campaign.

In free and fair elections, the joyful campaign is most likely to win the war.

Figure 13: Campaign copy for 2011 election in Nigeria (StateCraft)

25

EXPERTISE MATTERS

This is certainly a self-interested subject, but it is no less true for that.

The nature of African elections is fundamentally changing. The global movement towards democracy has permeated even the most hostile-to-freedom parts of Africa, upturning establishments, disgracing dictators and overwhelming incumbents. Something is giving way.

There is, of course, still much work left to be done from Uganda to Zimbabwe, but citizen-led change movements are steadily sweeping the continent, not just in presidential elections, but also in state and municipal contests.

This is deeply significant.

Africa's sit-tight leaders have routinely won elections based on five strategic pillars:

1. Control of the electoral system and commissions
2. Diversion of public funds to sponsor elections
3. Intimidation of opponents
4. Suppression of dissent
5. Manipulation of the media

"So how did Mugabe do it? The answer, according to his observers and opponents, is shameless electoral swindle at almost every level while maintaining the mere façade of an orderly poll on the day itself," the Independent reported in 2013. "The Zimbabwe Election Support Network (ZESN), a local observer group with 7,000 monitors, has listed a litany of offences, including state media bias, a campaign of intimidation in rural areas, and the rushed electoral process before key reforms the security services were in place. But the most effective measure was fiddling the electoral rolls. Held back until the day before the election – thus avoiding proper scrutiny – the roll revealed an estimated one million invalid names, including many deceased voters. And it excluded up to one million real ones, mostly in urban areas where the MDC support is strongest.

"This is much more subtle than past poll fixes, when ZANU-PF literally muscled out its opponents. By 2008, when Tsvangirai won the first round of the presidential election but was forced to withdraw after an outbreak of violence by Mugabe henchmen, this method was looking too crude.

"When Mugabe used violence in 2008, he lost legitimacy, so he found other ways to win," said Pedzisai Ruhanya, from the Zimbabwe Democracy Institute, a Harare-based think tank. "What we have seen is a masterclass in electoral fraud. It is chicanery, organised theft and electoral authoritarianism."

And these rulers continue to upgrade their methods.

"Uganda blocked social media and mobile money access for four tense days during the presidential polls in February 2016," Daniel Mwesigwa wrote in an opinion piece in May 2016 on iAfrikan.com. "The same thing happened again on 11th May 2016, a day before the swearing in ceremony of the 'old' new president, showing that the country's Internet infrastructure was subject to the whims of the ruling elite.

"The Republic of Congo was not going to be left behind. The government ordered a complete shutdown of telephone and internet services just a few days to their presidential polls in March."

But, ultimately, as we see everywhere from Gambia to Somalia, these power blocs have begun to crumble. The unfair advantages of incumbencies are steadily giving way to the sunlight of true competition. That levels the playing field.

"The old guard has plenty of experience in snatching ballot boxes, bribing electoral officials and intimidating opponents," the co-founder of our company, Adebola Williams correctly said to Forbes in February 2017. "When the system changes towards free and fair elections however, they are left out in the cold. They have nothing. And then we have the advantage."

What that means is that it is now possible to win on the merits.

And when merit applies, then experts and professionals become necessary.

Politics is at its base about competitiveness, and like all products and sales, competitiveness needs expertise.

In this case, and in a new world, expertise revolves around messaging, data, outreach, research, fundraising, getting out the vote, communication and technology.

The African elections that have managed to defeat establishments over the past three years have not taken any of these for granted, engaging local and international professionals routinely to develop strategy, co-create messaging, supervise outreach, and seal victory.

The reason for this is simple; many of the professionals have accumulated knowledge and experience that are not usually available to players used to a particular field of play. Much of this experience is gained on the job by engaging the realities of changing voter behaviour, the opportunities that open societies present, and the intersection between civil society, politics, media, and international consensus.

Also, the factors that come into play in modern campaigns have become more global that at any time in history, creating tools that can be shared and replicated across constituencies and demanding a synergy of ideas that can transplant global models into local realities.

In campaigns attacking behemoths, there can be very little room for error, and expertise routinely makes the difference.

The reason advanced democracies routinely engage experts is for the

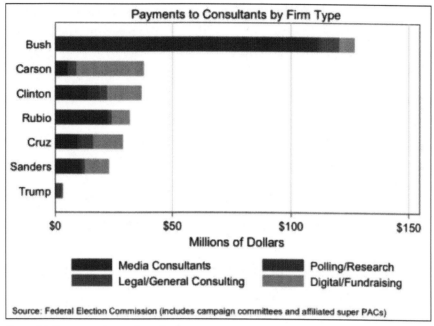

Figure 14: Payments to consultants by firm type

simple reason that the cross-functional experience that they gain from working on multiple campaigns in multiple contexts in and outside electoral politics equips them for situations and interplays that the flux of elections often present.

Elections are not straight lines; they are a massive interaction of history, current events, emotions, imagery, and personalities. Always too many parts moving at the same time, and in this atmosphere, instincts are not enough.

Many nations have engaged this imperative by mostly engaging players from America's robust election culture.

"Beginning in the 1960s with the adventurous activities of legendary pioneers, US overseas consultancy transformed into a global business by the end of the 1990s," the book *Global Political Campaigning: A Worldwide Analysis of Campaign Professionals* notes. "American consultants have been contracted by parties and candidates around the world, modifying or at least shaping campaign practices in foreign countries, as general strategists, media consultants, pollsters, direct marketing experts, or vendors of special campaign technologies and software."

As our firm has pioneered a 'for Africans, by Africans' model, combining international best practice, with a keen understanding of local aspiration by reason of living this experience, it has presented a compelling alternative for many political players, especially those working for insurgent campaigns.

Both options of international experience however underline the reality of expertise as an imperative.

In a time of great change, where players have very little room for error, relying simply on primitive methods of gut assumptions is not enough. Serious minded players must rely on the empiricism and experience that expertise usually brings.

26

SOCIAL MEDIA MATTERS AND WILL CONTINUE TO MATTER, EVEN MORE

Social media did this, said Trump, after he won the United States presidential elections in 2016.

According to him, his Twitter, Facebook and Instagram, where he had, at the time, over 28 million followers, helped him win the Republican primaries and the general elections despite his opponents spending "much more money than I spent."

"I won," he said. "I think that social media has more power than the money they spent, and I think maybe to a certain extent, I proved that."

There is very little argument about this in America these days. But then America is to all intent and purpose, a social media nation.

"On a total population basis (accounting for Americans who do not use the internet at all), that means that 68% of all U.S. adults are Facebook users, while 28% use Instagram, 26% use Pinterest, 25% use LinkedIn and 21% use Twitter," Pew Research data in November 2016 showed.

The question, however, is, how much does social media influence the elections in Africa, with still-low Internet penetration rates?

Let's look at the numbers.

"More than 16 million Nigerians sign in to Facebook every month. 7.2 million log in daily," TechCabal.com reported in February 2016. "As at Q4 2015, there were 5.2 million monthly active users of Facebook in Kenya. 5 million of them access the network from their mobile phones. In South Africa, 13 million log into Facebook every month. 7.8 million, are active every day."

At the time, the numbers showed that overall users – that is including non-active users – from the three countries averaged over 34 million.

It bears noting that the number of total Internet users in Africa as at March 2017 is estimated at 343,676,501, with 27.7% penetration.

Now, while 16 million users in Nigeria is not significant when you consider a population of well over 180 million, the more important number to track is the number that actually voted in elections. In 2015, that figure was a little shy of 30 million in its presidential elections. The number of Facebook users is therefore well above half of the voting population.

It is not for nothing that in the 2016 Ghanaian elections, our internal analysis from Facebook mostly correctly predicted the regions won by each candidate, by real-time tracking of user behaviour, and ultimately correctly predicted the ultimate winners of the elections in a country where there are at least 4.3 million users.

"In Ghana among the two major political parties – the National Democratic Congress (NDC) and the New Patriotic Party (NPP), the flagbearer of the NPP, Nana Addo Dankwa Akufo-Addo has the largest audience when it comes to top Facebook pages by politics as an industry than NDC's flagbearer President John Dramani Mahama," Ghanaweb. com noted days to the elections. "As at May 11, 2016 when it comes to the number of page likes NDC's John Mahama leads with 154,773. However, with just few days to the polls as at December 5, NPP's Nana Akufo-Addo currently leads with 188,396 making him generate more enthusiasm on social media than President John Mahama.

Gabby Otchere-Darko, one of the key actors in our campaign posted a message on 10th December crediting social media for the win. "NPP's social media army, a group of unpaid, ruthlessly smart loyalists, is mightily responsible for this victory. They helped to share our messages to every area of the country and helped to bypass the media establishment."

"While not everyone was convinced the online methods swung their vote, the potential is hard to argue with," Reuters wrote in the aftermath of Nigeria's 2015 elections. "Africa's most populous nation - with 170 million inhabitants - has some of the world's highest levels of mobile phone ownership. There are 127 million mobile phone subscriptions in Nigeria, the International Telecommunications Union says."

The report quoted StateCraft Inc's chief executive offer: "The digital strategy has been a lifeline of the campaign for young people. We needed to create an image that enabled people to connect with him. In the last four years it has become a lot easier and cheaper to get the Internet on your phone. It isn't exclusive anymore."

These tools are used to mobilise voters, to communicate issues, and to monitor elections.

"The Independent National Electoral Commission (INEC) encouraged citizens to use the hashtag to report on voting conditions across the country, to "provide a check on the legitimacy of the … elections", Quartz Africa reported in June 2016. "The 10,000 election observers across the country not only engaged in their traditional monitoring responsibilities, but also followed the social media posts to identify and address problems at polling stations. A report by Demos found that more than 12 million tweets about the Nigerian election were posted."

In 2015, a Twitter-based sentiment analysis report on the two leading parties in that election noted that the "PDP had a national penetration of 1.82%, while the APC's was 15.98%."

In reaction to this, a writer snorted on SaharaReporters.com. "Be that as it may, elections are not conducted on social media, neither is social media popularity a reliable pointer to or reflection of the support a candidate or a party enjoys," he said. "In more advanced countries where the Internet penetration is up to at least 80%, it could be a reliable barometer to gauge this, but this doesn't hold true in a developing country like Nigeria."

He was proved definitively wrong.

Little wonder many governments have declared war on social access before and during elections.

"Last week, Ghana, widely acknowledged as one of Africa's role models for best democratic practice, caught democracy watchdogs off guard when the country's police chief announced the government intends to shut down social media on voting day in November," the Quartz report continued. "The shutdown is to take place from 5 am to 7 pm "to ensure social media are not used to send misleading information that could destabilize the country."

"While it is a surprise Ghana is making this move, it has become more common for several other African countries who haven't been as courteous as to give voters notice before curtailing the use of social media and the right to free speech around elections."

Deji Olukotun of Internet freedom advocacy group Access Now, notes Ghana "was clearly looking to what other countries have done." Citizens in Ethiopia, Congo, Chad, Uganda, and elsewhere have found elections are a particularly popular time to crack down on social media."

Social media was at least influential in Gambia's elections in 2016, even doubters would admit.

"The effect of social media, including Facebook and WhatsApp, also helped close the gap between the opposing candidates' media presences, as mainstream outlets were dominated by the incumbent's information and propaganda during the campaign," WorldPolicy.org reported after the elections. "For example, the Gambia Youth and Women's Forum, a public Facebook group with 55,000 members, was very active leading up to the election. It regularly posted about and debated current issues, endorsing the opposition coalition and rallying voters.

"The opposition United Democratic Party (UDP), which came in second place in the 2001 and 2006 presidential elections, created over a dozen WhatsApp groups since April, when hundreds of people protested in the capital to call for political change and electoral reform. Many were arrested during the #GambiaRising campaign, and UDP secretary Solo Sandeng, along with two others, were killed in state custody. The

WhatsApp groups have been used over the past several months to communicate and discuss issues with the party's supporters. By the time the UDP joined an eight-party opposition coalition in October—an unprecedented effort to put forward a unity candidate after an unsuccessful attempt in 2006—the number of opposition WhatsApp groups nearly doubled and were collectively dubbed "the coalition forum." Members receive messages that they can share with their various contacts and can also post their own messages in the forums. Other social and community groups also became rallying tools for opposition voters.

"In reaction to this high volume of activity, WhatsApp was blocked in The Gambia. After users were advised to install virtual private networks (VPN) in order to circumvent the blockade, the government enforced a VPN blockade as well. Unable to completely block WhatsApp, the government soon instituted an entire internet shutdown before voters went to the polls."

Of course, in the absence of detailed mainstream studies that show the direct causal link between social media and votes, and with the difficulty in assessing whether social media users actually vote, serious campaign strategists want to be careful around the lines between causation and correlation.

And there is scholarly research that can, at least, dampen some of the rampaging enthusiasm.

Research by foremost Nigerian social communication scholar, AA Olorunnisola for instance establishes that the effect of social media in African social movements is often overblown in his paper, 'Influences of media on social movements: Problematizing hyperbolic inferences about impacts'.

"Pronouncements about the value of information and communication technology (ICT) (hereafter traditional, new, and social media) to social movements - hyperbolic in popular media references to new and social media (e.g., Facebook revolution, Twitter revolution, etc.) - invite scholarly inquiries that critically assess the implications of these assumptions for African countries," the abstract notes. "Sensing the tendency toward technological determinism, a position which Castells warns is fraught with failure to recognize complex interactions between society and technology; authors examined popular press vis-a-vis scholarly assumptions about the value of media during social movements. Questions that critically analyze the roles and power of old versus new media in social movements should be posed particularly about 21st century iterations with citizens increasingly doubling as creators and disseminators of news and information. For example: to what extent does various media comparatively facilitate or constrain activists in social movements? How have new ICTs assisted citizen activists in circumventing the power and reach of traditional media?

"How have the roles of traditional versus new media in social movements been framed in the popular press and academic journals? What contextual factors (e.g., communal networks; third-party- and foreign-interventions, digital divide, etc.) may be accountable for the takeoff and successes of social movements? In a continent fraught with cultural, political, and socio-economic divisions of historic proportions, authors critically assessed cases across Africa of variegated employment of old (i.e., radio, newspaper, television) and new media platforms (i.e., Facebook, Twitter, mobile telephone text messaging) by four social movements spanning 35years. Assessments underscore citizen empowerment and multiplier capabilities of new media but affirm the value of contextual factors that minimize hyperbolic assumptions about the contribution of new media to the formation and progression of social movements."

Speaking about the #OccupyNigeria protests of 2012, his paper with his student Nwachukwu Egbunike 'Framing the #Occupy Nigeria Protests in Newspapers and Social Media' advises caution: "Findings revealed that newspapers were better than social media in framing the motivation, diagnosis and prognosis of the protest," it says. "It also showed that the newspapers presented a more heterogeneous narration of the protest. This study holds that newspapers are better contributors to the discourse of the #OccupyNigeria Protests than social media."

These are important red flags about the true power of social media in today's continent. Despite its limitations however, social media will continue to be important to modern elections across Africa.

At the very least, it achieves the goal of democratising opinion, mapping flow of communication outside state-controlled bodies, supporting the less resourced and building international consensus. As we have seen from Ghana to Gambia, that is no small deal.

Social media and the world's new social sensibility will also be driving much of behaviour and much of political outcomes in the immediate and foreseeable future across the open world, and in fact beyond that.

The triage issues of short attention spans, fake news, and filter bubbles, vis a vis an informed and engaged citizenry will be an important influence on behaviours moving forward. Then there is, of course, the related matter of algorithm-driven behaviours in a social age.

"In an era of post-truth politics, driven by the 24-hour news cycle, diminishing trust in institutions, rich visual media, and the ubiquity and velocity of social networked spaces, *how do we identify information that is tinted*—information that is incomplete, that may help affirm our existing beliefs or support someone's agenda, or that may be manipulative—effectively driving a form of propaganda?" Gilad Lotan, Head of Data Science at Buzzfeed asked in a November 2016 piece.

"In a co-authored essay, John Borthwick and I define Media Hacking as the usage and manipulation of social media and associated algorithms to define a narrative or political frame. In that essay, we showed a few examples of ways in which individuals, states, and non-state actors are increasingly using Media Hacking techniques to advance political agendas.

"More recently I've written about another form of media hacking—where Trump supporters successfully gamed Twitter's trending topics algorithm to make the #TrumpWon hashtag trend worldwide after the first US presidential debate. As I was analyzing this data, it was striking for me just how organised this group of supporters seemed to be. They seemed to have been coordinating somewhere, all publishing to Twitter with the same unique keyword at the same time (a known tactic to get something to trend)."

Researcher Danah Boyd, also blogging at Data & Society, looks at another angle: "We've also seen the political establishment, law enforcement, marketers, and hate groups build capacity at manipulating the media landscape. Very little of what's happening is truly illegal, but there's no widespread agreement about which of these practices are socially and morally acceptable or not.

"The techniques that are unfolding are hard to manage and combat. Some of them look like harassment, prompting people to self-censor out of fear. Others look like "fake news", highlighting the messiness surrounding bias, misinformation, disinformation, and propaganda. Companies who built tools to help people communicate are finding it hard to combat the ways their tools are being used by networks looking to skirt the edges of the law and content policies. Institutions and legal instruments designed to stop abuse are finding themselves ill-equipped to function in light of networked dynamics.

"The Internet has long been used for gas lighting, and trolls have long targeted adversaries. What has shifted recently is the scale of the operation, the coordination of the attacks, and the strategic agenda of some of the players. A new form of information manipulation is unfolding in front of our eyes. It is political. It is global. And it is populist in nature. The news media is being played like a fiddle, while decentralized networks of people are leveraging the ever-evolving networked tools around them to hack the attention economy."

But then while these are all valid concerns, they are not new. They are simply the same extensions of historic power plays around the shaping of opinion that have now been enabled by technology on an unprecedented scale.

"Our understanding of media power (and of what it means to call something propaganda) must make room for a *variety* of potential collective and individual influences," media scholar Caroline Jack helpfully, and calmly, explains. "This includes corporations, interest groups, activist groups, and other traditional collectives; it should also include the new forms of individual and collective presence that digital communications facilitate. This includes state-sponsored online actors *and* ad-hoc user collectives.

"As these conversations unspool over the coming months and years, one way to avoid getting mired in is-it-or-isn't-it debates that serve as proxies for a fractured civic sphere is to ask what people get from using the epithet. People are referencing a disconcerting set of realizations about how media and power function in our society. In some cases, those realizations challenge the foundational beliefs of our constitutional democracy."

And ultimately, trying to control or even delegitimise the new flow of information amplified by social media is futile, no matter how many times we scream 'fake news'.

"While definitions of propaganda may vary, they generally have to do with power and persuasion," Jack says. "But propaganda (versus entertainment, versus education, versus activism…) is a matter of perspective. Almost any communication can be interpreted as propagandistic in nature. Outside of the most blatantly egregious, demagogic or hateful cases, attempting to stifle propaganda won't work. The emergence of propaganda as a media epithet, in practical use, isn't a cause but a symptom of deeper fissures."

These debates will continue as the power of social media continues to gallop into the future, and they are important conversations to have as society evolves tools to maintain equilibrium, but it is the larger point that is the more important one.

Headlines like PC Mag's 'Social media is ruining US elections' miss the point. That these are fundamentally value-neutral media like the printing press and the television, and that – like both – those are realities that we will have to contend with.

More important is to begin to assimilate the new order, that, "social platforms absolutely affected the election results," as The Verge wrote in 2016.

For many young Africans, and the generality of African voters in a time of great change, this fact is a net positive, whichever way you look at it.

"The APC campaign was consistent with their message on social media, they completely shaped the narrative there," a source within the Jonathan campaign famously told Quartz Africa in 2015. "By the time people here started to throw money at the social problem it was already too late. Then there was multiple messaging which was confusing for voters."

According to the report: "On Election Day, everyone with a social media account played a role in disseminating results. #NigeriaDecides was the top trending hashtag on Facebook and Twitter on March 30th as Nigeria and the rest of the world eagerly anticipated the results."

"Many people who stationed themselves at the polling centers until the close of election were able to know the results of those centers, record events and also photographed copies of results pasted," Tony Okeregbe, a professor at the University of Lagos told Quartz.

"Social media is creating a new generation of Nigerians who have neither power nor money but have influence. And this is what the old stock are afraid of," Nnenna Nwakanma, the Africa regional coordinator for the U.S.-based World Wide Web Foundation, told Aljazeera in March 2016. "Whatever trends on Twitter trends on traditional media. And whatever trends on traditional media trends in the policy space. So we are looking at a shift in paradigm, in which social media becomes a definer of social discourse."

That shift in paradigm has moved the balance of power to the side of the citizen. And at the end of every day, that is what democracy in its purest form should stand for.

27

THE MEDIA ABSOLUTELY MATTERS

"Did the media help Trump win?" the International Business Times asked in a piece just after the United States' presidential elections.

"Dear media, I really hope all the ratings were worth it," actor Josh Gad wrote on Twitter.

"Trump was handed a billion dollars in free media because he was entertaining and drew eyeballs," @TonyNormanPG tweeted.

And he had a point.

"Two weeks out from the election, Trump had spent $74 million on advertising, about a third of that spent by Clinton and less than half what Republican Mitt Romney had committed at the same time in the 2012 election cycle when he lost to then-incumbent Barack Obama," the Times report noted. "But Trump has been anything but absent from television screens in the 17 months since he announced his presidential bid.

"According to data-driven analytics firm mediaQuant, Trump received around $5 billion in free media coverage, more than twice that garnered by Clinton. From detailing his constant stream of headline-grabbing comments to regularly accepting phone-in interviews, Trump has been a virtual ever-present on cable news media for the past year and a half."

mediaQuant reached its figure by summing up the unpaid coverage across media and comparing that to what it would have cost if it was paid for.

"Relying heavily on an unorthodox mix of social media, unfiltered rhetoric, and a knack for winning free TV time, the New York real estate businessman likely paid less than $5 per vote during his insurgent White House bid, about half what Clinton paid, according to a Reuters analysis of campaign finance records and voting data," Reuters wrote in a report the morning after the elections. "Those figures assume the candidates spent all the funds they raised.

"Trump's cost-effective win has upended prevailing concepts about the influence of money in American politics and raised the question of whether a lean, media-savvy campaign can become the new model for winning office in the United States."

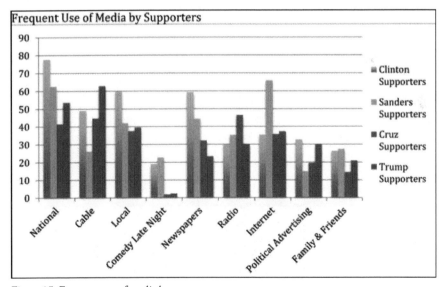

Figure 15: Frequent use of media by supporters

Well, duh.

Trump taught the world nothing that serious minded political engineers have not always known: the media is pivotal to winning elections, even in closed societies.

There is, after all, a reason Russia's president, Vladmir Putin has an 82% approval rating in his country.

"Russia's economy is staggering — the ruble is worth half of what it was three years ago — corruption is endemic and the country's south endures a persistent insurgency," the Associated Press has explained. "For some leaders such troubles could be fatal, but Putin has glided over them with a combination of steely control and personal aplomb.

"Under Putin, all major television channels came under state control and their reports — the main source of news for much of the country — either eschew criticism of the president or outright laud him. Although Putin now rarely engages in the televised stunts of his early years as president, such as bare-chested horse-riding or flying a motorized glider, he is never shown in the untoward moments that can befall anyone. Even the potential scandal of divorcing his wife was handled adroitly; Putin made the announcement during a TV interview in an anteroom between acts at a ballet."

According to one theory, it was the way that Trump forced the media to cover him that made the crucial difference – leveraging his expert, first-hand knowledge of how the media actually works.

"The best illustration of this came just days ago, when a media monitor tallied the amount of time nightly news broadcasts devoted to stories about Clinton's emails, and the amount of time they devoted to stories about *all policy matters combined,* and found that the former exceeded the latter," wrote Brian Beutler in The New Republic the day before the elections. "On any given Sunday morning, network news shows host panels of journalists, nearly all of whom are fluent in the esoteric details of Clinton's email practices, but many of whom couldn't tell you how Trump's tax plan works. As a result, if Trump were to win, millions of people would expect him to enact a populist agenda, even as his own campaign promises to raise taxes on millions of middle-income workers, privatize roads, and deregulate Wall Street.

"The final week of the campaign has been reminiscent of every relatively quiet stretch between Trump's serial implosions (attacking Gonza-lo Curiel, attacking the Khan family, attacking a former Miss Universe, or responding to the unearthing of the *Access Hollywood* video in which he boasted about committing sexual assault with impunity). When Trump wasn't in the midst of a self-inflicted crisis, we were treated to breathless commentary about how he was once again "sticking to script," as if this were a meaningful demonstration of competence for the hardest job in the world.

"These past 10 days have been no different. On the rare occasion when Trump stories eclipsed the din of chatter about Clinton's com-pletely irrelevant emails, they were frequently about how Trump had shown "discipline" in the final stretch. In reality, on every single one of those days, he was saying outrageous and false things at a dizzying clip."

Whether you agree with his judgement or not, the fact is the cov-erage went a long way into defining his image, and the pathway to his victory.

"The role of the mass media in the electoral process is not defined solely by the impact of media activities on the attitudes of voters," a Duke University paper 'Elections and the Mass Media' by Stanley Kelley Jr. notes. "The media also do things both for and to politicians, and to modes of political action, organization, and discourse.

"The modern candidate is acutely interested in gaining access to the media and in using that access effectively. He spends a large proportion of his campaign funds for the purchase of broadcast time. He adjusts the output of his statements to the rhythms of newspaper production. Even his whistle-stopping, and now his jet- stopping, is intended as much to capture the front pages of local newspapers as it is to expose the candi-date to local crowds."

We find in our work on the continent that many political operations are fundamentally ignorant about two crucial things: 1. What media platforms are most effective, and 2. How to use each media platform.

There is for instance the fact that many national campaigns in Nige-ria insist on national television network spends even in states where local radio spend is a more useful way to reach the people who actually show up at the polling booths.

Television often caters for specific upmarket audiences, but radio continues to do the job of microtargeting in spaces where data has yet to shine its light.

Of course this problem of mismatch comes because there is a dearth of reliable media measurement figures, including basic circulation numbers, demographic breakdown of viewers, and detailed analysis of timeslots and audience profiles.

So players who don't understand the nuance of the field are very likely to pour money down a hole, wasting time placing photos on front pages of national newspapers, when certain magazines hold the ace.

But beyond the what of media engagement, the how is often the bigger problem.

Most engagements with the media are ham-fisted, dictated by the understanding that the media is either corrupt or quality-deficient, and thus any relationship must either be transactional or driven by relationships only. Research underpins the validity of this worldview.

According to Agba P.C. in his 2007 paper 'Role of Mass Media in Electioneering Campaign in a Developing Context', "a European Union Election observation mission in respect of the 2003 general elections in Nigeria reported that: media performance during the Nigeria election was flawed as it failed to provide unbiased, fair and informative coverage of political parties and candidates contesting the elections. Federal and State owned (and even private owned) media were biased in favour of parties and candidates in power."

In the 2001 paper by John G.D and Enigbe J 'The Press in Nigerian Politics: An Historical Analysis Issues and Pattern of News Coverage', they noted that "there is recklessness and partisanship on the part of the press during elections. . . instead of restraint and responsible reporting of events; the principle of objectivity is always abandoned by the press in championing the causes of their masters political struggles."

While it is true that standards of journalism, especially across many parts of East and West Africa have fallen, it is a mistake to come to elections with a blanket understanding of media behaviour, or with a heavy-handed conclusion that critical coverage is sponsored by opposition and positive coverage engineered by friends.

The media, at least, in many of the democratic nations like Nigeria or Ghana or Kenya or Liberia is remarkably nuanced.

Yes, much of the media in the region can be transactional, but sometimes like all media in competitive and open markets, many times journalists are simply looking for a good story – that makes their editors happy, or that keeps the readers coming back.

Political operations that want to win must come to terms with this fact, and understand how to win the inevitable media war, because media attention is resolutely influential.

In analysis of available data in January 2016, Jonathan Stray of NiemenLab.com, the journalism platform from Harvard University, arrived at some interesting conclusions.

"There's an uncanny agreement between the media attention and each candidate's standing in national primary polls," he wrote. "It's a textbook correlation. Depending on what corner of the political universe you come from, it may surprise you to learn that both Trump and Sanders were covered in proportion to their poll results — at least online. Pretty much everyone was. The exceptions are Jeb Bush, who seems to have been covered twice as much as his standing would suggest, and Carson, who might have been slightly under-covered.

"By simply counting the number of mentions, we're completely ignoring what journalists are actually saying, including whether the coverage was positive or negative. This data doesn't say anything at all about tone or frame or even what issues were discussed. All of these things might be very important in the larger context of democracy, but they seem to be less important in terms of primary poll results. While the story surely matters, it doesn't seem to matter as much as the attention. In particular, Trump has received much more negative coverage than his GOP competitors, to little apparent effect."

He referenced data journalist, Nate Silver who had previously noted that this had been the trend for all primary elections since 1980.

"Understanding the dynamics of the modern media environment is an important skill for a candidate, and it's a skill that Trump has mastered," Silver wrote on his site FiveThirtyEight.com in December 2015. "But it's also important to understand the effects that media coverage can have on the campaign and on the polls. By one measure we'll get to in a moment, Trump has received about the most *disproportionate* media coverage ever for a primary candidate. The risk to Trump and candidates like him is that polling built on a foundation of media coverage can be subject to a correction when the news environment changes.

"The data I'll cite in this article comes from searches of NewsLibrary. com, an online archive of American newspapers from the 1980s onward.

"Since July, Trump has received 54 percent of the media coverage of the GOP primary — about six times more than Jeb Bush, who's in second place with just 8 percent of coverage. Trump isn't the only candidate to receive such a large fraction of coverage in his primary — Hillary Clinton is getting 77 percent of the media coverage in hers, far exceeding Bernie Sanders's 20 percent. Bob Dole dominated media coverage in the 1996 GOP race, and George W. Bush and Al Gore did in their respective races in 2000."

What was remarkable about this study was that it didn't matter if the coverage was affecting his favourability ratings, it just mattered that he was winning the coverage war.

"The interesting thing, as we've pointed out before, is that a candidate can potentially gain in the polls in the short term by increasing his media coverage, even if he potentially hurts his favorability rating. Trump seems to realize this," Silver shared. "So far in December — a month in which, among other things, he's proposed to ban Muslims from entering the United States — he's been the subject of 70 per cent of media coverage of the Republican race, even higher than his long-term average of 54 per cent. According to the regression, that extra media coverage is worth about 8 percentage points in the polls: almost exactly how much Trump has gained in national polls since the month began and enough to put him in the mid-30s in the polling average instead of the high 20s."

Then he asked: "Is such a strategy sustainable? Can Trump continue to dominate media coverage as much as he has already?"

Well, we know the answer now.

Trump knew precisely what he was doing, a formula he had shared in his 1987 bestseller, *The Art of the Deal*.

"One thing I've learned about the press is that they're always hungry for a good story, and the more sensational the better," he wrote. "It's in the nature of the job, and I understand that. The point is that if you are a little different, or a little outrageous, or if you do things that are bold or controversial, the press is going to write about you. I've always done things a little differently, I don't mind controversy, and my deals tend to be somewhat ambitious. Also, I achieved a lot when I was very young, and I chose to live in a certain style. The result is that the press has always wanted to write about me.

"I'm not saying that [journalists] necessarily like me. Sometimes they write positively, and sometimes they write negatively. But from a pure business point of view, the benefits of being written about have far out-weighed the drawbacks. It's really quite simple. If I take a full-page ad in the New York Times to publicize a project, it might cost $40,000, and in any case, people tend to be skeptical about advertising. But if the New York Times writes even a moderately positive one-column story about one of my deals, it doesn't cost me anything, and it's worth a lot more than $40,000.

"The funny thing is that even a critical story, which may be hurtful personally, can be very valuable to your business. Television City is a perfect example. When I bought the land in 1985, many people, even those on the West Side, didn't realize that those one hundred acres existed. Then I announced I was going to build the world's tallest building on the site. Instantly, it became a media event: the New York Times put it on the front page, Dan Rather announced it on the evening news, and

George Will wrote a column about it in Newsweek. Every architecture critic had an opinion, and so did a lot of editorial writers. Not all of them liked the idea of the world's tallest building. But the point is that we got a lot of attention, and that alone creates value."

Of course, there is a chicken and egg conundrum, especially in a social media age, where the question is: does media coverage follow attention, or does what the audience pay attention to depend on what the media chooses to focus on? Stray's thesis on this is very helpful.

"My sense is that what we have here is a feedback loop," he says. "Does media attention increase a candidate's standing in the polls? Yes. Does a candidate's standing in the polls increase media attention? Also yes. And everything else which sways both journalists and voters in the same direction just increases the correlation. The media and the public and the candidates are embedded in a system where every part affects every other.

"It's all of these forces acting in concert that tend to bind media attention and popularity together. It's not that media attention has no effect — we have good reason to believe it does, both from this data and from other research. It's just that the media is not all powerful, despite what the close correlation suggests."

The University of Oregon's School of Journalism and Communication shared a useful report in 2016 on the frameworks from which you can see the effects of media influence. Four of these factors correlate with our experience:

1. What it chooses to cover i.e. what it considers newsworthy.
2. How it chooses to cover – what frames does it impose on candidates, and what images and pieces are used to advance those frames.
3. The biases of journalists that lead to narrative slants (and we will treat narratives in more detail in the next chapter).
4. The volume (or lack of) of facts and data, and how this affects coverage.

A 2016 report by the Harvard Kennedy School's Shorenstein Center on Media, Politics and Public Policy noted that "journalistic bias" as to what story matters led to over-coverage of the Donald Trump campaign and under-coverage of Democrats.

In the work that StateCraft Inc does, we often take for granted that there are many factors that influence how journalists behave. Many of them are subconscious, including political bias, peer pressure and relationships with key actors. Therefore, very often, facts are different from the narratives that exist in the media.

"The problem, in retrospect, was that the socioeconomic class to which columnists, analysts, and speculators in political markets belonged had a heavy pro-Remain tilt to it," RealClearPolitics.com wrote for instance, on the 1st of November 2016 in speaking of media reportage in the American elections. "This infiltrated their analysis, as the supposedly objective measurements that they chose turned out to be massive exercises in confirmation bias."

The job of electoral politics therefore demands that professionals have a clear-eyed view about how the media operates in each context, what narratives it is sympathetic to, how important it is to show up in the first place, and how to align media expectations and audience desires to campaign imperatives.

It is always helpful to have the media sympathetic to the causes that are central to your campaign – to find out the point of convergence between your interests and their storytelling interests at any time.

When the elections were concluded in Ghana and the ruling National Democratic Congress refused to concede that it had lost the presidential elections, the media played a pivotal role. The results were splashed across all media platforms as the backdrop in post-election conversations. It ensured that results could not be changed without grievous consequences. One of our concerns pre-elections was the sanctity of the results and we engaged actively on that front.

It paid off handsomely, as the media ensured that it was difficult for the ruling party or the electoral commission to announce a different set of results.

So this much is obvious: it is impossible to win an election without prioritising effective engagement with media. It is impossible to persuade people without engaging new and traditional media effectively and consistently in modern societies. If messaging is the key tool for persuasion as the key political end, then the media becomes crucial as the tool to convey messaging.

Campaigns treat media as tangential to their strategies, or as solely transaction, at their own peril.

28

NARRATIVES MATTER

In April 2008, Hillary Clinton's campaign manager Geoff Garin wrote a piece, 'Fair is fair' from a place of deep frustration.

"What's wrong with this picture?" he asked, in the Washington Post. "Our campaign runs a TV ad Monday saying that the presidency is the toughest job in the world and giving examples of challenges presidents have faced and challenges the next president will face – including terrorism, the wars in Iraq and Afghanistan, mounting economic dislocation, and soaring gas prices. The ad makes no reference – verbal, visual or otherwise – to our opponent; it simply asks voters to think about who they believe is best able to stand the heat. And we are accused, by some in the media, of running a fear-mongering, negative ad.

"The day before this ad went on the air, David Axelrod, Barack Obama's chief strategist, appeared with me on 'Meet the Press.' He was asked whether Hillary Clinton would bring 'the changes necessary' to Washington, and his answer was 'no.' This was in keeping with the direct, personal character attacks that the Obama campaign has leveled against Clinton from the beginning of this race – including mailings in Pennsylvania that describe her as 'the master of a broken system'.

"So let me get this straight. On the one hand, it's perfectly decent for Obama to argue that only he has the virtue to bring change to Washington and that Clinton lacks the character and the commitment to do so. On the other hand, we are somehow hitting below the belt when we say that Clinton is the candidate best able to withstand the pressures of the presidency and do what's right for the American people, while leaving the decisions about Obama's preparedness to the voters."

Garin was running into a blockade that has frustrated many campaign professionals for decades: the power of narratives.

Narratives matter. They matter because the media is the primary tool for messaging, and messaging is the most important foundation of persuasion. The media runs based on narratives. It puts history and current events into particular frames, mostly without being conscious of it, and then proceeds based on that foundation.

In the United States Democratic Primary elections of 2008, the narrative was clear: Clinton was cynical, manipulative and negative and Obama was fresh, hopeful and positive. Media reportage flowed from these two basic frames, throughout the contest.

A Vox.com piece in July 2015 was very instructive in breaking down the headwinds of a negative narrative Clinton had always had to fight.

"After a quarter of a century on the national stage, there's no more comfortable political figure to afflict than Hillary Clinton," Jonathan Allen wrote. "And she's in for a lot of affliction over the next year and half.

"That's generally a good way for reporters to go about their business. After all, the more power a person wants in our republic, the more voters should know about her or him. But it's also an essential frame for thinking about the long-toxic relationship between the Clintons and the media, why the coverage of Hillary Clinton differs from coverage of other candidates for the presidency, and whether that difference encourages distortions that will ultimately affect the presidential race.

"The Clinton rules are driven by reporters' and editors' desire to score the ultimate prize in contemporary journalism: the scoop that brings down Hillary Clinton and her family's political empire. At least in that way, Republicans and the media have a common interest."

He went on to list the five pillars of her narrative:

1. Everything, no matter how ludicrous-sounding, is worthy of a full investigation by federal agencies, Congress, the "vast right-wing conspiracy," and mainstream media outlets.
2. Every allegation, no matter how ludicrous, is believable until it can be proven completely and utterly false. And even then, it keeps a life of its own in the conservative media world.
3. The media assumes that Clinton is acting in bad faith until there's hard evidence otherwise.
4. Everything is newsworthy because the Clintons are the equivalent of America's royal family.
5. Everything she does is fake and calculated for maximum political benefit.

"The media can definitely weigh down — and even destroy — a candidate. The emphasis on a candidate's flaws — real or perceived — comes at the cost of the candidate's ability to focus his or her message and at the cost of negative attention to the other candidates," he concluded. "This is a problem for Clinton, and it seems unlikely to go away. (She) is comfortable enough to be a target for a lot of journalistic affliction and powerful enough that no one needs to comfort her from that affliction. But these double standards are an important factor to keep in mind when judging her against her rivals for the presidency. Whether they're fair or not, the Clinton rules distort the public's perception of Hillary Clinton."

The University of Oregon's paper on 'Six ways the media influences elections' explained what was happening here.

"Aside from ideological bias, journalists across outlets also perpetuate biased views by distilling complex campaigns and issues into simplified "scripts."

"One popular election-coverage script is the "horserace" or "game frame" narrative. "We know from decades of research that the mainstream media tend to see elections through the prism of competition," said Lawrence. "Campaigns get covered a lot like sports events, with an emphasis on who's winning, who's losing, who's up, who's down, how they are moving ahead or behind in the polls."

"The media also perpetuate character-based scripts. "For example, in 2000, the script for Al Gore was that he was a pompous bore, and the script for George W. Bush was that he wasn't very smart," said Lawrence. In this year's presidential race, the narratives that Clinton is a corrupt politician and Trump is a racist, misogynist outsider have dominated election coverage."

Narratives are powerful. They are also difficult to fight. Actually, it can be a waste of time to fight them.

Donald Trump understood as much in the United States elections. He couldn't win the media narrative war painting him as a self-centered politician, and so he embraced it and re-focused it. Asked about his un-favourable leaked tax returns, he didn't miss a heartbeat: "I know our complex tax laws better than anyone who has ever run for president and am the only one who can fix them," he tweeted.

RealClearPolitics.com put the influence of narratives in stark relief in explaining the so-called failure of polling in America's 2016 elections.

"There is a fast-building meme that Donald Trump's surprising win on Tuesday reflected a failure of the polls," it wrote. "This is wrong. The story of 2016 is not one of poll failure. It is a story of interpretive failure and a media environment that made it almost taboo to even suggest that Donald Trump had a real chance to win the election.

"What occurred wasn't a failure of the polls. Instead, people gravitat-ed toward unreliable approaches such as reading the tea leaves on early voting or putting faith in Big Blue Walls, while ignoring things like the high number of undecided voters. They selected these data points rather than other possible indicators, such as the significant late break in the generic ballot that could have led them in a different direction. To be blunt, people saw what they wanted to see, and then found the data to support that view."

They forced the data to fit their prevailing narratives.

When StateCraft Inc arrives at a country for election work, we first spend a considerable period of time gathering information. Our first pre-strategy consideration in this regard is to decide what the narratives are: who are the bad and good guys, why are they the bad and good guys, how has the press calcified this narrative, and what is the voters' interaction with the narrative?

We don't engage the media without focus group, poll-driven understanding of this crucial media consensus. It is the foundation of all effective communication.

You can spend useful time fighting the unfairness of it, or you can instead empathise with its inevitability, and get to work aligning the reality with your campaign imperatives, unless of course publicly fighting unfairness is a well thought out media strategy on your part.

To be fair, the media narrative in 2015 was very sympathetic to the possibilities of a historical change in Nigeria's power structure, and we took full advantage of that. Journalists, editors and others had reached a consensus about the rudderless-ness of the Goodluck Jonathan government. Countless editorials had already demanded his resignation, following the almost weekly bombings in Northern Nigeria.

"Our results indicate strong significant score on media framing of conflict during the Nigerian 2015 Presidential elections and more news were framed to reflect crises in PDP than APC," concluded a paper 'Dimensions of Negativity in the Coverage of the Nigeria's 2015 Presidential Election' published in *The International Journal of International Relations, Media and Mass Communication Studies* by Emmanuel Sunday Nwofe. "Conflict has become a substantial part of news reporting as journalist's attitudes towards politics become increasingly cynical (Patterson 2009). Patterson argues that such attitude activate journalist's search for oppositional and conflictual information with little concern about the extent criticism is justified. On the incapability dimension, we also find that news that reflects incapability outweighs capability in the coverage of Nigerian 2015 Presidential election. And incapability frame was strongly significant toward President Jonathan/PDP than General Buhari/APC."

This frame coincided with an anti-Jonathan narrative pushed on social media by both opposition and general citizens about the president as 'clueless'. By the time the elections rolled by, this image was set in stone.

Of course, Buhari also had his narrative challenges. We decided to embrace them, rather than to fight them. The perceptions we thought needed to be changed, we decided to change subtly rather than wage a public war. It's the basic writing principle of 'show don't tell'.

So we embraced the image of the austere, stern General, plying that into a sub-messaging themed 'Who would you trust with your life?'

The subtext was clear – if the country was in danger, who would you trust best to protect it? The man the nation already concluded as clueless, or the disciplined, no-nonsense general who looked like he was ready to get it done?

The other small matter of him not being relatable was easy to dismiss, because it was a caricature. We easily re-directed his public image with a simple photo-shoot showing him in all the ways the public had never seen him before, including the viral photo of him in a suit, and convinced him to attend, in public, events that we realised in private he would enjoy. By seizing the main narrative, and dismissing the distractions, we set the course that made it easier for him to communicate the urgency of his candidacy.

Narratives work because they are strongly tied to how the human being processes information and makes decisions on a day-to-day basis.

"Consider the 2004 book, *Don't Think of an Elephant*, in which Berkeley linguistics professor George Lakoff applied the analytic techniques from his field to politics, explaining that all of what we know is physically embodied in our brains,' which process language through frames: 'mental structures that shape the way we see the world', Dave Gold wrote in a piece analyzing the Democratic Party's loss in the 2016 presidential elections.

"Convincing a voter—challenging an existing frame—is no small task. 'When you hear a word, its frame (or collection of frames) is activated in your brain," writes Lakoff. As a result, 'if a strongly held frame doesn't fit the facts, the facts will be ignored and the frame will be kept.' How then to persuade voters? How can we get them to change the way they see the world? Tell a story.

"Further evidence was put forward in 2007's *The Political Brain*, by Emory University psychologist Drew Westen. 'The political brain is an emotional brain,' Westen wrote, and the choice between electoral campaigns that run on an issue-by-issue debate versus those that embrace storytelling is stark: 'You can slog it out for those few millimeters of cerebral turf that process facts, figures and policy statements. Or you can take your campaign to the broader neural electorate collecting delegates throughout the brain and targeting different emotional states with messages designed to maximize their appeal'."

Of course, powerful as they are, narratives are not destiny. The narrative towards Trump in the elections, for instance, was uniformly and insistently negative, and yet he prevailed.

"I take a dim view of the idea that journalists successfully anoint political winners," the Vox piece noted. "The media might have been in the bag for Barack Obama, but he didn't win because he got positive coverage. He won because he had better strategy, a better message, and better skills at delivering that message — in the 2008 primary and in the two general elections he won."

Candidates can win despite the narratives that are thrown at them, and which they can do very little about.

But the key to overcoming this, where it is unfavourable, is not to ignore it, but to understand it, to engage it and then to align it with the messaging that the candidacy has decided on. As always, the messaging is the ultimate tool for winning the election.

29

HOPE MATTERS ABOVE ALL ELSE

"Hope is inexhaustible," former World Bank Vice President for Africa and co-founder of the #BringBackOurGirls campaign, Obiageli Ezekwesili, has routinely said to citizens as the inspiration for her unrelenting campaign to free the 254 girls who were kidnapped by the Boko Haram terrorist group in Nigeria's Chibok.

Indeed, at the time when the group's campaign began there was no hope that any of the girls would be found, and a former president (Olusegun Obasanjo) of Nigeria had indeed stated that they could never be found.

But in the period since the campaign began, the Nigerian army has recovered over 50 of the girls, at the time of writing this.

That same hope that Ezekwesili speaks about often, is precisely the driver that makes it possible for citizens of countries to take their destinies into their own hands and change their governments when they so decide.

Hope may not be a strategy, but it is a powerful driver of the human spirit.

In Dominique Moisi's book, *The Geopolitics of Emotion*, he notes that global politics is driven by three primary emotions today, two of which are hope and fear. According to him, "Asia has been able to concentrate on building a better future, so it is creating a new culture of hope."

Hope is not optimism, Archbishop Demond Tutu explains in *The Book of Joy* speaking of the primary emotion that drove the anti-apartheid struggle. In his telling, optimism is the belief that things will get better; hope is the understanding that things *can* get better.

Positive psychology specialist, Charles Richard Snyder in his paper 'Hope Theory' has said there are three main hangers for hope:

- Goals – Approaching life in a goal-oriented way.
- Pathways – Finding different ways to achieve your goals.
- Agency – Believing that you can instigate change and achieve these goals.

"In other words," according to analysis of the book. "Hope is defined as the perceived capability to derive pathways to desired goals, and motivate oneself via agency thinking to use those pathways. Snyder argues that individuals who are able to realize these 3 components and develop a belief in their ability are hopeful people who can establish clear goals, imagine multiple workable pathways toward those goals, and persevere, even when obstacles get in their way."

Replace 'individuals' with 'nations' and you can understand how a people can believe that a 20-year dictatorship can be overturned, that a 15-year political monopoly can be dislodged, and that a life presidency can be truncated.

The human capacity for hope is endless.

It is not for nothing that the 2008 Barack Obama 'Hope' poster quickly became iconic, and his slogan 'Change we can believe in' spoke not just to the possibility of change, but the possibility that this change could come to life.

Despite Somalia's 26-year-old ongoing war, in 2017 citizens came out to vote in historic elections.

Asked for the impetus, Bishop Giorgio Bertin, the apostolic administrator of Mogadishu and president of Caritas Somalia, told a newspaper it was hope.

"(The bishop) says Mass for only 15 people on Sunday because most are too scared to participate since the extremist crackdown in the area," Cruxnow.com reported in January 2017. "Even though there are challenges ahead, Bertin sees signs of hope."

We have said before that campaigns win when they effectively answer the questions that citizens are asking at that time. Whether those questions center on security, the economy, or culture wars at any time, it is apparent that the primary emotion driving the decision to come out and vote is hope – hope that the candidate can actually change the status quo, or make things better; hope that the candidate will do what he or she says.

Citizens are not stupid. They understand how intractable the challenges are and how near-to-impossible it can be for the status quo to change. But the basic driver of hope can often come down to the simple question: "What other choice do we have?"

It is important for players in the electoral space to understand both the beauty and the desperation of this question, and how primal it is a driver for decisions.

Hope is what drives people to come out and vote despite security challenges in their regions. Hope is what inspires voters despite the unending disappointment politicians have delivered to them.

Hope is what pushes people to pour out into the streets, despite the desperation of their affairs, to rejoice whenever a difficult election is won.

Hope is what will drive citizens of the Republic of Congo to the polls despite a lack of peaceful transition since it won independence in 1960.

It is always hope.

The candidate that best channels that hope and translates it into change that citizens can believe in more effectively is better positioned to carry the day.

"Not only jobs but also power has been in short supply. Mahama was nicknamed "Mr. Dumsor," which literally translates as Mr. Power Cut," FairObserver.com noted in December 2016 about Ghana's 2016 elections. "Power failures of six to 24 hours were common. Both power generation and distribution are in trouble. The country's biggest source

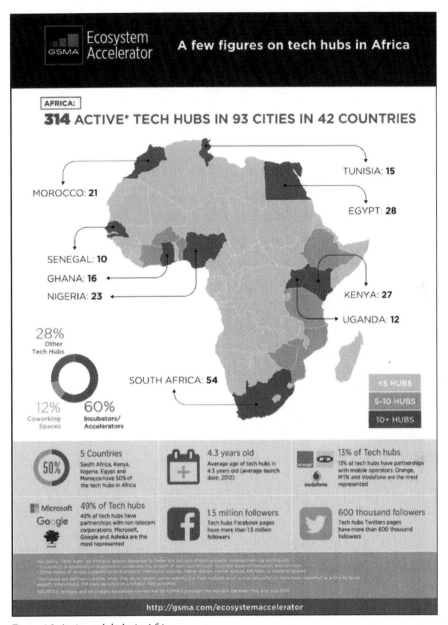

Figure 16: Active tech hubs in Africa

of power has been the Akosombo Dam. Climate change has led to decreasing rainfall, which has led to a diminishing amount of water in the dam. This, in turn, means the dam's electricity production has declined at a time when the population and demand for power in the country is on the rise.

"In the face of such daunting challenges, Mahama's government was ineffective and enmeshed in corruption scandals that gave Akufo-Addo's message a credible opening. He has promised to make Ghana the star of Africa again."

Of course, routinely, politicians have taken advantage of that hope, manipulating audiences in order to maintain strangleholds on power, or overselling capacity in order to secure a change in government, a depressing side-effect of an important aspiration.

But still hope must spring eternal. Because without it, it is impossible to galvanise people, especially those who are beaten down, to rise up and take charge of their destinies. And the times always call for politicians who have the visions and personas to lead a hopeful people to a new place of possibilities.

"I still believe in hope," Obama said in his last campaign rally for Hillary Clinton in 2016. "I'm still as optimistic as ever about our future. That's because of you, the American people."

There is no force on earth as powerful as an inspired, empowered people.

With the hope that remains in their hearts, they can do absolutely anything, including the transformation of their nations. And that, as examples from Rwanda to Botswana have shown for Africa, is absolutely no exaggeration.

30

EMPATHY MATTERS

"The Trump victory wasn't a mere expression of disdain or revenge, or an endorsement of the lesser of two evils," American media critic Jack Shafer wrote after the United States elections in 2016. "However negative Trump is—and you don't need a refresher course on that, do you?—he was selling a positive vision about greatness and restoration to voters. He slung praise upon a constituency that was starved for the respect of a plain-speaking candidate, and they rolled over on their backs and grinned, tongues akimbo, as he scratched their bellies. For these people he conveyed dignity and the rescue of lost honor. He delivered their payback. He embodied their grievances."

This point has been made before but it bears repeating, because it can stay at the crux of the matter: to win in contested elections, politicians need to answer the questions that voters are asking in their hearts.

That process demands that politicians must understand what is going on in the hearts and minds of voters.

The Merriam-Webster definition of empathy is anodyne: "Empathy refers to the ability to relate to another person's pain vicariously, as if one has experienced that pain themselves."

The Psychology Today definition gets closer to its true essence: "Empathy is the experience of understanding another person's condition from their perspective. You place yourself in their shoes and feel what they are feeling."

People wonder a lot about the thing that drove Muhammadu Buhari's continued chase after the presidency of Nigeria; that made him run for that office three times.

Despite everything that has happened in his presidency, this much was very apparent to the people around him throughout the campaign: he deeply empathised with the oppressed, depressed Nigerian voter.

"During one of Muhammadu Buhari's presidential campaign rallies, a huge crowd of supporters gathered around our campaign vehicle," Vice-President Yemi Osinbajo shared. "And General Buhari said to me, 'Yemi look at the people, what do you see?', and I said to him, 'I see our supporters'. Buhari said 'Look again, look into their eyes, what do you see?' And I said, 'Your excellency, I see Nigerians'. Then Buhari said, 'Can you see these people? Look into their eyes, they have high expectations and hopes on us, they expect us to turn Nigeria around positively the very first day we get to office, Yemi we've got a lot of work to do'."

That empathy permeated the entire campaign: he was angry on behalf of the many poor and destitute people, unpaid, that climbed on trees, besieged his cars, and wept at the sight of a man in whom they had invested dreams and hopes.

This isn't a statement about his politics or the quality of his governance. It is a statement about a key emotion that drove his ability to connect with the masses each election cycle, and to expand that base at a time of mass national frustration.

His campaign reflected that urgency of empathy.

"What is going on here?" he asked with feeling in one of our advert spots speaking directly to the camera, holding its gaze. "How can the terrorists of Boko Haram seize any part of Nigerian territory – a sovereign country?"

In contrast, the Goodluck Jonathan campaign looked like an exercise in chicanery – it felt and sounded distinctly disconnected from the depth of frustration that people were feeling, from the lack that defined the Nigerian experience right under his nose.

Whatever else was happening with the Jonathan campaign, this much was an underlying truth: it never, once, appeared that he understood how bad things had become for the country, or how bad it appeared (because he certainly was convinced he had made things better, and that was a valid sentiment) that things had become for the citizens of the country. And as an incumbent, with the maximum real and perceived power of the Nigerian presidency, his burden was even more enhanced: he needed to do more to prove that he did.

In January 2015, Obiageli Ezekwesili sounded this alarm at the Daily Trust Dialogue (themed '2015 Elections: How to Make Nigeria The Winner'), breaking down in tears over the many tragedies Nigerians have suffered, from the 1967 Civil War to the 2014 kidnap of 265 school girls.

"How could we pick up and move on?" she asked. "All agitations of being marginalised somehow never seemed to have persuaded Nigerians until Jos practically began to go up in smoke.

"Now our own military repels what started off as ragtag insurgency who, when their effect was not being felt in the whole of Nigeria, expanded their attack. It is time for the people to win. In the 54 years of fighting to control power, it is time to change that paradigm.

"Hello to the 170m citizen winners of the 2015 elections. You are more powerful than you look but that only happens when you make informed decisions."

When the elections came, the citizens overwhelmingly responded.

Of course, Jonathan had never been an emotive candidate; he was more likely to be removed and ceremonial. However, his campaign strategists had, in his first run, found a way to go round that challenge, coming down to the genius of his long-time aide and Special Assistant on Research and Strategy, Oronto Douglas: it was the narrative of the man who was so poor, he had no shoes when he was growing up in a backwater Nigerian village.

Whatever else happened, that simple narrative became the most memorable line from the entire 2011 campaign. It became a symbol of the candidate as 'every man' who had an understanding of what it means to live in a difficult country, and simultaneously aspirational because if he could do it – the message seemed to be to citizens who were paying attention to the subtext – then you could do it too.

And, it worked. Because empathy matters.

There are those who may call it pandering, and they completely miss the point. Again, unscrupulous politicians can take advantage of an electioneering essential, but it doesn't invalidate its necessity.

"Obama is probably the most empathy-focused President—or at least the President who uses the term the most—I've seen in my lifetime," Jamil Zaki, an Assistant Professor of Psychology at Stanford University, has written. "He often talks about there being an empathy deficit, and says that one of the ways that we need to improve our society and the fabric of our society, is by increasing our empathy. I bet there are a lot of people who would disagree with that as a policy for running a state.

"You saw this when Obama appointed Sotomayor as a Supreme Court justice and said this is a woman who has great empathy for the plight of many people. Well, that statement was vilified. He was pilloried for saying that, and people felt as though empathy is one of the worst features that you could select for when thinking about policy, when thinking about law, when thinking about government, because empathy is an emotion subject to all sorts of irrational biases. Justice should be blind, and presumably emotionally neutral.

"You see this a lot in a movement that's taken hold recently. Paul Bloom and a set of other psychologists have made what I think is a great and very interesting case that empathy is overrated, especially as a moral compass. Their view is that empathy generates kind and moral behaviors, but in fundamentally skewed ways, for instance, only towards members of your own group and not in ways that maximize well-being across the largest number of people. On this account, empathy is an inflexible emotional engine for driving moral behavior and if you want to do the right thing, you should focus on more objective principles to guide your decision-making.

"That's a great argument. It's not one that I agree with. It follows from somewhat of an incomplete view of what empathy is. If you believe that empathy is automatic and either just happens to you or doesn't, then sure, the biases that characterize empathy are inescapable and will always govern empathic decision-making. If you instead view empathy as something that people can control, then people can choose to align their empathy more with their values."

The question needs be asked in fact: If you don't feel the pain of the voter, why are you running to lead or represent them?

Indeed, there is research questioning whether empathy truly leads to ethical behaviour.

"Yale University psychologist Dr. Paul Bloom is a member of the camp that argues empathy is an "overrated" trait for a leader," a Huffington Post story has noted. "Although it can inspire altruism, he says, empathy can also be sullied by biases and doesn't necessarily translate to moral decision-making.

"Bloom and his colleagues conducted a study finding that volunteers who expressed the most empathy for terrorism victims in the Middle East also were more likely to favor military action. Other research has indicated that empathy may also lead us to care more about helping the one person we sympathize with the most rather than helping a group we aren't as intimately familiar with."

But the fact that still emerges is that human beings are drawn towards those they believe empathise with them. So whether empathy is useful in governance or not is a debate that will continue to rage, but there can be no doubt that in politics, it is very necessary.

Dr. Emma Seppala, scientific director of Stanford University's Center for Compassion and Altruism Research and Education, notes in the Post piece that voters are wont "to consider a candidate's capability to be empathetic before voting."

"I feel your pain." Bill Clinton famously won the heart of a nation when he said this to an AIDS activist in 1992.

"The biggest deficit that we have in our society and in the world right now is an empathy deficit," Obama said in 2007, underscoring why he was such a hit as a campaigner.

It is important to understand that this is not empathy with the entirety of the world, but empathy with the specific voters that are required in an election – being able to channel and reflect their challenges and hopes so intensely that you build lasting credibility with them.

"So Trump supporters get a full dose of cognitive empathy directed straight at them from the man at the campaign podium," journalist Emily Willingham wrote in an excellent piece for Forbes. "No one is reading those supporters and playing them better than Trump himself. His instinctive understanding of his fans' emotional state and his willingness to exploit them drive his success.

"And his skill with understanding his loyalists underlies his insouciance about outrage from other quarters: He knows his supporters will see anger targeted at him as attacks on themselves. With his ability to read his followers, he has magnetized them and their loyalty in a way that no amount of pointing out lies or potentially criminal behavior will weaken. Indeed, it just strengthens their bonds.

"Trump pivots effortlessly wherever his supporters' emotions point him. Like a giant mirror, he reflects those emotions back at his loyalists without seeming to truly share them himself. He is a master of projection, both of his own faults and his followers' anger, paranoia and fear."

Indeed, certain people can manipulate empathy for political gain. But that doesn't mean that empathy is unnecessary. It in fact doubles the necessity for politicians who are not manipulative to learn the pain points of their voters, and be sure that they are correctly understanding and addressing those issues.

"Empathy in this sense is essential; you can't act effectively in the world if you don't have some sense of what other people want," Paul Bloom, Professor of Psychology at Yale University, wrote in the Wall Street Journal in December 2016.

"EMPATHY is important for effective policies. How can U make good policies with results 4 people 4 whom you feel nothing?" Ezekwesili tweeted in November 2013. "EMPATHY is a huge subset of EMO-TIONAL INTELLIGENCE & critical for strategic/iconic LEADER-SHIP. Mostly inborn, [it] can be cultivated too."

If politicians with the best intentions don't learn this crucial skill, then talented politicians without it will continue to win.

It is human instinct to gravitate towards a nurse who takes the time to feel what we feel and administers the drug with the sensitivity that true concern brings.

Let no one blame the voter.

31

PEOPLE SHOULD NOT BE AFRAID OF THEIR GOVERNMENTS

"I shouldn't even be here," President Olusegun Obasanjo said to Nigerians who were grieving the deaths and injuries of their loved ones in the Ikeja Cantonment bomb blasts in 2004, expecting them to be grateful to have gotten a visit from their own president.

"If this how you want to talk to me," the governor of Oyo state said to students of a state polytechnic protesting the closure of their school for eight months, "then do your worst. Eight months. Eight months? Is that something we have not seen before?"

"My fate is in the hands of almighty Allah," Gambia's disgraced dictator, Yahya Jammer, told the BBC's Focus on Africa in 2011. "If I have to rule this country for one billion years, I will."

In 1998, Robert Mugabe famously boasted that he had "many degrees in violence". "Zanu PF will rule forever," his Vice President, Emmerson Mnangagwa has said as recently as 2017.

Africa's leaders have very little regard for their people.

They restrict their rights, they impose their will, they lock up opposition, they talk down at them, they dismiss their concerns, and they steal their votes.

	Leader	Country	Years
Africa's longest-serving leaders			
1	Jose Eduardo dos Santos	Angola	36
2	Teodoro Obiang Nguema	Equatorial Guinea	36
3	Robert Mugabe	Zimbabwe	35
4	Paul Biya	Cameroon	32
5	Denis Sassou Nguesso	Congo Brazzaville	31
6	Yoweri Museveni	Uganda	30
7	King Mswati III	Swaziland	29
8	Omar al-Bashir	Sudan	26
9	Idriss Deby	Chad	25

Figure 17: Africa's longest-serving leaders

"The respect, and, yes, the fear that leaders should have for citizens is mostly absent in the version of a social contract that Nigeria has," one of the authors of this book has written. "Unfortunately, the fault for this anomaly doesn't come only from those who lead.

"Today, we have citizens who have ceded their right to be treated with respect. You only need to pay attention to conversation online to see a citizenry that has not only ceded that right, but actively denigrates those who would exercise theirs. People who believe that political affiliation means blind loyalty. Those who believe that relationships with government mean silence whatever happens. Those who believe that those who make high demands of government are being 'troublesome' or 'unreasonable;.

"But if citizens want respect from their leaders, they have to demand it – and they have to demand it without reservation.

"In that case, it becomes imperative to turn up the heat. People should not be afraid of their governments. Governments should be afraid of their people.

"Governments should be worried about how the public receives their decisions and interprets their actions. Government activity would thence be made only against the background of what citizens thinks, what the voters' reaction will be, of the consequences of each step.

"Even if it leads to pandering – that is only a small price to pay for the bigger gain that comes. But it has to matter that the decision of those we have chosen to lead us must reflect our desires, our wishes, our imperatives and our preferences – and that their reactions must reflect an understanding of who truly calls the shots.

"That is how a functioning democracy works. Unfortunately, Nigeria is a long way from this balance of power."

You could replace Nigeria at this point with a large numbers of countries across the continent – Uganda, Cameroon, Zimbabwe, Equatorial Guinea, Angola, Sudan, Swaziland. The list can seem endless.

"Sudan's President seized power in 1989 in a bloodless military coup against the government of Prime Minister Sadiq al-Mahdi- a government which was democratically elected by the people of Sudan," a Forbes piece has said. "Soon after seizing power, Al-Bashir dispersed all political parties in the country, disbanded the country's parliament and shut down all privately-owned media outlets. His reign has been characterized by a civil war in which over one million have been killed, while several millions have been displaced. Al-Bashir is still wanted by the International Criminal Court for instigating crimes against humanity, particularly in directing and funding acts of violence against the Southern Sudan."

Of Swaziland, it says: "But for all the suffering of the Swazi people, King Mswati has barely shown concern or interest. He lives lavishly, using his kingdom's treasury to fund his expensive tastes in German automobiles, first-class leisure trips around the world and women. But his gross mismanagement of his country's finances is now having dire economic consequences."

And perhaps Angola is one of the strongest examples of the impunity and the disregard.

"José Eduardo dos Santos is Africa's second longest serving president," the piece notes. "To his discredit, Jose Eduardo has always run his government like it's his personal, privately-owned investment holding company. His cousin serves as Angola's vice president, and his daughter, Isabel Dos Santos is arguably the wealthiest woman in the country.

"For all its resource wealth, the vast majority of Angolans still live in the most horrid socio-economic conditions. 68% of the country's total population lives below the poverty line of $1.7 a day, while 28% live on less than 30 cents. Education is free, but it's practically worthless. Most of the schools are housed in dilapidated structures and there is a severe deficit of skilled and qualified teachers. According to the U.N. Children's Fund, 30% of the country's children are malnourished. The average life expectancy is about 41 years while child and maternal deaths are extremely high. Unemployment levels are very high. But José Eduardo Santos is unaffected. Rather than transforming Angola's economic boom into social relief for its people, he has channeled his energies towards intimidating the local media and diverting state funds into his personal and family accounts. Dos Santos's family controls a huge chunk of Angola's economy. His daughter, Isabel Dos Santos has amassed one of the country's largest personal fortunes by using proceeds from her father's alleged corruption to acquire substantial stakes in companies like Zon Multimedia, a Portuguese media conglomerate and in Portuguese banks Banco Espírito Santo and Banco Português de Investimento among others."

It is the reason many take a lot of solace in the misfortunes of many of Africa's brutal leaders like Liberia's Charles Taylor or Ivory Coast's Laurent Gbagbo presently on trial at the International Criminal Court after being forced out of power in 2011, and the reason so many were inflamed at the terms of Jemmah's exile from Gambia.

"Even before the cheers to celebrate the end of Yahya Jammeh's brutal 22-year rule of Gambia died down, there was fury that he was being allowed to flee into luxurious exile," the Star in Kenya reported. "Trader Aji Jagne, 32, had chanted "we are free" until her voice was hoarse on Sunday but by the end of the day, less than 24 hours after Jammeh flew out of the country and into exile, her toothy grin had disappeared.

""Why should he escape...? If he ever sets foot in Gambia again, we

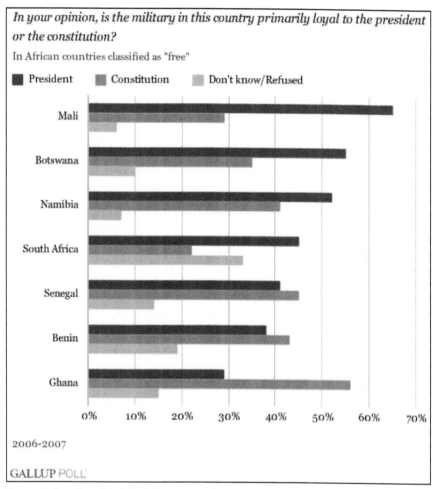

Figure 18: Presidential Rule Still Dominates African Politics

shall take him to the ICC," she said. For Jammeh's victims, the notion that he might never face justice and may have even escaped with his treasure is deeply troubling."

Thankfully, citizens across the continent are deciding they won't take it anymore, and that is an infinitively positive thing.

The overturning of establishments and incumbencies across the continent is making it clear that citizens are no longer having it from their leaders, and they are willing to make the sacrifices, sometimes at the cost of their lives, to bring change to their countries.

This is the battle of our lives, for the collective destinies of a troubled continent, and the citizens of these countries, especially the young people who have in their lifetimes never seen functioning, responsive governments, need all the help they can get, from neighboring countries, a global civil society and an international consensus of good governance.

This is a period of monumental change.

History always presents a multiplicity of chances for any nation to redirect its destiny. But there is no time as now to take advantage of the momentum in the land, and deliver to a vast number of countries, governments that understand how to put their people, front and center – with humility, with empathy and with goodwill.

These are truly exciting times.

32

THE NEW POLITICAL MARKETPLACE

"My colleague who led the team on the ground working on campaign communication for the Ghanaian presidential elections captured the crux of our learnings from two political campaigns to me on his return last month: the fatal mistake of entitled incumbents," Jideonwo wrote in a piece on YNaija.com recently, addressing a theme we have referred to in earlier chapters of this book.

"Many of them insist on telling citizens what they have already achieved. 'This is what I have done,' they announce, expecting voters to be grateful. 'These are the roads, these are the jobs.'

"But citizens no longer care about legacy, they care about tomorrow. What incumbents are supposed to do – a rule of thumb, really - is tie the past to the future. 'This is what I have done so far... and now this is what I am going to do." This, presented as if you were a new candidate, with no sense of entitlement, as if the voters owe you no gratitude – because they don't.'

It wasn't always like this. A (wo)man's track record should be the defining measure by which we gauge what she can do in the future. A lifetime of service and achievements should predict a future of service and achievement.

But disruption is not just for business and technology; it's a reality for all of society.

And this is the new reality: politics – the art of how voters make decisions – has been disrupted."

That's the reality: There is a new political marketplace and it has upturned all the rules about everything you know about how votes are won and how citizens interact with politicians.

Those players in the political space who are complaining are missing the entire point of how society has always evolved.

When disruption came to the phone industry, players were quick to adjust because the customer is always right. When disruption came to banking, players were quick to adjust because the customer is always right.

How is disruption fine when politicians are asking coal-miners to get with the programme, but on the matter of elite politicians adjusting to how their voters now behave – it is cause for global freak-out?

There is a cardinal rule political strategists worth their salt across the world know: Like the customer, the citizen is always right.

That means if the consumer decides that the way political decisions will be made moving forward is based on non-membership of the discredited elite, then that's the way it's going to be. If the consumer decides that the future is not just the major determinant, but the only the determinant for who gets their vote moving forward, then that is what it is going to be.

If in a democracy, policy makers need good politics to make good policy and policy is still the art of persuasion, then politicians and public office holders need to learn the new rules of persuasion.

That's the reality of the new political market place.*

Often disruption is the reality of a future that returns society to its original functions. In the case of communication, social media has led to the democratisation of information and voice, which in turn has restored the equilibrium of communication closer to its original structure: word of mouth.

Television, radio and newspapers can be said in a sense to have tools to amplify word of mouth, to amplify the ability for human beings to talk to each other in an atmosphere of trust, faith and mutual respect.

Instead, the media ultimately became a place for a new elite that over the years began to talk down at people and began to take advantage of the pulpit in a way that didn't align with public expectation. Along with other institutions developed over the past two centuries, it soon became about itself and its club rather than about an elevated purpose.

When technology brought disruption to that space, and citizens saw a tool to restore the instinctual purpose of communication, they abandoned the way they used to speak and access information, and welcomed a more intuitive way to share messages.

"Since the election, everyone has been obsessed with fake news, as experts blame 'stupid' people for not understanding what is 'real'," researcher Danah Boyd had written in Data and Society. "The solutionism around this has been condescending at best. More experts are needed to label fake content. More media literacy is needed to teach people how not to be duped. And if we just push Facebook to curb the spread of fake news, all will be solved.

"People believe in information that confirms their priors. In fact, if you present them with data that contradicts their beliefs, they will double down on their beliefs rather than integrate the new knowledge into their understanding. This is why first impressions matter. It's also why asking Facebook to show content that contradicts people's views will not only increase their hatred of Facebook but increase polarization among the network. And it's precisely why so many liberals spread "fake news" stories in ways that reinforce their belief that Trump supporters are stupid and backwards.

"Addressing so-called fake news is going to require a lot more than labeling. It's going to require a cultural change about how we make sense of information, whom we trust, and how we understand our own role in grappling with information. Quick and easy solutions may make the controversy go away, but they won't address the underlying problems.

"The reality is that my assumptions and beliefs do not align with most Americans. Because of my privilege as a scholar, I get to see how expert knowledge and information is produced and have a deep respect for the strengths and limitations of scientific inquiry. Surrounded by journalists and people working to distribute information, I get to see how incentives shape information production and dissemination and the fault lines of that process. I believe that information intermediaries are important, that honed expertise matters, and that no one can ever be fully informed. As a result, I have long believed that we have to outsource certain matters and to trust others to do right by us as individuals and society as a whole. This is what it means to live in a democracy, but, more importantly, it's what it means to live in a society."

She is right. But unfortunately, along with other vestiges of old-form institutions, citizens are re-negotiating the character and role of these once almighty mediators.

And that presents the reality of the new media marketplace. One in which the United States Secretary of State can be travelling on his first official state visit and rather than legacy institutions, choose a completely unknown – to the media establishment – online organisation that he considers best suited to his needs.

"The US State department caused a full-on brouhaha in Washington media circles when it said journalists wouldn't join secretary of State Rex Tillerson on his trip to South Korea, Japan and China, which began today," Quartz reported. "DC bureau chiefs sent an aggrieved letter, CNN anchor Jake Tapper called the move 'unusual and insulting.'"

But the media has changed. Like much of the free world, legacy doesn't mean much to the masses. And it is the masses who lie at the epicenter of democratic reality.

Like the media, politics has also changed and for the same reasons. The political establishment has become more about itself than about the people, and disruption has come to restore the balance.

"The dangers of a Hillary Clinton presidency are more familiar than Trump's authoritarian unknowns, because we live with them in our politics already," the New York Times' Ross Douthat captured the danger the establishment now presents to the public. "They're the dangers of elite groupthink, of Beltway power worship, of a cult of presidential action in the service of dubious ideals. They're the dangers of a recklessness and radicalism that doesn't recognize itself as either, because it's convinced that if an idea is mainstream and commonplace among the great and good then it cannot possibly be folly.

"Almost every crisis that has come upon the West in the last 15 years has its roots in this establishmentarian type of folly. The Iraq War, which liberals prefer to remember as a conflict conjured by a neoconservative cabal, was actually the work of a bipartisan interventionist consensus, pushed hard by George W. Bush but embraced as well by a large slice of center-left opinion that included Tony Blair and more than half of Senate Democrats.

"Likewise the financial crisis: Whether you blame financial-services deregulation or happy-go-lucky housing policy (or both), the policies that helped inflate and pop the bubble were embraced by both wings of the political establishment. Likewise with the euro, the European common currency, a terrible idea that only cranks and Little Englanders dared oppose until the Great Recession exposed it as a potentially economy-sinking folly. Likewise with Angela Merkel's grand and reckless open-borders gesture just last year: She was the heroine of a thousand profiles even as she delivered her continent to polarization and violence.

"This record of elite folly — which doesn't even include lesser case studies like our splendid little war in Libya — is a big part of why the United States has a "let's try crazy" candidate in this election, and why there are so many Trumpian parties thriving on European soil."

It is these tendencies, this collusion of the establishment across nations, across the world that has led to a year – 2016 – of the biggest political disruption that the world has ever seen; one that, despite the substance of the change in itself, has certainly returned power to the hands and will of citizens.

It is a rejection, and then a demolishment of the arrogant 'insider-trading' of the elite. A refusal by the commonality of peoples across the world to validate the necessity of national consensus that has not and does not work.

It is a decision to reject calm acquiesce with reckless resistance, in full understanding and ownership of the possible negative consequences of that electoral revolt.

The gentled, reasoned elite calls it counter-productive, and the everyday citizen responds: so is your way.

So now we have this: disrespect for orthodoxy that long stopped working for the majority of people and the willingness to try something (anything) different – validated by the fact of what is already not working.

It sounds primitive, but there is sophistication to the simplicity. The voters know what they are doing.

"Ten years ago, people were frustrated, but largely apathetic," a Harvard Kennedy School of Government study group noted in 2016. "Today, with economic discontent, foreign conflicts unresolved and pressing public policy issues unattended, increasingly citizens are engaging in organizations and movements designed to break the existing framework."

Canada's The Star echoed the same sentiments after the American elections: "But in a few short weeks, disruption has become the current paradigm as the world scrambles to adjust to a reordering of alliances and partnerships. Without question, global disruption (has) become the new norm, a norm which will challenge us all."

Then it advises calmly rather than declaring the end of the world: "We must confront this reality with pragmatic relationships."

Therein lies the demands of a new age for players in the space.

There is no sense in declaiming and decrying the realities of new marketplaces. It is more useful to create and road test models that can align with the demands of the marketplace.

"We cannot fall back on standard…approaches because the societal context has shifted," Boyd advised. "We need to get creative and build the social infrastructure necessary for people to meaningfully and substantively engage across existing structural lines."

In a world where tomorrow comes faster than at any other time in history, where factory jobs are being replaced by automatic cars faster than at any other time in history, adjusting to that reality should not be a hard thing. Or a bad thing.

Stop moaning. Innovate.

*This piece borrows substantially from a piece by Chude Jideonwo titled 'We should disrupt Africa's politics, learning just a little from Trump'.

33

THE CITIZEN IS ALWAYS RIGHT

"The most important office in a democracy," Obiageli Ezekwesili, former vice president of the World Bank for Africa and co-founder of the #BringBackOurGirls movement, told a national television audience at the '100,000 Voices' telethon in 2014, "is the office of the citizen."

And she should know; her leadership of the #BringBackOurGirls movement for three years now, has been the continent's most successful citizen-led campaign in recent history.

Unfortunately, while much of the world's political and economic elite had a theoretical understanding of what the office of the citizen means, and some pay some sort of lip service to the reality, it didn't mean they had come to terms with its implications. Until 2016.

In the aftermath of both 'Brexit' and Donald Trump, much of the elite world has declared the end of civilisation.

"Does Donald Trump's victory spell the end of the West?" a headline in the Nigerian Guardian just after the elections calmly asked.

This would be a valid question since, before the elections, Vanity Fair also had an equally dramatic headline: "Trump's ghostwriter speaks: If The Donald wins, it will be the end of civilization".

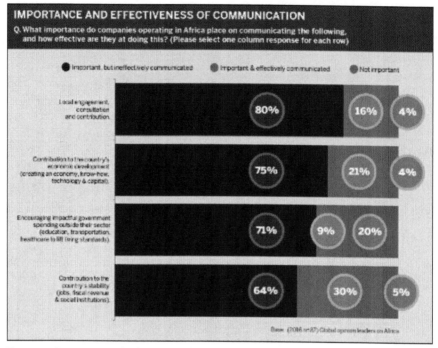

Figure 19: Importance and effectiveness of communication

For months, those who understood how angry citizens were had warned the elite in both countries that something seismic was going to happen, that the present elite consensus was not sustainable, that citizens were beyond angry and they wanted to burn it all down from frustration. But no one that mattered was really listening.

"It is not moral, not acceptable and not sustainable that the top one-tenth of one percent now own almost as much wealth as the bottom 90%," Bernie Sanders tweeted in July 2016.

He had expanded on these thoughts in the New York Times a month before. "Surprise, surprise," he wrote. "Workers in Britain, many of whom have seen a decline in their standard of living while the very rich in their country have become much richer, have turned their backs on the European Union and a globalized economy that is failing them and their children.

"And it's not just the British who are suffering. That increasingly globalized economy, established and maintained by the world's economic elite, is failing people everywhere. Incredibly, the wealthiest 62 people on this planet own as much wealth as the bottom half of the world's population — around 3.6 billion people. The top one per cent now owns more wealth than the whole of the bottom 99 per cent. The very, very rich enjoy unimaginable luxury while billions of people endure abject poverty, unemployment, and inadequate health care, education, housing and drinking water.

"Could this rejection of the current form of the global economy happen in the United States? You bet it could. During my campaign for the Democratic presidential nomination, I've visited 46 states. What I saw and heard on too many occasions were painful realities that the political and media establishment fail even to recognize.

"Nearly 47 million Americans live in poverty. An estimated 28 million have no health insurance, while many others are underinsured. Millions of people are struggling with outrageous levels of student debt. For perhaps the first time in modern history, our younger generation will probably have a lower standard of living than their parents. Frighteningly, millions of poorly educated Americans will have a shorter life span than the previous generation as they succumb to despair, drugs and alcohol.

"Let's be clear. The global economy is not working for the majority of people in our country and the world. This is an economic model developed by the economic elite to benefit the economic elite. We need real change."

Because those who should have were not listening, voters let out a primal scream.

"This was America's Brexit," the Independent figured out after the elections. "The similarity with Britain's shock vote in June to leave the European Union was uncanny. As with Brexit, America's divisions were on display: between the elite and ordinary people; between Wall Street and Main Street; between small town and urban America. There is the same distrust of globalisation, a feeling by white blue-collar workers – but not only them – that they had been forgotten by Washington. These divisions transcend conventional party divisions.

"Above all, they delivered a primal scream against Washington and all its works: a gridlocked Congress, and a dysfunctional self-perpetuating governing class of which Hillary Clinton is the living face. This was a raw yearning for change, that this other America believes only an outsider like Trump, whatever his faults, can bring. The American people 'expect the government to serve the people, and it will', Trump declared. 'The forgotten men and women of our country will be forgotten no longer.'"

An African-American Democrat who voted for Trump explained her decision to Politico.com: "It was my primal scream," Cohen says. "I wasn't gonna take it anymore.

"I wanted it burned down ... so that we could build a new, hopefully more equitable one that meets the needs of all, not only the super-rich."

A piece by Brendan O'Neill in The Spectator in July 2016 captured this sentiment after the Brexit vote: "By forcing Britain to quit the EU they have given a bloody nose to an elite that views them with contempt," he stated, correctly.

In return, the elite echo chambers blamed the voter.

"Britain's Brexit vote was a victory of the old over the young, of the less educated over the educated, of nationalism over internationalism," The Week sneered. "No wonder the presumed U.S. Republican presidential nominee, Donald Trump — who happened to be visiting one of his golf courses in Scotland when the result was announced on June 24 — was delighted. Polls show that both Brexit voters and Trump's grassroots supporters are motivated by a similar mix of fear and fantasy."

"Because we have entered an era of post-factualism," tweeted someone on the morning after Brexit. "The only era in which people like BoJo, Farage and Trump thrive."

He continued: "They [voters] made the arguments in favour of Brexit without an understanding of the consequences."

To which, Jideonwo responded: "This whole 'voters have become dumber' trend IS the reason many 'smart' politicians are losing the debate.

"There were very many intelligent people with sophisticated arguments in favour of leaving. If you don't respect them, you cannot influence them. It is disrespect to decide that because people choose different from you, they are unintelligent. They have lived in a world defined by experts and it has failed them."

And that's really the summary of the matter.

"Let's make no bones about this: Britain's poor and workless have risen up," the Spectator piece continued. "And in doing so they didn't just give the EU and its British backers the bloodiest of bloody noses. They also brought crashing down the Blairite myth of a post-class, Third Way Blighty, where the old ideological divide between rich and poor did not exist, since we were all supposed to be 'stakeholders' in society. Post-referendum, we know society is still cut in two, not only by economics but by politics too. This isn't just about the haves and have-nots: it's a war of views. The wealthier sections of society like it when politics involves detached cosmopolitan institutions and the poorer people don't. The less well-off have just asserted their stake in society and the chattering classes — who peddled all the nonsense about a 'stakeholder society' in the first place — aren't happy about it."

And then it delivered the summary of the case for those who continued to despise the voter: "This idea — that the poor are easy prey for demagogues — is the same claptrap the Chartists had to put up with in the 1840s. Their snooty critics frequently told them that, since the poor do not have a 'ripened wisdom' they are 'more exposed than any other class... to be converted to the vicious ends of faction'. Now, the metropolitan set once again accuse the little people of exactly the same thing.

"Surveys, however, dent this claim that the anti-EU throng was driven by disdain for foreigners. In a post-vote ComRes poll, only 34 per cent of Leave voters cited concern about immigration as their main reason for voting out (and concern about immigration isn't necessarily racism). A majority, 53 per cent, said they rejected the EU because they think Britain should make its own laws. So this swath of the country, defamed as a brainless pogrom-in-waiting, was actually voting for democracy.

"Then came the pitiers. Their diagnosis was a therapeutic one: that the less well-off suffered a spasm of anger. That they felt so ignored they decided to lash out crazily, but understandably. Don't be sucked in by this seemingly caring, Oprah-esque analysis of the masses, for it is also a way of demeaning their democratic choice by treating it as a primal scream rather than a political statement. It turns a conscious rebellion against the establishment outlook into a soppy plea for more listening exercises.

"But my take, from talking to numerous Leave voters, is not that they feel slighted by the political class but that they *oppose* it. People have a strong sense of being ruled over by institutions that fundamentally loathe them, or at least consider them to be in dire need of moral and social correction.

"They feel patronised, slandered and distrusted, not ignored."

Jideonwo wrote about this after the Americans elections:

"Unfortunately, citizens across the world are deciding that it shouldn't be so simple after all," he wrote. "They see something completely different, at least in the short term.

"They see benefits to businesses, but not to people. They see priviledged citizens enjoying the cost-savings but find no such benefits for themselves or their friends. They see median wage reducing because of pacts with low-wage countries. They see their jobs leaving because of trade deficits and the effects of 'global competitiveness'.

"And those promised better and higher paying jobs? They see so few of them that it makes no sense at all.

"What the experts say, and the reality they see in front of them every day are in such sharp conflict that every day from Nigeria to Britain, and from France to America, have decided to revolted against the experts. They have become deeply suspicious of their consensus – especially where that consensus disproportionally benefits those same experts.

"It is easy for those lucky to live amongst the elite to mouth the goodness of globalization, even if – like me – they only know it because they trust the experts. After all, there is no immediate consequence. As a businessperson with open lines of client acquisition from across the world, whatever is happening has only been good for me.

"But what if I were a South African with a job about to disappear? Or a trader in Kumasi whose life has only gotten worse as the one percent accumulates the benefits of global markets? Yeah, I wouldn't be so sanguine."

Now this next paragraph from the Spectator is crucial to creating understanding of how exactly voters made these decisions: "This rebellion wasn't caused by...a paroxysm of infantile anger. It was considered. The workers spied an opportunity to take the elite that despises them down a peg or two — and they seized it. They asserted their power, and in the process, blimey: they changed the world."

On ABC the night of the American election, its reporter Terry Moran noted that the election was "a rejection of the neoliberal world order that has been the consensus around the world."

In 2016, voters, all over the world made a calm, considered decision: to force politicians to pay attention to them.

For far too long, politicians have stopped listening to voters, assuming that they know much more than those who have hired them. And taking this sense of superiority to the extreme, they have stopped doing their primary job as politicians: to convince, to persuade and to build consensus. They expect voters simply to take for granted that the politicians know best, even when voters don't see the positive results of this supposed capacity.

And then when the voters react, they ask questions: why are the voters being so unreasonable?

Well, the voters have become 'unreasonable' because the politicians have become 'unreachable'.

"Because aneke the bird has learnt to fly without perching," an Igbo proverb reminds us, "the hunter in turn has learnt to shoot without missing."

Politics has a simple proposition the political elite need to be reminded of: voters are very busy living their daily lives and are unable – not because they are dumb, but because they are otherwise engaged – to focus on the fine detail of policy, of economics, of society. Often the fact of voting is a fundamental act of outsourcing: voters appoint representatives to take care of the problems that need to be solved, and they undertake the duty of paying those representatives to understand, to contend with and to solve those problems.

This social contract has an underpinning responsibility: 'ensure that you explain to us what you're doing, ensure that you win our support before you proceed and ensure that we have a frame of understanding because you act on my behalf. This contract is what is often defined by the twin imperatives of transparency and accountability.

The contract has been broken by one side of the bargain – and it is not the voter.

When voters make a choice that appears unreasonable, often it can come from desperation.

When there is a vacuum, demagogues rush to fill it. Leaders must take responsibility for that gap in options. Because it is the political elite that presents options, not the citizen.

Politicians must evolve as the people do. Politics is of no effect if it does not find itself responding to the cries, demands and hopes of the citizens.

That is why many who continue to be shocked that the youth of an African nation would choose a 70-year old ex-dictator to lead their nation have absolutely missed the point. They have missed the point of the statement that voters are trying to make – because votes and protests are the most effective tools they have to make important statements.

In Africa's case, the above statement has dealt a harsh rebuke to the collective establishment.

"The populist wave that carried Donald Trump to the American presidency is a global phenomenon. Nowhere is this more apparent than in West Africa, over the past two years," Jideonwo has written. "The sense is the same—there is now a deep suspicion of the established economic and political order (you could add to that, media) across much of West Africa, with citizens suspicious of the elite consensus that appears to benefit only a handful at the expense of the many.

"The backlash led to a dramatic change of government in Nigeria in 2015, and an equally dramatic change to Ghana in 2016.

"It's odd to see so many engaged, empowered and angry youth turn to symbols of the same old order to make change happen in countries desperate for a turnaround. Leading the communication agency that worked on the campaigns of the two winnings candidates however, I know the narrative is not that simple.

"Above all else, there's a ferocious mix of anger and hope. As always, compared to the alternative at the time, many young Nigerians insist they had no choice. And as all political strategists know, hope is inexhaustible. The idea of movement from what doesn't already work is a more powerful incentive than the age of candidates.

"More than that, the collective capacity of a people to punish a failed government is one that has become a powerful motivation for a frustrated generation—witness the downfall of Jammeh and the animus against the presidents of South Africa and Kenya (opposition candidate, Ralia Odinga is 72).

"Since rebuilding our nations will ultimately be a long-term march, then a change in government represents an important step in making revolution happen."

When citizens make these choices, it is foolish to blame them for exercising their rights in the ways they deem fit. These decisions do not come from stupidity, these decisions often come from well-considered sentiments developed over time, and most of them rest on a simple reality – the status quo is not working for them.

"Should citizens for instance simply take for granted that open and closed economies have some kind of moral undertone that is ultimately good for them, irrespective of what their eyes see and their hear?"

Politicians need to get back to their primary jobs: listening to citizens, building frames of understanding and convincing voters of agenda and decisions. Citizens across the world deserve better than the current media, cultural, political and economic elite posture of arrogance, petulance and deafness.

Leaders need to start paying attention to citizens.

If they don't do this, it is the duty of citizens to force them to listen, and it is the prerogative of voters to punish them for failure to engage. Whatever citizens decide to do in that process, as long as popular will remains in their hands, they are resolutely right and justified.

Unless the global economic and political elite find the humility to answer questions that citizens are asking of them and the world with the clarity and simplicity that popular consensus requires, the burning down of the system – from Nairobi to Paris – will continue.

These upheavals across the world, and especially across Africa, are destined to continue as long as they are necessary.

34

WHY AFRICA NEEDS DEMOCRACY

The induction document for our parent group, RED makes a very clear – perhaps unusual – statement of purpose within its first 10 slides: "We believe resolutely in democracy and capital giving society the best outcomes."

We believe this in the depths of our hearts, because we believe in competition: we believe that a robust, fair competition between ideas and services drives human beings to approach and fulfill their best impulses.

Of course we don't believe that these tools must be left alone. Like very many social phenomena, they are likely to be manipulated by the selfish and the unscrupulous, which is why the form and shape of these two imperatives have to be defined, protected and sustained. Capitalism's faultiness, for instance, has evolved into a global clarion call for inclusive capitalism.

To discuss this and our commitment, in this particular case, to democracy, we will in this one chapter, step out of the frame of research and data and focus on our own intrinsic ideas about why democracies are deeply important for the nations of Sub-Saharan Africa, at the very least.

The first is a basic fact of history: No other system of government since political independence has worked for the majority of people in two crucial areas – the economy and the dignity of the person.

The history of the continent is littered with failures, with strong men and freedom fighters who won independence for their nations, or who sought through military coups to change the government supposedly for the good of the people, but fell prey to their own egos and became the very problems they were supposed to solve.

Zambia's Mobutu Sese-Seko, Uganda's Yoweri Museveni, Sudan's Omar al-Bashir, Cameroon's Paul Biya, Angola's Jose Eduardo dos Santos, Equitorial Guinea's Tedoro Obiang, Liberia's Charles Taylor, Nigeria's Sani Abacha and of course, Zimbabwe's Robert Mugabe are only some the highlights of a culture that prizes people and personality over systems and institutions. And the one thing that democracies across the world have proven is that effective institutions are best built under flourishing democracies.

However, these dictators have taken nations of incredible wealth and promise and decimated them, supervising administrations of vast corruption, accumulating obscene personal wealth, and even worse, adding insult to injury by attacking fundamental human rights and creating climates of fear whose only purpose is to perpetuate their power.

They have done these because the freedoms they won for their people were not followed by institutions that could ensure those freedoms.

"Two structural features that are driving this bad behavior in many of Africa's countries: rich resources and weak political institutions," University of California political scientist, Barbara F. Walter, has correctly, in our opinion, noted. "Countries like Uganda and the DRC hold substantial resources that tempt leaders to line their pockets and use the money to easily buy off opponents. These countries also have few institutional restraints on their executives, making it easy for leaders to behave as they will. Most revolutionaries, when put in this structural situation, would likely behave the same way.

"The revolutionaries who do become democrats, such as the IRA in Ireland, are the ones who already operate in a highly institutionalized environment where executive power is checked. In unrestrained environments where wealth is there for the taking and one's time in office is uncertain, the incentives to plunder are often too strong to resist."

Constitutional democracy appears to be the best tool to generate the other imperatives that help society function as the best version of itself: a free press, a flourishing civil society, an independent judiciary and free enterprise.

Second, the nations that have either been role models of hope on the continent, or that have transmuted into symbols of hope have been those nations that have found their way to true democracies through free and fair elections and have maintained that stand –Senegal, Botswana, Namibia, Mozambique and, until now at least, Rwanda.

It is surely not by accident that peace continues to define Senegal and Botswana, two nations with leaders who have willingly sought constitutional adjustments to limit their terms in office. And it is not an accident that Liberia which turned out to be a model of post-conflict transformation is led by Ellen Johnson-Sirleaf, who is actively looking forward to completing her term and handing over office.

It can't be sheer luck that Namibia has become a success story thanks to a chain of leaders after independence (even after a 25-year war) in 1990 including the recent Hifikepunye Pohamba who have ensured that this prosperous nation is a stark African symbol of democracy and freedom. All its leaders have respected their term limits and the country has responded with economic growth.

"Political stability and sound economic management have helped anchor economic growth and poverty reduction in Namibia," the World Bank notes. "Namibia has enjoyed a sustained period of strong growth. Between 2010 and 2014, the economy grew at an average annual rate of 5.6% per annum. Growth was driven by massive investment in extractive projects, strong export prices, rapid private credit growth, and a program of deficit-financed fiscal stimulus."

Mozambique's second president, Joaquim Chissano has been praised for "his decision not to seek a third presidential term (which) reinforced Mozambique's democratic maturity and demonstrated that institutions and the democratic process were more important than personalities."

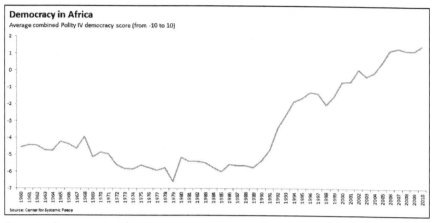

Figure 20: Democracy in Africa

He left behind a nation averaging economic growth of seven per cent for years, and one that continued to flourish in the United Nations Human Development Index.

The evidence is overwhelming.

In fact, outside of that there is the simple argument that, having tried everything else, it makes sense for Sub-Saharan Africa as a collective to try something else and that thing is undoubtedly democracy. It is the one thing we have not experimented with, as a group of nations, for a consistent, sustained period of time.

"Africa is not a dark continent, yet it has more blackouts than any other continent," Jideonwo said in a speech at The Future Awards Africa in 2015. "We protest Africa is not a theatre of war, but it has more national coups than any part of the world today. Yes, Africa is not a dark continent of poverty, but we have more poor people with no pathway to rising than any continent existing in 2015.

"Yes, Africa is not a continent of disease, but polio was just eradicated in Nigeria this year. And not because we told better stories. But because a foreign donor worked with local change-makers to make it happen. And it did not occur to our government officials, celebrating this news and claiming credit, that the fact that such a simple matter should have lingered this long should become instead a reason for reflection, not backslapping.

"Brothers and sisters of Africa, 329 million mobile phone users is not growth, it is consumption. 200 million people when there are no roads for them to move goods and service is not a market. Luxury motor shops opening in Lagos is not development, it is alternative reality.

"We must stop, stop! Stop this lowering of the bar, where we declare progress for six per cent growth rate over the past 10 years while countries like China have sustained 11 per cent growth for most of the last 30 years, pulling millions out of poverty in the process.

"Because this rising tide has not lifted all boats. What is rising instead is the number of Africa's children out of school – 18 million as at last count, the number of young people living below two dollars a day – 72 per cent at last count, the percent of our GDP that goes only to less than 10 per cent, the number of people who have to hold their hands over their heads to pass into the airport in Kenya, and the sheer number of jobless youth – over 75 million between ages 15 and 24 – who have no jobs. It is not a sexy story. But it is a true story."

Change is possible, he said, but only if the character of our governments will first fundamentally change.

"Of course, this story can change. And in some countries, like in my favourite Rwanda, it is in fact changing. And from countries like this come a powerful message of hope, but it is one that does not have to rely on a lie.

"That message is simple: Africa CAN rise. But it can rise if only we can urgently scale up the work that governments and then civil society are doing. Government first – because one thousand NGOs cannot take the place of a single functioning government."

We need functioning, responsive governments country to country, and we have an urgent duty to ensure free and fair elections lead to flourishing functional democracies that give us the option and liberty to co-create these solutions.

The co-founders of StateCraft Inc were born in a time of intense hopelessness across much of the continent. Both of them were born under violent dictatorships in Nigeria and witnessed the same anomaly across the continent. Like much of the aware, engaged, angry citizenry

– they are absolutely set in their hearts that it is time for something to give and have given their lives to build the systems and structures that empower citizens to give their societies that push that they need.

Above all else, to make this happen, they have governments in their sights: highly functioning, people-centered governments.

There is that thing they say: Democracy is the worst form of government, except for all the others.

Until a better, more intuitive, more functional system of leading a people is evolved – and there is nothing to say that the future will not bring innovations to this essential function – Africans must cast their lots with constitutional democracy. We should start from there as the very basic minimum.

35

WHY IT'S STILL TOO SOON TO CELEBRATE AN AFRICAN DEMOCRATIC WAVE

The greatest pro-democracy event in the last decade has been the Arab Spring.

Or has it?

A silent but more formidable series of democratic events are taking place in Sub Saharan Africa. Between 2010 and 2011, an exceptionally high number of elections had been held. By mid-2011 presidential and/or parliamentary elections had taken place in 20 countries.

This period represents the highest number of elections that have been held across the continent till date. But it continues. Barring the creation of new countries before this book is published, every country has held elections with the exception of Eritrea.

Civil society is awakening and has begun to mobilise (through the democratisation of technology) a semblance of opposition to a political elite that have failed to reflect their aspirations; and African regional institutions, led by the African Union, have begun to take their roles as custodians of electoral democracy with the seriousness of action.

The proliferation of elections across the continent is good news for democracy and even better news is the recent occurrence of elections overturning entrenched incumbencies that have been hailed as further proof of electoral democracy gaining a solid foothold on the continent.

The success of opposing parties forming coalitions to displace dominant parties and strongmen (Senegal 2000, Kenya 2002, Nigeria 2015, Gambia 2016) is no mean feat and deserves the media attention that these events have received. The one problem however is the narrative of triumphalism.

The narrative of these elections being seen as consolidation of democratic principles is early and might be misguided. Of course, the triumphalism is understandable, and legitimate. In a continent mostly defined by the darkness of dictatorship, even this book can hardly resist the allure of pushing a new narrative of overwhelming people power. And this narrative is powerful; striking fear in the hearts of an unsophisticated elite that relies more on guts more than evidence.

A global interest in the world's so-called last frontier is in no small way behind this triumphal narrative. International players – governments, scholars, civil society and journalists – in a globalised world are susceptive to the drama that events in Africa since the Arab Spring across Tunisia, Egypt, Libya and Yemen presents. This leads to a re-doubled international liberal consensus that Africa's problem has been as a result of its epileptic relationship with democracy and for true progress to emerge democratic principles must be strengthened across the continent. The extent of the (welcome) obsession with long serving African leaders is typified by Quartz Africa's headline on the recent Confederation of Africa Football (CAF) elections: "One of Africa's longest serving strongmen just got voted out of power".

"Since December 2010 the world has watched as demonstrations and protests spread across countries in North Africa and the Middle East," Cornell University's project on 'Arab Spring: A Research & Study Guide' captures breathless excitement. "These pro-democracy movements rose up against the dictatorial regimes and corrupt leaders that had ruled for decades in some cases. Someone called these revolutionary events "Arab Spring," and the phrase stuck. The specificity of these Arab revolutions is that they have been popular uprisings, leaderless and uncompromising in demanding total change."

A 2011 Amnesty International Report 'Middle East and North Africa: Year of rebellion: The state of human rights in the Middle East and North Africa echoes these sentiments: "2011 was a year without precedent for the peoples of the Middle East and North Africa region. It was a year in which millions of people of all ages and backgrounds flooded on to the streets to demand change. Dubbed the "Arab Spring", in fact the protests brought together in common cause people from many different communities. This report describes the events of this tumultuous year, one which saw much suffering and sadness but also spread hope within the region and beyond, to countries where other people face repression and everyday abuse of their human rights."

That excitement has redoubled as the movement appears to have spread beyond the North of the continent.

Still, we must temper – every step of the way – excitement with realism.

In the paper 'The Economic Prospects of the 'Arab Spring': A Bumpy Road Ahead' by Hassan Hakimian, Director of the London Middle East Institute and Reader, Economics Department, SOAS, he underscored "the underlying importance of the economic conditions facing the new republics, such as Egypt and Tunisia, which are emerging as a result of the 'Arab Spring' in the Middle East and North Africa. His analysis suggests that they will face difficult challenges in trying to both bring about lasting transformations in the livelihoods of ordinary citizens and avoiding the burden of conditionalities likely to be linked to future external assistance and investment."

And there is the fact that democracy hasn't automatically given good governance to some of the countries.

Senegal's Abdoulaye Wade, supported by a coalition of opposition candidates and parties to win the 2000 elections, rode into power and set about aggrandising power as a governing philosophy and seeking a third term in office.

241

The proliferation of elections in Sub Saharan Africa is good news on the surface, but the waters run deeper.

In essence we need to be careful when ascribing meaning to the high number of elections that have occurred within the continent. Sub Saharan Africa possesses a long history of elections being used as tools of promoting the veneer of legitimacy of unpopular governments that have seized power by the back door. A favourite tool of military dictators across the continent has been seizing power by the barrel of the gun and then using the ballot box to portray legitimacy. These autocrats have grown adept at using the arms of government that they either directly control, or have been able to utilise their patronage network to induce, to extend their terms in power.

For every Burkina Faso where a Blaise Campore has been forced out by popular revolt after his attempt to extend his term in office, there is a Burundi which has been unsuccessful in getting out Pierre Nkurunziza, chalked down – ironically – to the failure of the military to impose the will of the people. Relying on the military to act as custodians of democracy is of course a fool's errand. If the institutions that administer the elections, electoral bodies and judicial systems, cannot judiciously decide irregularities and maintain impartiality, then the road ahead may be long and winding.

There is also the fact that liberation movements that gained post-colonial power via the ballot box such as the People's Movement for the Liberation of Angola, the Zimbabwe African National Union – Patriotic Front in Zimbabwe and the African National Congress in South Africa are under pressure by a younger generation who owe no allegiance to these movements turned political parties, seeing them rightly as legacy-validated tools for elite enrichment.

"The party that has a modern conception of society does not look at itself first... its starting point is society and asks what kind of society do we want to create? What is it that we must put in place in society?" South African political analyst Prince Mashele said of the ANC at the launch of the book *Unmasked: Why the ANC Failed to Govern*

While those like Jose Eduardo Dos Santos, reading the handwriting on the wall, have announced his plan to not contest the next Angolan elections and in his stead has attempted to push the limelight towards his deputy and his daughter as possible replacements, others are still hanging tight, like Robert Mugabe whose Zimbabwe was rocked by its first major united protest – #ThisFlag – against the ruling party in recent memory. Others like Jacob Zuma are trying to read the signs – just as this book was going to press, the nation was demanding his resignation, and he was conceding some ground by promising party members he would resign if they asked. Factions inside the party had already tried to remove him as party leader after its municipality elections.

The use of seemingly legitimate state structures to carry out actions apathetic to democratic principles or good governance outcomes is therefore the bane of African democracies.

We should be very worried that Western (and African) darling and Rwandan strongman Paul Kagame whose nation has been labelled the "African Silicon Valley" has also held and won a referendum to extend his term limit, with an avalanche of intellectual work struggling to draw parallels with Lee Kuan Yew of Singapore.

The problem is not the decision to increase term limits, the issue is a leader who has been at the helm of the country for 17 years using tools of the state to direct outcomes, and the dangerous background of other such leaders who have lost their way. When we encourage the optimism of incumbencies being overturned in The Gambia and Nigeria, we must temper it by recalling the entrenchment of power in Burundi and Rwanda overturning presidential term limits and repressing political parties.

Then, in a trend we have addressed in another chapter, with citizen mobilisation has come citizen repression; from Zimbabwe's crackdown on internet use, to Cameroons shutdown of internet in the English speaking parts of the country. Even seemingly liberal South Africa with its long democratic history currently has an ANC sponsored bill being debated at Parliament on "Cybercrime and Cyber security" that has been decried by local activists as regressive.

So this is the sum of our thesis: there is ample reason to celebrate. There is little or no doubt that the continent has come far from 2001 where 5 leaders across the continent governed as a result of the coup d'etats that brought them to power compared to the last three years without a successful coup.

The barrel of the gun as a path to governance at least seems to be coming to an end. Even the autocrats that are currently in power have attempted to reform themselves as democrats and have held the appearance of elections. At the barest minimum in the most regressive of states in the region, leaders understand they must hold elections (or postpone them if you're Joseph Kabila and can, in a bit of gallows humour, use your poor economic situation as rationale for not holding elections). That is no small progress.

African countries, especially under the guidance of the African Union (AU), have taken a strong dislike to unelected leaders with the suspension of Burkina Faso and AU's threat to impose sanctions on it unless the coup leaders returned power to the interim government that was to hold elections. ECOWAS has been quick to tout its military and economic strength against the illegitimate governments of Mali, Guinea Bissau and recently The Gambia. Its swift response and desire to ensure mandates are secured from the civilian population that the leaders seek to govern is commendable. Whilst reasons for African regional institutions seeming insistence on representative democracy among its member states vary dependent on the respondent asked to provide an opinion.

However, political freedom is yet to be understood as a central tenet and authoritarian practices such as repressing civil society and censuring the press mean that a level playing field is lacking. Democracy is not about the holding of elections alone.

Strongmen might be losing their place in Africa. However, the narrative of Africa's democracy being strengthened requires restraint, if for nothing, at least for the necessity of eternal vigilance.

Then, even where free and fair elections are won, citizens must remain on guard to ensure the fruits of their struggles are not hijacked, as Nigerians have figured out, protesting and organising against a government that has overseen a downturn in economic conditions.

We cannot replace one simple story with another simple story. Joseph Conrad's *Heart of Darkness* fell into the trap of evidence-free preju- diced narratives just as much as the Economist's 'Africa rising' cry comes from a place of peer-pressured simplicity.

There is still a far stretch of the road remaining to be walked, and the work has only just begun. Local and international players have earned the right to celebrate the small victories our continent has won, but they cannot spend more than a minute in festivity. This journey has only just begun.

REFERENCES

Legacy doesn't matter, as much as it used to

Eberstadt, N. (2017). *Our Miserable 21st Century.* [online] Commentary Magazine. Available at: https://www.commentarymagazine.com/articles/our-miserable-21st-century/ [Accessed 19 Apr. 2017].

Harvard IOP (2017). *Trust in Institutions and the Political Process.* [online] Iop.harvard.edu. Available at: http://iop.harvard.edu/trust-institutions-and-political-process [Accessed 19 Apr. 2017].

Jonathan, G. (2010). *SPEECH BY PRESIDENT GOODLUCK EBELE JONATHAN DECLARING HIS CANDIDACY FOR THE PDP PRESIDENTIAL PRIMARIES.* [online] Facebook. Available at: https://www.facebook.com/notes/goodluck-jonathan/speech-by-president-goodluck-ebele-jonathan-declaring-his-candidacy-for-the-pdp-/155774224450221/ [Accessed 19 Apr. 2017].

Martin, J. and Haberman, M. (n.d.). *2016 election: Hillary Clinton vs. Jeb Bush?.* [online] POLITICO. Available at: http://www.politico.com/news/stories/1112/83550_Page2.html [Accessed 19 Apr. 2017].

Nsude, C. (2013). *Goodluck Jonathan had no shoes..* [online] YouTube. Available at: https://www.youtube.com/watch?v=-jJXxAkVb3Y [Accessed 19 Apr. 2017].

Obama, B. (2008). *The Audacity of Hope.* 1st ed. New York: Vintage bei Random House.

Stokols, E. (2016). *Inside Jeb Bush's $150 Million Failure.* [online]

POLITICO Magazine. Available at: http://www.politico.com/ magazine/story/2016/02/jeb-bush-dropping-out-set-up-to-fail-213662 [Accessed 19 Apr. 2017].

Change matters. Period.

Crockett, E. (2016). *Obama: "Not me, not Bill, nobody" has been more qualified for president than Hillary.* [online] Vox. Available at: http://www.vox.com/2016/7/27/12306702/democratic-con-vention-obama-hillary-clinton-bill-qualified [Accessed 19 Apr. 2017].

Nelson, L. (2016). *Is Hillary Clinton really the most qualified candidate ever? An investigation..* [online] Vox. Available at: http://www. vox.com/2016/8/1/12316646/hillary-clinton-qualified [Accessed 19 Apr. 2017].

The Nigerian Voice (2015). *Buhari did not buy a single rifle for military as Head of State - Jonathan.* [online] The Nigerian Voice. Available at: https://www.thenigerianvoice.com/news/166104/ buhari-did-not-buy-a-single-rifle-for-military-as-head-of-st.html [Accessed 19 Apr. 2017].

Anger matters, more than you know

Benac, N., Swanson, E. and Associated Press (2017). *Americans are angry at the government, desire change, exit polls show.* [online] PBS NewsHour. Available at: http://www.pbs.org/newshour/ rundown/americans-angry-government-desire-change-ex-it-polls-show/ [Accessed 17 Apr. 2017].

Eberstadt, N. (2017). *Our Miserable 21st Century - Commentary Magazine.* [online] Commentary Magazine. Available at: https://www.commentarymagazine.com/articles/our-misera-ble-21st-century/ [Accessed 17 Apr. 2017].

France-Presse, A. (2017). *Anger, Determination As South Africa Votes.* [online] NDTV.com. Available at: http://www.ndtv.com/world-news/anger-determination-as-south-africa-votes-560590 [Accessed 17 Apr. 2017].

Grose, T. (2017). [online] Available at: https://www.usnews.com/ news/best-countries/articles/2016-06-16/anger-at-immigra-tion-fuels-the-uks-brexit-movement [Accessed 17 Apr. 2017].

Martin, J. and Haberman, M. (2017). *2016 election: Hillary Clinton vs. Jeb Bush? - Jonathan Martin and Maggie Haberman.* [online] POLITICO. Available at: http://www.politico.com/news/stories/1112/83550_Page3.html [Accessed 17 Mar. 2017].

Msimang, S. (2017). *South Africa's local election shock down to anger and apathy.* [online] the Guardian. Available at: https://www.theguardian.com/world/2016/aug/05/anger-and-apathy-behind-south-africas-shock-local-election [Accessed 17 Apr. 2017].

NOI Polls (2012). *NOI-Polls: Most Married Nigerians claim to be Happily Married.* [online] Noi-polls.com. Available at: http://www.noi-polls.com/root/index.php?pid=140&ptid=1&parentid=14 [Accessed 17 Mar. 2017].

Page, S. and Crescente, F. (2017). *USA TODAY poll: Americans see Brexit anger as widespread.* [online] USA TODAY. Available at: https://www.usatoday.com/story/news/politics/elections/2016/06/30/poll-americans-brexit-anger-widespread/86546786/ [Accessed 17 Apr. 2017].

Polls, N. (2012). *NOI-Polls: Reports of Pensions' Fraud and other corruption cases make Nigerians sad.* [online] Noi-polls.com. Available at: http://www.noi-polls.com/root/index.php?pid=240&ptid=1&parentid=14 [Accessed 17 Mar. 2017].

Powell, A. (2017). *Violent Protests Mount Ahead of South African Municipal Vote.* [online] VOA. Available at: http://www.voanews.com/a/south-africa-pretoria-riots/3385268.html [Accessed 17 Apr. 2017].

Reilly, K. (2017). *Americans Are Happy With Their Lives but Angry at Government, Poll Shows.* [online] Time.com. Available at: http://time.com/4296805/american-anger-poll-donald-trump/ [Accessed 17 Mar. 2017].

Smith, S. (2017). *Young people express anger over PM's Brexit strategy, study finds.* [online] Evening Standard. Available at: http://www.standard.co.uk/news/uk/young-people-express-anger-over-theresa-mays-brexit-strategy-study-finds-a3443746.html [Accessed 17 Apr. 2017].

The Institute of Politics at Harvard University (2017). *Trust in Institutions and the Political Process.* [online] Iop.harvard.edu. Available at: http://iop.harvard.edu/trust-institutions-and-political-process [Accessed 17 Apr. 2017].

Vox (2017). *Is Hillary Clinton really the most qualified candidate ever? An investigation.*. [online] Vox. Available at: http://www.vox.com/2016/8/1/12316646/hillary-clinton-qualified [Accessed 17 Mar. 2017].

Establishments Matters

BBC (2017). *Botswana profile - Timeline - BBC News.* [online] BBC News. Available at: http://www.bbc.com/news/world-africa-13041658 [Accessed 17 Apr. 2017].

Parsons, N. (2016). *Festus Mogae | president of Botswana.* [online] Encyclopedia Britannica. Available at: https://www.britannica.com/biography/Festus-Mogae#ref1185973 [Accessed 17 Apr. 2017].

Perry, A. (2008). *Festus Mogae: Africa's Good Leader.* [online] TIME.com. Available at: http://content.time.com/time/world/article/0,8599,1852066,00.html [Accessed 17 Apr. 2017].

Whitehead, E. (2012). *Interview: Festus Mogae, former president of Botswana.* [online] Thisisafricaonline.com. Available at: http://www.thisisafricaonline.com/News/Interview-Festus-Mogae-former-president-of-Botswana?ct=true [Accessed 17 Apr. 2017].

Wikipedia (2017). *President of Botswana.* [online] En.wikipedia.org. Available at: https://en.wikipedia.org/wiki/President_of_Botswana [Accessed 17 Apr. 2017].

Candidates matter, first and foremost

Trende, S. (2014). *Midterm Demographics Didn't Sink the Democrats.* [online] Realclearpolitics.com. Available at: http://www.realclearpolitics.com/articles/2014/11/19/midterm_demographics_didnt_sink_the_democrats_124701.html [Accessed 17 Apr. 2017].

Weigel, D. (2016). *How voters who heavily supported Obama switched over to Trump.* [online] Washington Post. Available at: https://www.washingtonpost.com/politics/how-voters-who-heavily-supported-obama-switched-over-to-trump/2016/11/10/65019658-a77a-11e6-ba59-a7d93165c6d4_story.html?utm_term=.6b5d93ce743d [Accessed 17 Apr. 2017].

Persuasion matters

Horn, B. (2013). *Top Five Rules of Political Persuasion.* [online] Daily Kos. Available at: http://www.dailykos.com/story/2013/5/23/1211036/-Top-Five-Rules-of-Political-Persuasion [Accessed 17 Apr. 2017].

Marshall, W. (2016). *What Democrats Can Learn From Hillary Clinton's Tragedy.* [online] The Daily Beast. Available at: http://www.thedailybeast.com/articles/2016/12/07/what-democrats-can-learn-from-hillary-clinton-s-tragedy.html?via=twitter_page [Accessed 17 Apr. 2017].

Progressive Majority Action (n.d.). *How to Persuade.* [online] Progressive Majority Action. Available at: http://www.progressivemajorityaction.org/how_to_persuade [Accessed 17 Apr. 2017].

Willer, R. and Feinberg, M. (2015). *Opinion | The Key to Political Persuasion.* [online] Nytimes.com. Available at: https://www.nytimes.com/2015/11/15/opinion/sunday/the-key-to-political-persuasion.html?_r=1 [Accessed 17 Apr. 2017].

Messaging matters above all else

Chozick, A. and Confessore, N. (2016). *Hillary Clinton's Campaign Strained to Hone Her Message, Hacked Emails Show.* [online] Nytimes.com. Available at: https://www.nytimes.com/2016/10/11/us/politics/hillary-clinton-emails.html [Accessed 17 Apr. 2017].

Clark, P. (2016). *Hillary's weak economic messaging is to blame for President Trump.* [online] Mashable. Available at: http://mashable.com/2016/11/13/hillary-clinton-messaging-trump/#w-guYH12r8qq9 [Accessed 17 Apr. 2017].

Gold, D. (2017). *'Data-Driven' Campaigns Are Killing the Democratic Party.* [online] POLITICO Magazine. Available at: http://www.politico.com/magazine/story/2017/02/data-driven-campaigns-democrats-need-message-214759 [Accessed 17 Apr. 2017].

Inspiration absolutely matters

Brooks, D. (2017). *Opinion | The Unifying American Story.* [online] Nytimes.com. Available at: https://www.nytimes.com/2017/03/21/opinion/the-unifying-american-story.html [Accessed 17 Apr. 2017].

Cahn, J. and Cahn, D. (2016). *Millennials to Hillary Clinton: Inspire us or we won't vote.* [online] chicagotribune.com. Available at: http://www.chicagotribune.com/news/opinion/commentary/ct-hillary-clinton-millennials-bernie-sanders-perspec-20160727-story.html [Accessed 17 Apr. 2017].

Gross, D. (2016). *What Bernie Sanders Is Doing With All that Money He's Raising.* [online] Fortune.com. Available at: http://fortune.com/2016/05/12/bernie-sanders-fundraising-donations-spent/ [Accessed 17 Apr. 2017].

The New York Times (2016). *Which Presidential Candidates Are Winning the Money Race.* [online] Nytimes.com. Available at: https://www.nytimes.com/interactive/2016/us/elections/election-2016-campaign-money-race.html [Accessed 17 Apr. 2017].

Tully, M. (2016). *How can you not love Bernie Sanders?.* [online] Indianapolis Star. Available at: http://www.indystar.com/story/opinion/columnists/matthew-tully/2016/04/28/tully-bernie-sanders-inspires-young-love-iu/83644786/ [Accessed 17 Apr. 2017].

Zeren, O. (2017). *What makes Bernie Sanders so inspirational, and persuasive?.* [online] Quora. Available at: https://www.quora.com/What-makes-Bernie-Sanders-so-inspirational-and-persuasive [Accessed 17 Apr. 2017].

Authenticity Matters

Ambinder, M. (2015). *No One Knows Whether Hillary Clinton Is Authentic.* [online] FiveThirtyEight. Available at: https://fivethirtyeight.com/features/no-one-knows-whether-hillary-clinton-is-authentic/ [Accessed 17 Apr. 2017].

Nyhan, B. (2015). *Hillary Clinton's Authenticity Problem, and Ours.* [online] Nytimes.com. Available at: https://www.nytimes.com/2015/10/02/upshot/hillary-clintons-authenticity-problem-and-ours.html [Accessed 17 Apr. 2017].

Pro Bono Statistics (2017). *Sanders's name recognition.* [online] Pro Bono Statistics. Available at: https://probonostats.wordpress.com/2016/02/01/sanderss-name-recognition/ [Accessed 17 Apr. 2017].

Seifert, E. (2012). *The politics of authenticity in presidential campaigns, 1976-2008.* 1st ed. Jefferson, N.C.: McFarland & Co.

Shafer, J. (2016). *Trump Was Not a Media Fail.* [online] POLITICO Magazine. Available at: http://www.politico.com/magazine/story/2016/11/donald-trump-wins-2016-media-214442 [Accessed 17 Apr. 2017].

Corruption matters

Dogbevi, E. and Odonkor, E. (2015). *Ghana not second most corrupt country in Africa - TI official - Ghana Business News.* [online] Ghana Business News. Available at: https://www.ghanabusinessnews.com/2015/12/03/ghana-not-second-most-corrupt-african-country-transparency-international-official/ [Accessed 17 Apr. 2017].

export.gov (2016). *Ghana - Corruption.* [online] Export.gov. Available at: https://www.export.gov/article?id=Ghana-Corruption [Accessed 17 Apr. 2017].

Mike, U. (2017). *Corruption in Nigeria: Review, Causes, Effects and Solutions.* [online] Soapboxie. Available at: https://soapboxie.com/world-politics/Corruption-in-Nigeria [Accessed 17 Apr. 2017].

PWC (2016). *Impact of Corruption on Nigeria's Economy.* [online] pwc.com/ng. Available at: https://www.pwc.com/ng/en/assets/pdf/impact-of-corruption-on-nigerias-economy.pdf [Accessed 17 Apr. 2017].

The economy, of course, matters – but not just in the way you think

Guo, J. (2016). *A new theory for why Trump voters are so angry — that actually makes sense.* [online] Washington Post. Available at: https://www.washingtonpost.com/news/wonk/wp/2016/11/08/a-new-theory-for-why-trump-voters-are-so-angry-that-actually-makes-sense/?utm_term=.4324c21b8f2a [Accessed 17 Apr. 2017].

Hoffman, R. (2016). *How the Left Created Trump.* [online] POLITICO Magazine. Available at: http://www.politico.com/magazine/story/2016/11/how-the-left-created-donald-trump-214472 [Accessed 17 Apr. 2017].

Levitz, E. (2016). *Trump Won a Lot of White Working-Class Voters Who Backed Obama.* [online] Daily Intelligencer. Available at:

http://nymag.com/daily/intelligencer/2016/11/trump-won-a-lot-of-white-working-class-obama-voters.html [Accessed 17 Apr. 2017].

Moore, M. (2016). *5 Reasons Why Trump Will Win.* [online] MICHAEL MOORE. Available at: http://michaelmoore.com/trumpwillwin/ [Accessed 17 Apr. 2017].

Schwartz, I. (2016). *David Brooks: "Us Enlightened People" Should Give Trump Voters Dignity, "Condescension Is What Fueled This".* [online] Realclearpolitics.com. Available at: http://www.realclearpolitics.com/video/2016/11/12/david_brooks_us_enlightened_people_should_give_trump_voters_dignity_condescension_is_what_fueled_this.html [Accessed 17 Apr. 2017].

Scola, N. (2017). *Silicon Valley sends ambassador to Trump's coal country.* [online] POLITICO. Available at: http://www.politico.com/story/2017/03/trump-election-silicon-valley-ambassador-appalachia-ro-khanna-236486 [Accessed 17 Apr. 2017].

Mobilisation matters, and so (big) data will matter

Confessore, N. and Hakim, D. (2017). *Data Firm Says 'Secret Sauce' Aided Trump; Many Scoff.* [online] The New York Times. Available at: https://www.nytimes.com/2017/03/06/us/politics/cambridge-analytica.html?mtrref=undefined&mtrref=www.nytimes.com&gwh=C630CDADA2E55B9CA601A0D9353F-9CE9&gwt=pay [Accessed 17 Apr. 2017].

Gold, D. (2017). *'Data-Driven' Campaigns Are Killing the Democratic Party.* [online] POLITICO Magazine. Available at: http://www.politico.com/magazine/story/2017/02/data-driven-campaigns-democrats-need-message-214759 [Accessed 17 Apr. 2017].

Green, D. and Gerber, A. (2008). *Get Out The Vote.* 1st ed. Washington, D.C.: Brookings Institution Press, pp.1-11.

Plouffe, D. (2017). *What I Got Wrong About the Election.* [online] The New York Times. Available at: https://www.nytimes.com/2016/11/11/opinion/what-i-got-wrong-about-the-election.html?smid=tw-share&_r=1&mtrref=undefined&gwh=5F53F7DA1E3D98E221102A3CE7F-B6203&gwt=pay&assetType=opinion [Accessed 17 Apr. 2017].

Wagner, J. (2016). *Clinton's data-driven campaign relied heavily on an algorithm named Ada. What didn't she see?*. [online] Washington Post. Available at: https://www.washingtonpost.com/news/post-politics/wp/2016/11/09/clintons-data-driven-campaign-relied-heavily-on-an-algorithm-named-ada-what-didnt-she-see/?utm_term=.f48eaec24176 [Accessed 17 Apr. 2017].

Technology doesn't matter as much as it will soon

Akwagyiram, A. (2015). *How technology eased Buhari's path to power in Nigeria.* [online] Reuters. Available at: http://www.reuters.com/article/nigeria-election-technology-idUSL6N0WZ2JF20150402 [Accessed 17 Apr. 2017].

Bodoni, S. (2014). *Google to Facebook Seen as Too Big for EU Nations' Privacy Czars.* [online] Bloomberg. Available at: https://www.bloomberg.com/news/articles/2014-05-09/google-to-facebook-seen-as-too-big-for-eu-nations-privacy-czars [Accessed 17 Apr. 2017].

Cadwalladr, C. (2017). *Revealed: how US billionaire helped to back Brexit.* [online] the guardian. Available at: https://www.theguardian.com/politics/2017/feb/26/us-billionaire-mercer-helped-back-brexit [Accessed 17 Apr. 2017].

Confessore, N. and Hakim, D. (2017). *Data Firm Says 'Secret Sauce' Aided Trump; Many Scoff.* [online] The New York Times. Available at: https://www.nytimes.com/2017/03/06/us/politics/cambridge-analytica.html?_r=0&mtrref=undefined&gwh=CC20D167F0F83287DE9C8C12ADC65006&gwt=pay [Accessed 17 Apr. 2017].

Data & Society (2017). *Media, Technology, Politics.* [online] Data & Society: Points. Available at: https://points.datasociety.net/media-technology-politics-258f4cfce87c [Accessed 17 Apr. 2017].

Doward, J., Cadwalladr, C. and Gibbs, A. (2017). *Watchdog to launch inquiry into misuse of data in politics.* [online] the guardian. Available at: https://www.theguardian.com/technology/2017/mar/04/cambridge-analytics-data-brexit-trump [Accessed 17 Apr. 2017].

Evans-Pritchard, A. (2017). *The powerful 'corporate state' is the new global villain.* [online] The Telegraph. Available at: http://

www.telegraph.co.uk/business/2017/01/18/powerful-corpo-rate-state-new-global-villain/ [Accessed 17 Apr. 2017].

Smith, M. (2016). *Theresa May launches thinly veiled attack on Apple, Facebook and Philip Green.* [online] Mirror. Available at: http://www.mirror.co.uk/news/uk-news/theresa-may-apple-face-book-bhs-8982954 [Accessed 17 Apr. 2017].

Waterson, J. (2016). *Vote Leave, The Canadian IT Company, And The £725,000 Donations.* [online] BuzzFeed. Available at: https://www.buzzfeed.com/jimwaterson/vote-leave-the-ca-nadian-it-company-and-the-ps725000-donation?utm_term=.asaQ5VV44#.hpm6GNNvv [Accessed 17 Apr. 2017].

Wright, B. and Marlow, B. (2017). *Tech giants in the crosshairs as Davos elite faces up to new global realities.* [online] The Telegraph. Available at: http://www.telegraph.co.uk/business/2017/01/22/tech-companies-new-whipping-boys-davos-threat-jobs/ [Accessed 17 Apr. 2017].

Demographics always matter

Bremmer, I. (2016). *These 5 Facts Show Why Demographics Are Destiny.* [online] TIME. Available at: http://time.com/4218169/demographics-global-economy-immigrants-china/ [Accessed 17 Apr. 2017].

Gonchar, M. (2016). *Demography Is Destiny? Teaching About Cause and Effect With Global Population Trends.* [online] The Learning Network. Available at: https://learning.blogs.nytimes.com/2016/03/23/demography-is-destiny-teach-ing-about-cause-and-effect-with-global-population-trends/ [Accessed 17 Apr. 2017].

Enten, H. (2016). *'Demographics Aren't Destiny' And Four Other Things This Election Taught Me.* [online] FiveThirtyEight. Available at: https://fivethirtyeight.com/features/demographics-arent-destiny-and-four-other-things-this-election-taught-me/ [Accessed 17 Apr. 2017].

Kirk, A. and Dunford, D. (2016). *EU referendum: How the results compare to the UK's educated, old and immigrant populations.* [online] The Telegraph. Available at: http://www.telegraph.co.uk/news/2016/06/24/eu-referendum-how-the-results-compare-to-the-uks-educated-old-an/ [Accessed 17 Apr. 2017].

Kirk, A. and Scott, P. (2016). *US election: How age, race and education are deciding factors in the race for President.* [online] The Telegraph. Available at: http://www.telegraph.co.uk/news/0/us-election-how-age-race-and-education-are-deciding-factors-in-t/ [Accessed 17 Apr. 2017].

Kotkin, J. (2016). *The Improbable Demographics Behind Donald Trump's Shocking Presidential Victory.* [online] Forbes. Available at: https://www.forbes.com/sites/joelkotkin/2016/11/09/don-ald-trumps-presidenti-victory-demographics/#5de16ccb3b96 [Accessed 17 Apr. 2017].

Roberts, S. (2008). *Minorities in U.S. set to become majority by 2042.* [online] The New York Times. Available at: http://www.nytimes.com/2008/08/14/world/ameri-cas/14iht-census.1.15284537.html?mtrref=undefined&g-wh=937F8FD39483595044B862F94EC04A7F&gwt=pay [Accessed 17 Apr. 2017].

Scott, P. and Kirk, A. (2016). *Hillary Clinton failed to win over black, Hispanic and female voters - the charts that show why she lost the presidential election.* [online] The Telegraph. Available at: http://www.telegraph.co.uk/news/2016/11/09/hillary-clinton-failed-to-win-over-black-hispanic-and-female-vot/ [Accessed 17 Apr. 2017].

Tyson, A. and Maniam, S. (2016). *Behind Trump's victory: Divisions by race, gender, education.* [online] Pew Research Center. Available at: http://www.pewresearch.org/fact-tank/2016/11/09/behind-trumps-victory-divisions-by-race-gender-education/ [Accessed 17 Apr. 2017].

Psychographics will matter as much as demographics

Samuels, A. (2016). *Psychographics Are Just as Important for Marketers as Demographics.* [online] Harvard Business Review. Available at: https://hbr.org/2016/03/psychographics-are-just-as-import-ant-for-marketers-as-demographics [Accessed 17 Apr. 2017].

Of course, youth matter

Chutel, L. (2016). *Bill Gates thinks Africa's youth are vital for driving in-novation.* [online] Quartz. Available at: https://qz.com/734799/

bill-gates-thinks-africas-youth-are-vital-for-driving-innovation/ [Accessed 17 Apr. 2017].

GE (n.d.). *This is how sub-Saharan Africa will cash in on its youth.* [online] Quartz. Available at: https://qz.com/473032/this-is-how-sub-saharan-africa-will-cash-in-on-its-youth/ [Accessed 17 Apr. 2017].

International Institute for Environment and Development (n.d.). *African youth in participatory politics.* [online] International Institute for Environment and Development. Available at: https://www.iied.org/african-youth-participatory-politics [Accessed 17 Apr. 2017].

Kuo, L. (2015). *A quarter of the world's population will live in Africa by 2050.* [online] Quartz. Available at: https://qz.com/467755/a-quarter-of-the-worlds-population-will-live-in-africa-by-2050/ [Accessed 17 Apr. 2017].

Resnick, D. and Casale, D. (2011). *The Political Participation of Africa's Youth: Turnout, Partisanship and Protest - GSDRC.* [online] GSDRC. Available at: http://www.gsdrc.org/document-library/the-political-participation-of-africas-youth-turnout-partisanship-and-protest/ [Accessed 17 Apr. 2017].

Political parties will continue to matter for a very long time

Barone, M. (2009). *No Permanent Majorities in America.* [online] RealClearPolitics. Available at: http://www.realclearpolitics.com/articles/2009/01/no_permanent_majorities_in_ame.html#ixzz4cbSD8kh5 [Accessed 17 Apr. 2017].

Cost, J. and Trende, S. (2009). *Election Review: Moving Beyond "Permanent Majorities".* [online] RealClearPolitics. Available at: http://www.realclearpolitics.com/articles/2009/01/election_review_moving_beyond.html#ixzz4cbR82SY0 [Accessed 17 Apr. 2017].

Epstein, R. and Hook, J. (2017). *Bernie Sanders Loyalists Are Taking Over the Democratic Party One County Office at a Time - Bernie Sanders.* [online] Bernie Sanders. Available at: https://bernie-sanders.com/bernie-sanders-loyalists-taking-democratic-party-one-county-office-time/ [Accessed 17 Apr. 2017].

Flanders, S. (2007). *Political Parties.* [online] Scholastic.com. Available at: https://www.scholastic.com/teachers/articles/teaching-content/origins-and-functions-political-parties/ [Accessed 17 Apr. 2017].

Friedersdorf, C. (2016). *Donald Trump Is Steve Bannon's Latest Weapon in His Crusade to Destroy the Left.* [online] The Atlantic. Available at: https://www.theatlantic.com/politics/archive/2016/08/the-radical-anti-conservatism-of-stephen-bannon/496796/ [Accessed 17 Apr. 2017].

Guilford, G. and Sonnad, N. (2017). *Steve Bannon has a grand vision for remaking America.* [online] Quartz. Available at: https://qz.com/898134/what-steve-bannon-really-wants/ [Accessed 17 Apr. 2017].

Jideonwo, C. (2007). *What is WRONG with these people!.* [online] Chudesblog.blogspot.com.ng. Available at: http://chudesblog.blogspot.com.ng/2007/04/come-on-people.html [Accessed 17 Apr. 2017].

Jideonwo, C. (2017). *The irony of the youth-led frustration that keeps electing old men into office across Africa.* [online] Quartz. Available at: https://qz.com/904665/donald-trump-joins-buhari-in-nigeria-and-akufo-addo-in-ghana-as-70-year-olds-leading-young-electorates/ [Accessed 17 Apr. 2017].

Lind, M. (2016). *This Is What the Future of American Politics Looks Like.* [online] POLITICO Magazine. Available at: http://www.politico.com/magazine/story/2016/05/2016-election-realignment-partisan-political-party-policy-democrats-republicans-politics-213909 [Accessed 17 Apr. 2017].

Rabin-Havt, A. (2016). *The Hostile Takeover Of The GOP Is Now Complete.* [online] The Huffington Post. Available at: http://www.huffingtonpost.com/ari-rabin-havt/the-hostile-takeover-of-t_b_11572846.html [Accessed 17 Apr. 2017].

Riotta, C. (2017). *Sanders supporters are taking over the Democratic Party.* [online] Rawstory.com. Available at: http://www.rawstory.com/2017/02/sanders-supporters-are-taking-over-the-democratic-party/ [Accessed 17 Apr. 2017].

Shivani, A. (2016). *Millennials are ripe for socialism: A generation is rising up against neoliberal oppression.* [online] Salon. Available at: http://www.salon.com/2016/07/04/millennials_are_ripe_for_

socialism_a_generation_is_rising_up_again_partner/ [Accessed 17 Apr. 2017].

Political Instincts Matter

360Nobs.com (2015). *Fashola And Tinubu At War*. [online] 360Nobs.com. Available at: https://www.360nobs.com/2015/08/fashola-and-tinubu-at-war/ [Accessed 17 Apr. 2017].

CBS NEWS (2008). *Obama's Political "Godfather" In Illinois*. [online] CBS NEWS. Available at: http://www.cbsnews.com/news/obamas-political-godfather-in-illinois/ [Accessed 17 Apr. 2017].

Cost, J. and Trende, S. (2009). *Election Review: Moving Beyond "Permanent Majorities"*. [online] RealClearPolitics. Available at: http://www.realclearpolitics.com/articles/2009/01/election_review_moving_beyond.html#ixzz4PhvGRWyU [Accessed 17 Apr. 2017].

Lawal, D. (n.d.). *After listening to Gov. Fashola yesterday we need to ask: Is he the most loyal party man or what? - The ScoopNG*. [online] The Scoop. Available at: http://www.thescoopng.com/2014/12/17/listening-gov-fashola-yesterday-need-ask-loyal-party-man/ [Accessed 17 Apr. 2017].

Makinwa, E. (2017). *Peter Obi - contradictory ex-governor of Anambra State - Who is he?*. [online] Naij.com. Available at: https://www.naij.com/1089765-peter-obis-net-worth-achievements.html [Accessed 17 Apr. 2017].

Stein, J. (2016). *Why Bernie Sanders is lobbying superdelegates — even though they won't save his campaign*. [online] Vox. Available at: http://www.vox.com/2016/5/2/11571480/bernie-sanders-superdelegates-campaign [Accessed 17 Apr. 2017].

Ideology simply doesn't matter yet

Bamikole, L. (2002). Nkrumah and the Triple Heritage Thesis and Development in Africana Societies. *International Journal of Business, Humanities and Technology*, 2(2).

Bienen, H. (1969). *An Ideology for Africa*. [online] Foreign Affairs. Available at: https://www.foreignaffairs.com/articles/tanzania/1969-04-01/ideology-africa [Accessed 17 Apr. 2017].

Chotiner, I. (2016). *A Historian of Fascism on How Trump's Rhetoric Will Permanently Affect American Politics.* [online] Slate Magazine. Available at: http://www.slate.com/articles/news_and_politics/interrogation/2016/10/donald_trump_s_fascism_is_rooted_in_his_own_self_interest.html [Accessed 17 Apr. 2017].

Duignan, P. and Gann, L. (1994). *Communism in sub-Saharan Africa.* 1st ed. Stanford, CA: Hoover Institution on War, Revolution, and Peace, Stanford University.

Nneji, A. (2015). *Devolution of Power: Atiku, Buhari lock horns.* [online] Post-Nigeria. Available at: http://www.post-nigeria.com/devolution-of-power-atiku-buhari-lock-horns/ [Accessed 17 Apr. 2017].

Odusote, O. (2013). *AWOISM and the AWOIST: The Battles over a Political Philosophy.* [online] Odusote Oluwakayode. Available at: https://actionkay.wordpress.com/2013/02/09/awoism-and-the-awoist-the-battles-over-a-political-philosophy/ [Accessed 17 Apr. 2017].

Ross, J. (2012). *China's economic success sets an example to the rest of the world.* [online] the guardian. Available at: https://www.theguardian.com/commentisfree/2012/jul/13/china-economic-success-example-world [Accessed 17 Apr. 2017].

Ross, J. (2012). *Deng Xiaoping and John Maynard Keynes.* [online] Key Trends in Globalisation. Available at: http://ablog.typepad.com/keytrendsinglobalisation/2012/02/deng-xiaoping-and-john-maynard-keynes-1.html [Accessed 17 Apr. 2017].

Shapiro, B. (2016). *Is Donald Trump a Pragmatist?.* [online] National Review. Available at: http://www.nationalreview.com/article/442221/donald-trump-pragmatist-not-conservative [Accessed 17 Apr. 2017].

Shilgba, L. (2014). *Ideological fundamentals of the APC.* [online] ScanNews. Available at: http://scannewsnigeria.com/politics/ideological-fundamentals-of-the-apc/ [Accessed 17 Apr. 2017].

Young, C. (1982). *Ideology and Development in Africa.* 1st ed. Yale University Press.

Money doesn't matter as much as you think it does

360Nobs.com (2015). *President Jonathan Demands Refund of N2 Tril-*

lion Of His Campaign Funds. [online] 360Nobs.com. Available at: https://www.360nobs.com/2015/04/president-jonathan-demands-refund-of-n2-trillion-of-his-campaign-funds/ [Accessed 17 Apr. 2017].

Allison, B., Rojanasakul, M., Harris, B. and Sam, C. (2016). *Tracking the 2016 Presidential Money Race.* [online] Bloomberg Politics. Available at: https://www.bloomberg.com/politics/graphics/2016-presidential-campaign-fundraising/ [Accessed 17 Apr. 2017].

Goidel, K. and Gaddie, K. (2016). *Money Matters (in Presidential Elections).* [online] The Huffington Post. Available at: http://www.huffingtonpost.com/kirby-goidel/money-matters-in-presiden_b_9190198.html [Accessed 17 Apr. 2017].

Gold, M. (2016). *Trump stops holding high-dollar fundraisers that were raising big cash for the GOP.* [online] The Washington Post. Available at: https://www.washingtonpost.com/news/post-politics/wp/2016/10/25/trump-halts-big-money-fundraising-cutting-off-cash-to-the-party/?utm_term=.16e76052fdd9 [Accessed 17 Apr. 2017].

Haskell, J. and Kreutz, L. (2016). *Hillary Clinton Has Headlined More Than 350 Fundraisers Since Launching Campaign.* [online] ABC News. Available at: http://abcnews.go.com/Politics/hillary-clinton-headlined-350-fundraisers-launching-campaign/story?id=43055539 [Accessed 17 Apr. 2017].

Idowu, O. (2017). *The Buhari Narrative.* [online] Stears. Available at: https://www.stearsng.com/article/the-buhari-narrative [Accessed 17 Apr. 2017].

Kayode-Adedeji, D. (2015). *Jonathan campaign money tears Ogun support group apart - Premium Times Nigeria.* [online] Premium Times. Available at: http://www.premiumtimesng.com/news/top-news/178721-jonathan-campaign-money-tears-ogun-support-group-apart.html [Accessed 17 Apr. 2017].

NPR (2010). *Talk of the Nation.* [podcast] 'Drive' Not Always Explained By Rewards. Available at: http://www.npr.org/templates/story/story.php?storyId=122221202 [Accessed 17 Apr. 2017].

Post-Nigeria (2016). *Fani-Kayode breaks silence on Goodluck Jon-*

athan's Campaign Funds. [online] Post-Nigeria. Available at:
http://www.post-nigeria.com/fani-kayode-breaks-silence-on-goodluck-jonathans-campaign-funds/ [Accessed 17 Apr. 2017].

Smith, B. (2007). *Money matters.* [online] POLITICO. Available
at: http://www.politico.com/blogs/ben-smith/2007/07/money-matters-002046 [Accessed 17 Apr. 2017].

Tankersley, J. (2016). *The advertising decisions that helped doom Hillary Clinton.* [online] The Washington Post. Available at: https://www.washingtonpost.com/news/wonk/wp/2016/11/12/the-advertising-decisions-that-helped-doom-hillary-clinton/?utm_term=.0c4c9777f5bb [Accessed 17 Apr. 2017].

Civil society matters

Aljazeera (2016). *The Gambia president warns against election protest.* [online] Aljazeera. Available at: http://www.aljazeera.com/news/2016/11/gambia-president-warns-election-protest-161130163024674.html [Accessed 17 Apr. 2017].

Atabong, A. (2016). *Mass protests in Cameroon are exposing the fragility of its dual French-English system.* [online] Quartz. Available at: https://qz.com/845783/cameroon-protests-are-growing-over-the-anglophone-francophone-split/ [Accessed 17 Apr. 2017].

Atabong, A. (2017). *Political tensions are growing in Cameroon's troubled English-speaking regions.* [online] Quartz. Available at: https://qz.com/936788/cameroons-anglophone-protestors-are-facing-a-government-crackdown/ [Accessed 17 Apr. 2017].

BBC News (2016). *Why are South African students protesting? - BBC News.* [online] BBC News. Available at: http://www.bbc.com/news/world-africa-34615004 [Accessed 17 Apr. 2017].

Camara, S. (2016). *Gambia: Social Media Overwhelms a 20-Year Dictator | World Policy Institute.* [online] Worldpolicy.org. Available at: http://www.worldpolicy.org/blog/2016/12/09/gambia-social-media-overwhelms-20-year-dictator [Accessed 17 Apr. 2017].

Chutel, L. (2016). *South Africa's intensifying protests could lead to electoral violence in August.* [online] Quartz. Available at:

https://qz.com/717716/south-africas-intensifying-pro-tests-could-lead-to-electoral-violence-in-august/ [Accessed 17 Apr. 2017].

Dahir, A. (2017). *How Cameroon pressured mobile operators to shut down the internet and stifle dissent.* [online] Quartz. Available at: https://qz.com/893401/cameroon-pressured-mtn-and-other-operators-to-shut-down-internet-in-bamenda-buea-regions/ [Accessed 17 Apr. 2017].

Ibeh, N. (2015). *Why I remained calm while Orubebe misbehaved - Ex-INEC Chair, Jega.* [online] Premium Times. Available at: http://www.premiumtimesng.com/features-and-inter-views/188174-why-i-remained-calm-while-orubebe-misbehaved-ex-inec-chair-jega.html [Accessed 17 Apr. 2017].

Jollofnews (2017). *Gambia: Barrow Urges Jammeh To End Crackdown Of Activists.* [online] Jollofnews. Available at: https://jollofnews.com/2017/01/03/gambia-barrow-urges-jammeh-to-end-crack-down-of-activists/ [Accessed 17 Apr. 2017].

Laccino, L. (2016). *Gambia jails opposition leader and 18 other pro-testers for demanding electoral changes.* [online] International Business Times UK. Available at: http://www.ibtimes.co.uk/gambia-jails-opposition-leader-18-other-protesters-demand-ing-electoral-changes-1571752 [Accessed 17 Apr. 2017].

Nimarkoh, J. (2014). *Ghana: New Dawn for Social Activism in Gha-na.* [online] allAfrica. Available at: http://allafrica.com/sto-ries/201409191227.html [Accessed 17 Apr. 2017].

Shaban, A. (2017). *Gambia's election chief slips into exile following death threats | Africanews.* [online] Africanews. Available at: http://www.africanews.com/2017/01/03/gambia-s-election-chief-slips-into-exile-following-death-threats// [Accessed 17 Apr. 2017].

Sunday, S. (2016). *2000 Immigration recruits to protest in Abuja.* [online] Daily Trust. Available at: https://www.dailytrust.com.ng/news/general/2000-immigration-recruits-to-protest-in-abu-ja/139484.html [Accessed 17 Apr. 2017].

YNaija (2016). *Why Gambia's election chairman is a true African hero - YNaija.* [online] YNaija. Available at: https://ynaija.com/gambias-election-chairman-true-african-hero/ [Accessed 17 Apr. 2017].

Electoral commissions are increasingly beginning to matter

Ibeh, N. (2015). *Why I remained calm while Orubebe misbehaved - Ex-INEC Chair, Jega.* [online] Premium Times. Available at: http://www.premiumtimesng.com/features-and-interviews/188174-why-i-remained-calm-while-orubebe-misbehaved-ex-inec-chair-jega.html [Accessed 17 Apr. 2017].

Mwere, D. and Gathara, P. (2016). *Is IEBC really prepared for the challenge of the 2017 elections.* [online] The Star. Available at: http://www.the-star.co.ke/news/2016/03/12/is-iebc-really-prepared-for-the-challenge-of-the-2017-elections_c1310915 [Accessed 19 Apr. 2017].

Shaban, A. (2017). *Gambia's election chief slips into exile following death threats | Africanews.* [online] Africanews. Available at: http://www.africanews.com/2017/01/03/gambia-s-election-chief-slips-into-exile-following-death-threats// [Accessed 17 Apr. 2017].

YNaija (2016). *Why Gambia's election chairman is a true African hero - YNaija.* [online] YNaija. Available at: https://ynaija.com/gambias-election-chairman-true-african-hero/ [Accessed 17 Apr. 2017].

International consensus matters

Adeniyi, O. (2017). *Obazee, Accountability and the Church.* [online] THISDAY. Available at: https://www.thisdaylive.com/index.php/2017/01/12/obazee-accountability-and-the-church/ [Accessed 17 Apr. 2017].

Agutu, N. (2016). *Kenyans 4th most active Twitter users in Africa, politics among hot topics.* [online] The Star. Available at: http://www.the-star.co.ke/news/2016/04/06/kenyans-4th-most-active-twitter-users-in-africa-politics-among-hot_c1326926 [Accessed 17 Apr. 2017].

Emmanuel, O. (2013). *Nigerians fiercely reject Jonathan's electricity claim in CNN Superbowl follow-up -.* [online] Premium Times. Available at: http://www.premiumtimesng.com/news/118784-nigerians-reject-jonathans-electricity-claim-in-cnn-superbowl-follow-up.html [Accessed 17 Apr. 2017].

Gaffey, C. (2017). *Gambia's Yahya Jammeh may have taken a golden farewell before leaving the country*. [online] Newsweek. Available at: http://www.newsweek.com/gambias-yahya-jammeh-looted-11-million-two-weeks-official-546880 [Accessed 17 Apr. 2017].

Mahr, K. (2017). *How a Washington consultancy helped force Gambia's dictator from power*. [online] Newsweek. Available at: http://www.newsweek.com/2017/02/10/gambia-yahya-jammeh-ada-ma-barrow-vanguard-550031.html [Accessed 17 Apr. 2017].

Sieff, K. (2017). *Senegal sends troops into Gambia to force longtime leader to step down*. [online] The Washington Post. Available at: https://www.washingtonpost.com/world/despite-expired-term-gambias-president-refuses-to-leave-office-even-as-troops-close-in/2017/01/19/eccaf29c-ddde-11e6-8902-610fe486791c_story.html?utm_term=.a11e98dbc400 [Accessed 17 Apr. 2017].

Seriously, joy really matters

Bruni, F. (2015). *Jeb Bush's Slog: The Tortoise and the Hair*. [online] The New York Times. Available at: https://www.nytimes.com/2015/08/19/opinion/jeb-bushs-slog-the-tortoise-and-the-hair.html?_r=0&mtrref=undefined&gwh=DC3A9BC8219B5B-DAFFAD1B10B4A47107&gwt=pay&assetType=opinion [Accessed 17 Apr. 2017].

Coppins, M. (2015). *Jeb Bush Embarks On Least Joyful Campaign Ever*. [online] BuzzFeed. Available at: https://www.buzzfeed.com/mckaycoppins/jeb-bush-embarks-on-least-joyful-campaign-ever?utm_term=.qoj25BBee#.xhmMENN22 [Accessed 17 Apr. 2017].

Debenedetti, G. (2016). *Hillary Clinton's joyless victory*. [online] POLITICO. Available at: http://www.politico.com/story/2016/05/hillary-clinton-kentucky-joyless-victory-223310 [Accessed 17 Apr. 2017].

Eggers, D. (2016). *'Could he actually win?' Dave Eggers at a Donald Trump rally*. [online] the guardian. Available at: https://www.theguardian.com/books/2016/jun/17/could-he-actually-win-dave-eggers-donald-trump-rally-presidential-campaign [Accessed 17 Apr. 2017].

Ehiabhi, V. (2015). *Fayose Gets More Knocks As Another APC Chieftain Reacts*. [online] Naij.com. Available at: https://politics.naij.

com/366865-fayose-gets-more-knocks-over-ad-on-buhari.html [Accessed 17 Apr. 2017].

Freedland, J. (2008). *The end of attack politics*. [online] the guardian. Available at: https://www.theguardian.com/commentisfree/cifamerica/2008/oct/16/obama-mccain-debate-attacks [Accessed 17 Apr. 2017].

Goddard, T. (2016). *The Candidate Having the Most Fun Usually Wins - Political Wire*. [online] Political Wire. Available at: https://politicalwire.com/2016/01/11/the-candidate-having-the-most-fun-usually-wins/ [Accessed 17 Apr. 2017].

Indiatoday (2016). *Trump is enjoying campaign trail: aide*. [online] Indiatoday. Available at: http://indiatoday.intoday.in/story/trump-is-enjoying-campaign-trail-aide/1/743703.html [Accessed 17 Apr. 2017].

Karni, A. and Thrush, G. (2016). *22 toxic days for Hillary Clinton*. [online] POLITICO. Available at: http://www.politico.com/story/2016/10/hillary-clinton-trump-wikileaks-229864 [Accessed 17 Apr. 2017].

Killough, A. (2016). *Jeb Bush, the 'joyful tortoise,' gives out tiny toy turtles*. [online] CNN. Available at: http://edition.cnn.com/2016/01/06/politics/jeb-bush-turtle-tortoise-joyful/ [Accessed 17 Apr. 2017].

Kizenko, P. (2016). *Uncensored: an inside look at a Donald Trump rally*. [online] The Duran. Available at: http://theduran.com/uncensored-an-inside-look-at-a-donald-trump-rally/ [Accessed 17 Apr. 2017].

Lizza, R. (2015). *How to Beat Hillary Clinton*. [online] The New Yorker. Available at: http://www.newyorker.com/news/newsdesk/how-to-beat-hillary-clinton [Accessed 17 Apr. 2017].

Mehta, S. (2015). *Jeb Bush sets aside his 'joyful tortoise' persona to go after Donald Trump*. [online] latimes.com. Available at: http://www.latimes.com/nation/politics/la-na-bush-trump-20150904-story.html [Accessed 17 Apr. 2017].

Moore, M. (2016). *5 Reasons Why Trump Will Win*. [online] MICHAEL MOORE. Available at: http://michaelmoore.com/trumpwillwin/ [Accessed 17 Apr. 2017].

Olapoju, K. (2015). *'Jog round a stadium to prove you're fit' - PDP tells*

Buhari. [online] YNaija. Available at: https://ynaija.com/jog-round-a-stadium-to-prove-youre-fit-pdp-tells-buhari/ [Accessed 17 Apr. 2017].

Paulinus, O. (2015). *Full video of AIT controversial documentary of Buhari's evil deeds.* [online] TheInfo.NG. Available at: http://www.theinfong.com/2015/01/full-video-of-ait-controversial-documentary-of-buharis-evil-deeds/ [Accessed 17 Apr. 2017].

Post On Politics (2015). *Jeb Bush declares himself the 'joyful tortoise' in Republican race.* [online] Post On Politics. Available at: http://postonpolitics.blog.palmbeachpost.com/2015/07/28/jeb-bush-the-joyful-tortoise/ [Accessed 17 Apr. 2017].

Siollun, M. (2015). *How Goodluck Jonathan lost the Nigerian election.* [online] the guardian. Available at: https://www.theguardian.com/world/2015/apr/01/nigeria-election-goodluck-jonathan-lost [Accessed 17 Apr. 2017].

Expertise matters

Cendrowicz, L. (2013). *Robert Mugabe's Zimbabwe election victory was a 'masterclass in.* [online] The Independent. Available at: http://www.independent.co.uk/news/world/africa/robert-mugabes-zimbabwe-election-victory-was-a-masterclass-in-electoral-fraud-8744348.html [Accessed 18 Apr. 2017].

Mwesigwa, D. (2016). *Why African Dictators are Excited by China's Tough Stance on Internet Usage.* [online] iAfrikan. Available at: https://www.iafrikan.com/2016/05/26/why-african-dictators-are-excited-by-chinas-highhandedness-on-internet-use-2/ [Accessed 18 Apr. 2017].

Nsehe, M. (2017). *Meet The 30 Year-Old Nigerian Entrepreneur Who Helped 3 African Presidents Get Elected.* [online] Forbes. Available at: https://www.forbes.com/sites/mfonobongnsehe/2017/02/17/meet-the-30-year-old-nigerian-entrepreneur-who-helped-3-african-presidents-get-elected/4/#5bc5662f4108 [Accessed 18 Apr. 2017].

Plasser, F. and Plasser, G. (2002). *Global Political Campaigning: A Worldwide Analysis of Campaign Professionals and Their Practices (Praeger series in political communication, 1062-5623).* 1st ed. Westport: Praeger.

Webb, D. (2013). *Campaign Guru: The Basic Elements of a Political Campaign*. [online] utahpolicy.com. Available at: http://utah-policy.com/index.php/topics/campaign-guru/70-campaign-gu-ru-the-basic-elements-of-a-political-campaign [Accessed 18 Apr. 2017].

Social media matters and will continue to matter, even more

Akwagyiram, A. (2015). *How technology eased Buhari's path to power in Nigeria*. [online] Reuters. Available at: http://www.reuters.com/article/nigeria-election-technology-idUSL6N0WZ2JF20150402 [Accessed 18 Apr. 2017].

Bankole, O. (2016). *There are 16 million Nigerians on Facebook*. [online] Techcabal.com. Available at: http://techcabal.com/2016/02/05/there-are-16-million-nigerians-on-facebook/ [Accessed 18 Apr. 2017].

Boyd, D. (2017). *Hacking the Attention Economy*. [online] Data & Society: Points. Available at: https://points.datasociety.net/hacking-the-attention-economy-9fa1daca7a37 [Accessed 18 Apr. 2017].

Camara, S. (2016). *Gambia: Social Media Overwhelms a 20-Year Dictator*. [online] World Policy Blog. Available at: http://www.worldpolicy.org/blog/2016/12/09/gambia-social-media-over-whelms-20-year-dictator [Accessed 18 Apr. 2017].

Dvorak, J. (2016). *Social Media Is Ruining US Elections*. [online] PCMAG. Available at: http://www.pcmag.com/commen-tary/349599/social-media-is-ruining-us-elections [Accessed 18 Apr. 2017].

Edozien, F. (2015). *Social media was the other big winner at Nige-ria's historic elections*. [online] Quartz. Available at: https://qz.com/377777/social-media-was-the-other-big-winner-at-nige-rias-historic-elections/ [Accessed 18 Apr. 2017].

Egbunike, N. (2015). Framing the Occupy Nigeria Protests in Newspapers and Social Media. *OALib*, [online] 02(05), pp.1-13. Available at: http://www.oalib.com/articles/3144955#.WPb1T-FKZMy5 [Accessed 19 Apr. 2017].

George, C. (2017). *Elections 2015: Why the Social Media is Highly Overrated*. [online] Sahara Reporters. Available at: http://saharareporters.com/2015/03/01/elections-2015-why-social-media-highly-overrated-chinedu-rylan-george [Accessed 18 Apr. 2017].

GhanaWeb (2016). *Can Facebook really predict Ghana's next president?*. [online] GhanaWeb. Available at: http://www.ghanaweb.com/GhanaHomePage/NewsArchive/Can-Facebook-really-predict-Ghana-s-next-president-493002 [Accessed 18 Apr. 2017].

Greenwood, S., Perrin, A. and Duggan, M. (2016). *Social Media Update 2016*. [online] Pew Research Center: Internet, Science & Tech. Available at: http://www.pewinternet.org/2016/11/11/social-media-update-2016/ [Accessed 18 Apr. 2017].

Internet World Stats (2017). *Africa Internet Users, Facebook and 2017 Population Statistics*. [online] Internet World Stats. Available at: http://www.internetworldstats.com/stats1.htm [Accessed 18 Apr. 2017].

Jack, C. (2017). *What's Propaganda Got To Do With It?*. [online] Data & Society: Points. Available at: https://points.datasociety.net/whats-propaganda-got-to-do-with-it-5b88d78c3282 [Accessed 18 Apr. 2017].

Lotan, G. (2016). *Fake News Is Not the Only Problem*. [online] Data & Society: Points. Available at: https://points.datasociety.net/fake-news-is-not-the-problem-f00ec8cdfcb [Accessed 18 Apr. 2017].

Matfess, H. (2016). *More African countries are blocking internet access during elections*. [online] Quartz. Available at: https://qz.com/696552/more-african-countries-are-blocking-internet-access-during-elections/ [Accessed 18 Apr. 2017].

Morin, R. (2016). *Trump says social media was key to victory.* [online] POLITICO. Available at: http://www.politico.com/story/2016/11/donald-trump-social-media-231285 [Accessed 18 Apr. 2017].

Newton, C., Robertson, A. and Tiffany, K. (2016). *How social platforms influenced the 2016 election*. [online] The Verge. Available at: http://www.theverge.com/2016/11/14/13626694/election-2016-trending-social-media-facebook-twitter-influence [Accessed 18 Apr. 2017].

Olorunnisola, A. and Martin, B. (2013). Influences of media on social movements: Problematizing hyperbolic inferences about impacts. *Telematics and Informatics*, [online] 30(3), pp.275-288.

Available at: http://www.sciencedirect.com/science/article/pii/
S0736585312000226 [Accessed 19 Apr. 2017].

O'Reilly, T. (2016). *Media in the Age of Algorithms – What's The
Future?*. [online] Medium. Available at: https://medium.com/
the-wtf-economy/media-in-the-age-of-algorithms-63e80b9b0a73
[Accessed 18 Apr. 2017].

Reid, S. (2015). *Nigerians look to social media amid information scarcity
ahead of election*. [online] Aljazeera America. Available at: http://
america.aljazeera.com/articles/2015/3/19/social-media-plays-
key-role-in-nigerian-elections.html [Accessed 18 Apr. 2017].

Stannard, J. (2017). *Does Gambia's Election Redefine Social Media's Political Role?*. [online] Social Songbird. Available at: http://www.
socialsongbird.com/2016/12/does-gambias-election-redefine-so-
cial.html [Accessed 18 Apr. 2017].

The media absolutely matters

Agba, P.C, (2007) "Role of Mass Media in electioneering Campaign
in a developing context," in Ikechukwu Nwosu et al (eds). Communication for sustainable human development. Engugu. African
Council for Communication Education.

Bamidele, G. (2015). *The Role Of Media In The Democratic Process
In Nigeria*. [online] Newsdiaryonline.com. Available at: https://
newsdiaryonline.com/the-role-of-media-in-the-democratic-pro-
cess-in-nigeria-by-gbemiga-bamidele/ [Accessed 19 Apr. 2017].

Beutler, B. (2016). *Shame on Us, the American Media*. [online] New
Republic. Available at: https://newrepublic.com/article/138502/
shame-us-american-media [Accessed 18 Apr. 2017].

Brichacek, A. (2016). *Six ways the media influence elections*. [online]
School of Journalism and Communication. Available at: http://
journalism.uoregon.edu/news/six-ways-media-influences-elec-
tions/ [Accessed 18 Apr. 2017].

Childress, S. (2016). *Study: Media Biased in Primary Campaign Coverage*. [online] FRONTLINE. Available at: http://www.pbs.org/
wgbh/frontline/article/study-election-coverage-skewed-by-jour-
nalistic-bias/ [Accessed 18 Apr. 2017].

Gibson, G. and Smith, G. (2016). *At under $5 each, Trump's votes
came cheap*. [online] Reuters. Available at: http://www.reuters.

com/article/us-usa-election-spending-idUSKBN1341JR [Accessed 18 Apr. 2017].

Heintz, J. (2016). *Putin's popularity: the envy of other politicians.* [online] The Big Story. Available at: http://bigstory.ap.org/article/3c87367986df4fac9a27cbdadc86e7a0/putins-popularity-envy-other-politicians [Accessed 18 Apr. 2017].

John G.D and Enigbe J (2001) "The Press in Nigerian Politics: An historical analysis issues and pattern of news coverage." The Nigerian Journal of Communications (1), 6.67, 2001.

Kelley, S. (1962). Elections and the Mass Media. *Law and Contemporary Problems,* [online] 27(2), pp.307-326. Available at: http://scholarship.law.duke.edu/cgi/viewcontent.cgi?article=2926&context=lcp [Accessed 18 Apr. 2017].

Le Miere, J. (2016). *Did The Media Help Donald Trump Win? $5 Billion In Free Advertising Given To President-Elect.* [online] International Business Times. Available at: http://www.ibtimes.com/did-media-help-donald-trump-win-5-billion-free-advertising-given-president-elect-2444115 [Accessed 18 Apr. 2017].

Lozada, C. (2015). *How Donald Trump plays the press, in his own words.* [online] Washington Post. Available at: https://www.washingtonpost.com/news/book-party/wp/2015/06/17/how-donald-trump-plays-the-press-in-his-own-words/?utm_term=.d158b615c216 [Accessed 18 Apr. 2017].

Silver, N. (2015). *Trump Boom Or Trump Bubble?.* [online] FiveThirtyEight. Available at: https://fivethirtyeight.com/features/trump-boom-or-trump-bubble/ [Accessed 18 Apr. 2017].

Stray, J. (2016). *How much influence does the media really have over elections? Digging into the data.* [online] Nieman Lab. Available at: http://www.niemanlab.org/2016/01/how-much-influence-does-the-media-really-have-over-elections-digging-into-the-data/ [Accessed 18 Apr. 2017].

Trende, S. (2016). *Brexit Surprise Due to Analysts' Bias, Not Numbers.* [online] RealClearPolitics. Available at: http://www.realclearpolitics.com/articles/2016/11/01/brexit_surprise_due_to_analysts_bias_not_numbers.html [Accessed 18 Apr. 2017].

Trump, D. and Schwartz, T. (1987). *Trump: The Art of the Deal.* 1st ed. New York: Random House.

Narratives Matter

Allen, J. (2015). *The 5 unspoken rules for covering Hillary Clinton*. [online] Vox. Available at: http://www.vox.com/2015/7/6/8900143/hillary-clinton-reporting-rules [Accessed 18 Apr. 2017].

Brichacek, A. (2016). *Six ways the media influence elections*. [online] School of Journalism and Communication. Available at: http://journalism.uoregon.edu/news/six-ways-media-influences-elections/ [Accessed 18 Apr. 2017].

Gold, D. (2017). *'Data-Driven' Campaigns Are Killing the Democratic Party*. [online] POLITICO Magazine. Available at: http://www.politico.com/magazine/story/2017/02/data-driven-campaigns-democrats-need-message-214759 [Accessed 18 Apr. 2017].

Inyang, I. (2012). *PUNCH Editorial: Jonathan, Enough Is Enough!*. [online] Daily Post. Available at: http://dailypost.ng/2012/12/04/punch-editorial-jonathan-enough-is-enough/ [Accessed 18 Apr. 2017].

Jideonwo, C. (2008). *Fair is Fair....* [online] Chude!. Available at: https://chudesblog.blogspot.com.ng/2008/04/fair-is-fair.html [Accessed 18 Apr. 2017].

Nwofe, E. (2016). Dimensions of Negativity in the Coverage of the Nigeria's 2015 Presidential Election. *European - American Journal*, [online] 2(2), pp.6-29. Available at: http://www.eajournals.org/wp-content/uploads/Dimensions-of-Negativity-in-the-Coverage-of-the-Nigeria--s-2015-Presidential-Election.pdf [Accessed 18 Apr. 2017].

Trende, S. (2016). *It Wasn't the Polls That Missed, It Was the Pundits*. [online] RealClearPolitics. Available at: http://www.realclearpolitics.com/articles/2016/11/12/it_wasnt_the_polls_that_missed_it_was_the_pundits_132333.html [Accessed 18 Apr. 2017].

Hope matters above all else

Catholic News Service (2017). *As elections approach in Somalia, bishop sees signs of hope*. [online] Crux. Available at: https://cruxnow.

com/cns/2017/01/17/elections-approach-somalia-bishop-sees-signs-hope/ [Accessed 18 Apr. 2017].

Chen, S. (2016). *In his last campaign speech for Clinton, President Obama says he still has hope for America.* [online] Quartz. Available at: https://qz.com/830981/election-2016-president-obama-says-he-still-has-hope-for-america-in-his-last-campaign-speech-for-hillary-clinton/ [Accessed 18 Apr. 2017].

Ollunga, S. and Singh, A. (2016). *Africa This Month: The Season of Elections, Hope and Change.* [online] Fair Observer. Available at: https://www.fairobserver.com/region/africa/africa-election-news-gambia-drc-ghana-43450/ [Accessed 18 Apr. 2017].

Snyder, C., Rand, K. and Sigmon, D. (2002). Hope Theory. In: C. Snyder and J. Lopez, ed., *Handbook of Positive Psychology*, 1st ed. New York: Oxford University Press, pp.257-276.

Empathy Matters

Bloom, P. (2016). *The Perils of Empathy.* [online] The Wall Street Journal. Available at: https://www.wsj.com/articles/the-perils-of-empathy-1480689513 [Accessed 18 Apr. 2017].

Gregoire, C. (2016). *How Important Is It For Politicians To Have Empathy?.* [online] The Huffington Post. Available at: http://www.huffingtonpost.com/entry/empathy-leadership_us_56f-04d40e4b09bf44a9e1b9d [Accessed 18 Apr. 2017].

Nairaland (2016). *What Buhari Told Osinbajo During Campaign.* [online] Nairaland. Available at: http://www.nairaland.com/3052051/what-buhari-told-osinbajo-during [Accessed 18 Apr. 2017].

OAK TV (2015). *Daily Trust Dialogue: Oby Ezekwesili weeps for Nigeria's lost empathy.* [online] OAK TV. Available at: http://oak.tv/daily-trust-dialogue-oby-ezekwesili-weeps-for-nigerias-lost-empathy/ [Accessed 19 Apr. 2017].

Shafer, J. (2016). *Trump Was Not a Media Fail.* [online] POLITICO Magazine. Available at: http://www.politico.com/magazine/story/2016/11/donald-trump-wins-2016-media-214442 [Accessed 18 Apr. 2017].

Willingham, E. (2016). *Yes, Donald Trump Is A Master Of Empathy.* [online] Forbes. Available at: https://www.forbes.com/sites/

emilywillingham/2016/11/03/yes-donald-trump-is-a-master-of-empathy/2/#5920be31dab2 [Accessed 18 Apr. 2017].

Zaki, J. (2015). *Choosing Empathy*. [online] Edge. Available at: https://www.edge.org/conversation/jamil_zaki-choosing-empathy [Accessed 18 Apr. 2017].

People should not be afraid of their governments

BBC News (2011). *Gambia's Yahya Jammeh ready for 'billion-year' rule.* [online] BBC News. Available at: http://www.bbc.com/news/world-africa-16148458 [Accessed 18 Apr. 2017].

Jideonwo, C. (2017). *Office Of The Citizen with Chude Jideonwo: Remember that thing Governor Ajimobi said?.* [online] YNaija. Available at: https://ynaija.com/office-citizen-chude-jideonwo-remember-thing-governor-ajimobi-said/ [Accessed 18 Apr. 2017].

Mukori, W. (2017). *"Zanu PF will rule forever!" boast Mnangagwa oblivious of the "Dead End Ahead!".* [online] Zimbabwe Social Democrats. Available at: http://zsdemocrats.blogspot.com.ng/2017/02/zanu-pf-will-rule-forever-boast.html [Accessed 18 Apr. 2017].

Reuters (2017). *In Gambia, relief turns to anger at Yahya Jammeh's luxurious exile.* [online] The Star. Available at: http://www.the-star.co.ke/news/2017/01/24/in-gambia-relief-turns-to-anger-at-yahya-jammehs-luxurious-exile_c1493709 [Accessed 18 Apr. 2017].

Tendi, B. (2010). *Making history in Mugabe's Zimbabwe.* 1st ed. Oxford: Peter Lang.

The new political marketplace

Collenette, P. (2017). *In politics, disruption is the new normal.* [online] thestar.com. Available at: https://www.thestar.com/opinion/commentary/2017/01/29/in-politics-disruption-is-the-new-normal-collenette.html [Accessed 18 Apr. 2017].

Douthat, R. (2017). *The Dangers of Hillary Clinton.* [online] The New York Times. Available at: https://www.nytimes.com/2016/10/23/opinion/sunday/the-dangers-of-hillary-clinton.html?mtrref=undefined&gwh=E37D0A60F88D-

422DE832268E19A35292&gwt=pay&assetType=opinion [Accessed 18 Apr. 2017].

Haldevang, M. (2017). *The only journalist going to Asia with Rex Tillerson works for the "Buzzfeed for conservatives"*. [online] Quartz. Available at: https://qz.com/933157/rex-tillerson-is-traveling-to-asia-with-just-one-journalist-from-independent-journal-review/ [Accessed 18 Apr. 2017].

McKinnon, M. (2017). *Political Disruption: Where It's Coming From & Why We Need It.*. [online] Iop.harvard.edu. Available at: http://iop.harvard.edu/get-involved/study-groups/political-disruption-where-its-coming-why-we-need-it-led-mark-mckinnon [Accessed 18 Apr. 2017].

The citizen is always right

@SenSanders (2016). *Bernie Sanders on Twitter*. [online] Twitter. Available at: https://twitter.com/sensanders/status/758746109103661056 [Accessed 18 Apr. 2017].

AFP (2016). *Does Donald Trump's victory spell the end of the West?*. [online] The Guardian. Available at: https://guardian.ng/news/does-donald-trumps-victory-spell-the-end-of-the-west/ [Accessed 18 Apr. 2017].

Akers, M. (2016). *'It Was My Primal Scream'*. [online] POLITICO Magazine. Available at: http://www.politico.com/magazine/story/2016/12/progressive-trump-vote-214534 [Accessed 18 Apr. 2017].

Boyd, D. (2017). *Did Media Literacy Backfire?*. [online] Data & Society: Points. Available at: https://points.datasociety.net/did-media-literacy-backfire-7418c084d88d [Accessed 18 Apr. 2017].

Cornwell, R. (2016). *Donald Trump's supporters let out a primal scream against Washington*. [online] The Independent. Available at: http://www.independent.co.uk/voices/donald-trump-wins-us-presidential-election-2016-supporters-primal-scream-against-washington-a7406841.html [Accessed 18 Apr. 2017].

Gainor, D. (2016). *Trump triumphs – Media's 'primal scream' is heard round the world*. [online] Fox News. Available at: http://www.foxnews.com/opinion/2016/11/09/trump-triumphs-medias-primal-scream-is-heard-round-world.html [Accessed 18 Apr. 2017].

Jideonwo, C. (2017). *The irony of the youth-led frustration that keeps electing old men into office across Africa*. [online] Quartz. Available at: https://qz.com/904665/donald-trump-joins-buhari-in-nigeria-and-akufo-addo-in-ghana-as-70-year-olds-leading-young-electorates/ [Accessed 18 Apr. 2017].

Matthews, O. (2016). *Europe's primal scream*. [online] The Week. Available at: http://theweek.com/articles/632850/europes-primal-scream [Accessed 18 Apr. 2017].

O'Neill, B. (2016). *Brexit voters are not thick, not racist: just poor*. [online] The Spectator. Available at: https://www.spectator.co.uk/2016/07/brexit-voters-are-not-thick-not-racist-just-poor/# [Accessed 18 Apr. 2017].

Sanders, B. (2016). *Bernie Sanders: Democrats Need to Wake Up*. [online] The New York Times. Available at: https://www.nytimes.com/2016/06/29/opinion/campaign-stops/bernie-sanders-democrats-need-to-wake-up.html?_r=1&mtrref=undefined&gwh=C097A1803257C28B36BE8C5AC2792E-B1&gwt=pay&assetType=opinion [Accessed 18 Apr. 2017].

Why Africa needs democracy

African Development Bank Group (2016). *Mozambique Economic Outlook*. [online] African Development Bank Group. Available at: https://www.afdb.org/en/countries/southern-africa/mozambique/mozambique-economic-outlook/ [Accessed 18 Apr. 2017].

BBC News (2016). *Namibia country profile*. [online] BBC News. Available at: http://www.bbc.com/news/world-africa-13890726 [Accessed 18 Apr. 2017].

BBC NEWS (2007). *Mozambique ex-leader wins prize*. [online] BBC NEWS. Available at: http://news.bbc.co.uk/2/hi/africa/7056159.stm [Accessed 18 Apr. 2017].

Spatz, B. (2013). *Liberia, a remarkable African success story, still needs help*. [online] The Christian Science Monitor. Available at: http://www.csmonitor.com/Commentary/Opinion/2013/0923/Liberia-a-remarkable-African-success-story-still-needs-help [Accessed 18 Apr. 2017].

The World Bank (2017). *Namibia Overview*. [online] The World Bank. Available at: https://www.worldbank.org/en/country/namibia/overview [Accessed 18 Apr. 2017].

Walter, B. (2012). *Why Africa's Rebels Become Dictators.* [online] Political Violence at a Glance. Available at: https://politicalvio-lenceataglance.org/2012/08/16/why-africas-rebels-become-dic-tators/ [Accessed 18 Apr. 2017].

Why it's still too soon to celebrate an African democratic wave

Aljazeera (2015). *African Union suspends Burkina Faso after military coup.* [online] Aljazeera. Available at: http://www.aljazeera. com/news/2015/09/african-union-suspends-burkina-faso-mili-tary-coup-150919073352770.html [Accessed 19 Apr. 2017].

BBC News World (2013). *Arab uprising: Country by country - Libya.* [online] BBC News World. Available at: http://www.bbc.com/ news/world-12482311 [Accessed 19 Apr. 2017].

Cheesman, N. (2017). *Africa's real story of 2017 will be of close elections and activists struggling to hold governments accountable.* [online] African Arguments. Available at: http://africanarguments. org/2017/01/10/africas-real-story-of-2017-will-be-of-close-elec-tions-and-activists-struggling-to-hold-governments-accountable/ [Accessed 19 Apr. 2017].

Cornell University Library (n.d.). *Arab Spring: A Research & Study Guide * الربيع العربي: Libya.* [online] Cornell Universi-ty Library. Available at: http://guides.library.cornell.edu/c. php?g=31688&p=200751 [Accessed 19 Apr. 2017].

Kazeem, Y. (2017). *One of Africa's longest serving strongmen just got voted out of power.* [online] Quartz. Available at: https:// qz.com/934102/issa-hayatous-29-year-reign-as-africas-football-president-is-over/ [Accessed 19 Apr. 2017].

Makhafola, G. (2017). *#ZumaBirthday: President says he would step down if asked by ANC.* [online] IOL. Available at: http://www. iol.co.za/news/politics/zumabirthday-president-says-he-would-step-down-if-asked-by-anc-8645522 [Accessed 19 Apr. 2017].

Ngcobo, Z. (2017). *Analyst: ANC has no conception of modern soci-ety.* [online] EYEWITNESS NEWS. Available at: http://ewn. co.za/2017/04/13/analyst-slams-anc-led-government-for-looting [Accessed 19 Apr. 2017].

Songwe, V. (2015). *African Leadership Transitions Tracker.* [online]

Brookings. Available at: https://www.brookings.edu/interactives/african-leadership-transitions-tracker/ [Accessed 19 Apr. 2017].

Vorrath, J. (2011). *African developments: political trends in recent elections in Sub-Saharan Africa*. [online] Deutsches Institut fur Entwicklungspolitik. Available at: https://www.die-gdi.de/en/briefing-paper/article/african-developments-political-trends-in-recent-elections-in-sub-saharan-africa/ [Accessed 19 Apr. 2017].

REFERENCES FOR FIGURES

AFROBAROMETER (2016). Does less engaged mean less empowered? Political participation lags among African youth, especially women. http://afrobarometer.org/publications/youth-day-2016 [Accessed 17 Apr. 2017].

Aid Data (2014). *THIS WEEK: A SMORGASBORD FOR AN OPEN DATA, CITIZEN ENGAGEMENT AND CLIMATE CHANGE ENTHUSIAST.* http://aiddata.org/blog/this-week-a-smorgasbord-for-an-open-data-citizen-engagement-and-climate-change-enthusiast [Accessed 17 Apr. 2017].

Ernst & Young's (n.d.). *Ernst & Young's 2012 Africa attractiveness survey Africa.* http://www.ey.com/za/en/issues/business-environment/2012-africa-as-it-is-perceived–emerging-and-developed-market-views [Accessed 17 Apr. 2017].

FTI Strategy Consulting & Research (2016). *Confidence in the Continent: Research with Opinion Leaders on Investment Sentiments in Africa.* http://research.ftistratcomm.com/2016/07/29/confidence-in-the-continent-research-with-opinion-leaders-on-investment-sentiments-in-africa/ [Accessed 17 Apr. 2017].

Gallup (2008). *Presidential Rule Still Dominates African Politics.* http://www.gallup.com/poll/106486/presidential-rule-still-dominates-african-politics.aspx [Accessed 24 Apr. 2017].

Iowa State University News Service (2016). *TV a top source of political information for caucus-goers, according to ISU/WHO-HD poll.* http://www.news.iastate.edu/news/2016/01/29/politicalinformation [Accessed 24 Apr. 2017].

NerdWallet (2013). *Hillary Clinton: An Infographic.* https://www.nerdwallet.com/blog/investing/hillary-clinton-political-legacy-infographic/ [Accessed 17 Apr. 2017].

NPHR New Hampshire Public Radio (2015). *The 2016 Primary Money Race, in Two Charts.* http://nhpr.org/post/2016-primary-money-race-two-charts#stream/0 [Accessed 24 Apr. 2017].

RealClearPolitics (n.d.). *General Election: Bush vs. Clinton.* http://www.realclearpolitics.com/epolls/2016/president/us/general_election_bush_vs_clinton-3827.html [Accessed 17 Apr. 2017].

Statista (2016). *Number of Millennial social network users in the United States from 2012 to 2018 (in millions).* https://www.statista.com/statistics/372650/us-millennial-social-network-users/ [Accessed 17 Apr. 2017].

The Electoral Commission (2016). *25% of single people are not registered to vote.* http://www.electoralcommission.org.uk/__data/assets/image/0005/194297/Infographic-25-percent-of-single-people-are-not-registered-to-vote-England-and-London.jpg [Accessed 24 Apr. 2017].

Washington Post (2017). *These former Obama strongholds sealed the election for Trump.* https://www.washingtonpost.com/graphics/politics/2016-election/obama-trump-counties/ [Accessed 17 Apr. 2017].